I0893779

RECONCILABLE DIFFERENCES

MILLER CENTER STUDIES ON THE PRESIDENCY

GUIAN A. MCKEE AND MARC J. SELVERSTONE, EDITORS

Reconcilable Differences

The Unlikely Political Alliance of John F. Kennedy and Eleanor Roosevelt

BARBARA A. PERRY

UNIVERSITY OF VIRGINIA PRESS
Charlottesville and London

Published in association with the University of Virginia's Miller Center of Public Affairs

The University of Virginia Press is situated on the traditional lands of the Monacan Nation, and the Commonwealth of Virginia was and is home to many other Indigenous people. We pay our respect to all of them, past and present. We also honor the enslaved African and African American people who built the University of Virginia, and we recognize their descendants. We commit to fostering voices from these communities through our publications and to deepening our collective understanding of their histories and contributions.

University of Virginia Press
© 2026 by the Rector and Visitors of the University of Virginia
All rights reserved
Printed in the United States of America on acid-free paper

First published 2026

9 8 7 6 5 4 3 2 1

ISBN 978-0-8139-5553-7 (hardback)
ISBN 978-0-8139-5554-4 (ebook)

Library of Congress Cataloging-in-Publication Data
is available for this title.

Cover art: Eleanor Roosevelt and John F. Kennedy just after their Val-Kill lunch meeting, 1960. (Courtesy of FDRL/Gurewitsch)
Cover design: Kelley Galbreath

For Jay and Lossie Wilkinson
and Bob Brill,
cherished friends, wise counselors, unstinting supporters

CONTENTS

ACKNOWLEDGMENTS

Many friends and colleagues know the story of my life-long interest in John F. Kennedy, whom my mother took me to see as he ran for president in 1960. Little did she know that her preschool daughter's career path as a political scientist who studies the presidency would be determined that October day at a Louisville, Kentucky, political rally. Both of my parents introduced me to the Roosevelts' legacies with stories of how FDR saved the country during the Great Depression (especially appreciated after my dad's family lost their home) and World War II (in which he served as an Army officer).

So when my friends Rose and Rob Capon offered to drive me to New York to interview Ted Sorensen for my book on Rose Kennedy, I asked if we could add a visit to Hyde Park. Neither they nor I expected that I would burst into tears when the National Park Service ranger pointed out the room where FDR was born at the Springwood mansion high above the Hudson River. Fortunately, I maintained my emotions at Eleanor's Val-Kill Cottage and was immediately drawn to a photo there of ER with JFK, both smiling broadly as they emerged from their lunch meeting in August 1960. I had to know the entire backstory of that historic gathering of two of the twentieth century's most powerful political influencers from the nation's two most consequential modern political dynasties.

Happily, my UVA Miller Center colleagues, historians Marc Selverstone, Guian McKee, and Elizabeth Rees, along with the UVA Press's

Editor in Chief Nadine Zimmerli, immediately embraced the book when I presented the proposal to them. Their informed edits, combined with those from Professors Mark White and Myra Gutin, who served as outside reviewers, smoothed the narrative and its themes. David Woolner, resident historian at the Roosevelt Institute, provided the earliest support for this project by suggesting that it focus on the impact of religion, race, and gender in the midcentury Democratic Party.

The Miller Center's Executive Director Bill Antholis and my former UVA colleague Professor Philip Zelikow supported my request for a 2020 sabbatical, when I hoped to return to the FDR Presidential Library and visit the Schlesinger Library at Harvard to fill in research gaps. Alas, both libraries had to close when the COVID pandemic hit, but thanks to historian Allida Black's monumental efforts to digitize Eleanor Roosevelt's papers, I was able to stay safe at home while accessing this treasure trove of primary sources and superb annotations.

Alfred Reaves IV, the Miller Center's faculty coordinator and a stalwart friend, provided crucial research for several chapters. Our superb Miller Center editor, Jeni Crockett-Holme, applied her exquisite desktop publishing skills to my idiosyncratic file "management" with expertise and humor. Compatriots of more decades than we care to admit, Debra DeCamillis and Dr. Julia McDonough were ever at the ready to read drafts (in Debra's case) and provide a historian's expertise on race and gender (as did Julia). Debra's Raleigh, North Carolina, book club served as an enthusiastic focus group for titles and ideas.

Longtime AV archivist at the John F. Kennedy Presidential Library, James Hill, has now assisted me in acquiring photographs for four books on the Kennedy family, and Maura Hammer of the JFKL Foundation remains a valued friend and contact for linking me to research assistance. Supervisory Archivist Abigail Malangone is my newest connection at the library. Equally helpful were FDR Library Archivist Sarah Navins, who provided photos in record time, as did Truman Library Digital Archivist Lindsay Closterman. The National Archives' presidential libraries are stellar research facilities, staffed by dedicated public servants.

Three steadfast friends, Jay and Lossie Wilkinson and Bob Brill, always knew just when to ask the universal question for authors everywhere, "How's your book coming?" Their diplomacy and genuine concern, in addition to gentle suggestions for breaking through obstacles, kept me on task and in good spirits. That is why this tome is dedicated to them with deepest gratitude.

RECONCILABLE DIFFERENCES

INTRODUCTION

Tête-à-Tête at Val-Kill

AUGUST 14, 1960, DAWNED SUNNY and warm in Hyde Park, New York. Staff at Franklin Roosevelt's birthplace, high above the Hudson River, readied a podium on the lawn outside Springwood mansion, adjacent to the president's rose garden gravesite. About two miles east, at Val-Kill cottage, FDR's widow Eleanor busied herself in preparation for lunch with the day's featured speaker, Sen. John F. Kennedy, Democratic presidential nominee. She did so with a heavy heart. Just two days earlier, her son, John, had phoned with news that Eleanor's beloved teenaged granddaughter Sally had succumbed to injuries suffered in a horseback-riding accident at an upstate New York camp.[1]

"Life is a strange thing, and the only thing we can ever be sure of is the unexpected," Mrs. Roosevelt reflected in her newspaper column a few days later. She recalled her memories of the vibrant thirteen-year-old Sally, who lived near Val-Kill with her parents: "The slim young figure that was so graceful and so quick, such a good swimmer, such a good horsewoman." Eleanor tried to find meaning in the accident: "There is no explanation for tragedies as we feel them in the loss of a young life, but we must believe there is a reason which wisdom beyond

Eleanor Roosevelt and granddaughters Sally and Nina Roosevelt, near Val-Kill, walking Fala, 1951. (Courtesy of Franklin D. Roosevelt Presidential Library)

our own can understand. We have to know that those who suffer in life are those who have the most understanding and love to give and who can help others more because they know what suffering is from personal experience."[2]

Perhaps ER thought of her late husband and how his battle with polio solidified his character and commitment to progressive policies for the disadvantaged.[3] As Eleanor expressed in 1956 about FDR's experience with infantile paralysis, he had "time to think about a great many things that he probably might never have had time to think about. He actually grew spiritually. And I felt that the latent powers and abilities were all there. They would have developed perhaps in a little different way, but that development [was] more quickly and decisively than anything else would have [produced]."[4]

ER also knew that the tragedies throughout her life, including the deaths of her parents by the time she was ten, the curse of alcoholism that led to the loss of her father and brother, the death of her baby son, and her husband's marital infidelities, had molded her career as a humanitarian and advocate for the impoverished. She believed that "Franklin had had, in a way, an easier life than I had." While Mrs. Roosevelt was rarely given to bouts of self-pity, she believed that a "sense of obligation" had been "bred" into her.[5]

John F. Kennedy, no stranger to sudden family calamities, having lost his brother and brother-in-law four weeks apart in World War II and his sister in a plane crash a few years later, offered to postpone lunch, but the former First Lady insisted that it proceed because she knew how busy presidential candidates were. Never one to fuss over her appearance, the now slightly stooped seventy-five-year-old piled her white curls on top of her head, held them in place with a hairnet, donned a modest shirtwaist dress, added a necklace and pin at her décolletage, and adjusted her hearing aids and matronly eyeglasses.

The ostensible reason for Kennedy's appearance at Hyde Park gratified Mrs. Roosevelt. After lunch, he would speak at an event sponsored by the Golden Ring Club, a senior citizens' organization that had gathered to lay a wreath on FDR's grave to celebrate the twenty-fifth anniversary of President Roosevelt's signing the Social Security Act.

Yet JFK had an even more compelling motivation for visiting Hyde Park and luncheoning with FDR's widow that day. She had earned the label "First Lady of the World" from her husband's successor, Harry Truman, for her tireless efforts on behalf of peace and human rights around the globe. From a shy and awkward surrogate for her husband after paralysis struck him in 1921, she leveraged her keen intellect, shrewd political instincts, genuine empathy, boundless energy, and international celebrity to become one of the Democratic Party's most influential power brokers by the 1950s. She modestly, but inaccurately, claimed in 1956 that she wasn't a power broker but simply knew many people, possessed effective listening skills, and served as a useful sounding board for political aspirants to clarify their policy arguments in conversations with her.[6]

Her modesty could turn condescending, however, as when she addressed Senator Kennedy, young enough to be her son, as "my dear boy" in a 1959 telegram.[7] The maternalism inherent in that salutation reflected not only the generational difference between the two Democrats but a deeper schism for Eleanor. As a young woman, she had been a shrinking violet, while her husband displayed all the attributes of a charming extrovert. "Adulation bothered Eleanor. It intoxicated her husband," biographer Joseph Lash observed of their personality differences, and she occasionally chastised Franklin for his impertinence.[8] She particularly disliked FDR's flirtatious nature—even before she discovered his extramarital affair with Lucy Mercer in 1918. During her lengthy engagement to Franklin, young Eleanor had fretted that she might lose her fiancé because he was so "attractive."[9]

JFK's well-known reputation as a womanizer, indeed playboy, might well have rankled FDR's widow. Perhaps the callowness she perceived in Kennedy reminded her of Franklin's immaturity in the early years of their marriage or the irresponsibility of their five children, who numbered nineteen marriages among them. Eleanor thought that Kennedy's prodigious ambition to become the youngest man ever elected president (at age forty-three) far outstripped his knowledge and experience.[10] Yes, her beloved uncle, Theodore Roosevelt, had become president at forty-two, but he had ascended to the position from the vice presidency, upon President William McKinley's 1901 assassination.

"Mrs. R," as her secretaries endearingly dubbed Eleanor, also maintained a suspicion toward JFK that sprang, in part, from her mistrust of his father Joseph's isolationism and appeasement as FDR's ambassador to the Court of St. James's. In fact, the last time a Kennedy had lunched with the First Lady was two decades earlier. FDR had called his wife to his study in the Roosevelts' Hyde Park mansion just after a 1940 meeting with Ambassador Kennedy, whose policies toward World War II had diverged too markedly from his appointing president. "I never want to see that son of a bitch again as long as I live," the president sputtered. "Give him lunch and put him on the train," President Roosevelt declared. The First Lady followed the commander in chief's order and remembered the incident as one of the most "dreadful" of her life.[11]

Twenty years later, Mrs. Roosevelt had amassed other reasons to oppose Ambassador Kennedy's son, including his moderation on civil rights and acquiescence in Sen. Joseph McCarthy's anticommunist witch-hunt. These specific policy differences reflected a general tension between Kennedy and the more liberal wing of the Democratic Party in the 1950s, especially its tie to the New Deal. "I'm not a liberal at all," newly elected Senator Kennedy observed in 1953, reflecting both his strategic electoral moderation and unemotional affect toward what he viewed as liberals' mawkish morality. Like other Kennedy opponents, Eleanor undoubtedly knew of the controversy over the authorship of Jack's 1957 Pulitzer Prize–winning book *Profiles in Courage*. Had he penned it or relied on his speechwriter Ted Sorensen and several historians to expand his ideas into the final manuscript?[12] The latter possibility would have been especially galling to Mrs. Roosevelt, who never relied on ghostwriters to produce her daily newspaper columns or memoirs, as many public figures did. Moreover, she didn't consider JFK to be a courageous leader on the issues most important to her. In addition, she had received a letter from an individual she didn't know claiming that JFK suffered from Addison's disease, a potentially fatal deficiency of the adrenal glands.[13] Thus, for a host of varied reasons—personal, political, ideological, and medical—she mistrusted Kennedy and had refused to support his candidacy in the race for the 1960 Democratic presidential nomination.

Now that he had garnered his party's spot at the top of the ticket, Kennedy had to request Eleanor's crucial endorsement as he commenced his general election campaign for president. Without the support of the most powerful woman in the Democratic Party, who had played a key role in anointing the candidacy of the party's standard bearer, Adlai Stevenson, in 1952 and '56, JFK's victory over the formidable GOP candidate, Vice President Richard Nixon, was anything but assured. Kennedy not only needed Roosevelt's endorsement, he knew that her active campaigning for him through personal appearances, advertisements, and her newspaper column could make the difference in November. The widow of his party's patron saint of the New Deal could launch his New Frontier presidency. Selling his candidacy to the former First Lady would not be easy, however, even for the preternaturally charming senator.

Although countless volumes have been published on these two giants of the middle third of twentieth-century American politics, none has focused on their political relationship, how it developed through the Roosevelt and Kennedy dynasties, how Cold War issues at home and abroad shaped it, what it meant for the 1960 presidential election's outcome, why religion, age, race, and gender influenced it, and what the duo's two different approaches to public policy reveal about timeless lessons of political partnerships and leadership.

JFK arrived at Hyde Park in August 1960 as the ultimate pragmatist (especially in domestic policy), who placed political convenience above principle, which was how he garnered the Democratic presidential nomination in a fractious party riven by geography and race. Although an asset in his five successful Massachusetts congressional races, his Roman Catholicism counted as an obstacle among Protestants nationally, so he compartmentalized his religion into the personal and private sphere of life. His economic privilege, heroic military service, youthful charisma, and rhetorical skills emboldened him to seek the presidency and ask the party's "grande dame" for her support in the general election.

Mrs. Roosevelt represented the very essence of idealism, compromising only when absolutely necessary to achieve her goals. Her name had never appeared on a ballot. Thus, she had advocated principled positions on rights for women, children, Blacks, Jews, Asians, labor unions, farmers, and the impoverished. Operating from a position of high socioeconomic status, near the apex of American government, ER nevertheless faced constraints of gender and lack of official power, even as First Lady, and certainly after her tenure ended as a UN delegate in 1953.

Kennedy and Roosevelt met at the fulcrum of the 1960 campaign, when it was unclear whether each might evolve on the pragmatism-idealism spectrum and tip the levers of politics and government toward convenience or principle, especially on issues of race and gender. Both would die before the Great Society and the third wave of feminism answered those questions for American politics—at least until the rightward turn of the Reagan era. Yet in the time that each had remaining, would they become at least transitional figures, serving as a bridge to further progress? Would they be able to compromise on their differences, providing roadmaps for effective leadership and governance? Could a potential combination of the New Deal and New Frontier result in a whole that was greater than the sum of the two platforms' parts?

Their venue for this momentous meeting, Val-Kill (the name derived from a corruption of the property's Fall Kill stream), existed because of Eleanor's fraught personal life and her desire to maintain independence. To create a retreat for Eleanor and her Greenwich Village friends, life partners Nancy Cook and Marion Dickerman,[14] FDR had designed and contracted the construction of the Dutch colonial Stone Cottage in 1925. He added a pool, where they could all enjoy swims, which he found therapeutic for his polio-afflicted legs. Val-Kill Pond surrounded the wooded property. Eleanor could escape her intrusive mother-in-law, Sara Delano Roosevelt, who would remain the dowager of the Hyde Park manor until her death there in 1941.

ER and her friends added a bigger building in 1926 to house their new venture, Val-Kill crafting. The enterprise lasted a decade until the Great Depression shut its doors. Eleanor, now First Lady, converted the factory into what would be called Val-Kill Cottage, a home for her and her secretary, Malvina (Tommy) Thompson. Dickerman and Cook remained in Stone Cottage until 1947.

Val-Kill Cottage on Hyde Park estate. (Courtesy of Robert S. Capon)

When Franklin died in 1945, Springwood, his familial mansion, passed to the federal government. Eleanor happily made her country home at Val-Kill, where she would entertain all visitors—from myriad grandchildren to Shirley Temple to boys from a nearby reform school to candidate-supplicants (like JFK) to heads of state (Khrushchev, Tito, Nehru, and Selassie).[15] She was never happier than when celebrating Thanksgiving, Christmas, and Independence Day at her homey cottage with family and friends, unless it was taking solitary walks in the nearby woods with Fala or the Scotties who succeeded FDR's celebrity pooch.

As Eleanor awaited the arrival of Senator Kennedy for lunch at this historic, yet modest, cottage, the former First Lady contemplated what she wanted from the young candidate in return for her support. Political shrewdness was firmly embedded in these two lunch partners' DNA, yet neither knew how the Val-Kill showdown would end. Would they bury their political hatchets in the bucolic grounds surrounding Val-Kill Cottage—or in each other?

1

DYNASTIES CONVERGE

ELEANOR ROOSEVELT'S AND JOHN KENNEDY'S individual biographies reveal the personal grit and determination that each brought to the Val-Kill table. Eleanor had overcome a tragic childhood, limited higher education, a meddlesome mother-in-law, an unfaithful husband, and societal misogyny to seize opportunities in public life rarely available to women of any socioeconomic status. Although avoiding the handicap of gender, Jack had faced multiple medical challenges, an aloof mother and demanding father (both of whom favored his elder brother), family tragedies, and a near-death experience in World War II. Yet each player in the Val-Kill drama possessed the benefits of hailing from the twentieth century's two most powerful American political dynasties.

Their differences, however, had set them on a collision course. Eleanor Roosevelt, born in 1884, was a full generation older than Kennedy, who was just in his early forties when he ran for president in 1960. At seventy-five, she was nearly the same age as his mother, Rose, which gave JFK one advantage in his relationship with Eleanor. For more than four decades, he had endured his mother's Victorian criticisms of his tardiness, irresponsibility, and carelessness and bucked her irritating attempts to impose discipline. Yet he appreciated her effective campaign appearances for him from 1946 onward. Whether hosting intimate tea parties, appearing at large receptions, speaking at conventions, meeting with journalists, or recording televised commercials, Rose was an even more experienced campaigner than Eleanor, though the Kennedy matriarch never embraced policy activism.[1]

By 1960, JFK had to absorb Mrs. Roosevelt's harsh political critiques and find a way to earn her endorsement, despite the obstacles she posed. One of Kennedy's favorite books on the office he sought was Richard Neustadt's 1960 pathbreaking work, *Presidential Power.* JFK devoured the thin volume and then recommended it to his advisors. Whereas most scholars had focused on the chief executive's formal powers, granted in the Constitution and laws, Neustadt argued that "presidential power is the power to persuade": first, party power brokers and the electorate, then Congress, the media, the military, foreign leaders, and administration officials.[2] Could Kennedy put Neustadt's theory into practice by persuading Eleanor to support his candidacy? Both would have to engage in the delicate dance of discernment that makes for successful politicians when they size up opponents, plead their respective cases, apply personal magnetism, search for common beliefs, and join forces to win office and achieve shared policy goals.

Kennedy and Roosevelt came from two completely different cultures: the Episcopalian Roosevelts—to the manner born in Manhattan, Oyster Bay, and Hyde Park—descended from seventeenth-century Dutch settlers, while the Roman Catholic Kennedys were just a few generations removed from potato-famine Irish refugees in mid-nineteenth-century Boston. Yet Joseph P. Kennedy Sr.'s meteoric rise through the socioeconomic ranks, based on wealth accumulated in pre-Depression Wall Street stocks, movie distribution, and Hollywood film production and his escape from parochial New England to New York City destined the two families to meet in the political arena.

The Roosevelts' Dutch ancestors started the family's two famous branches: one based in Oyster Bay on Long Island, the other in the Hudson Valley's Hyde Park. President Theodore Roosevelt descended from the Oyster Bay branch. His brother's daughter, Anna Eleanor, would marry her fifth cousin, once removed, Franklin Delano Roosevelt of the Hyde Park clan, in 1905. TR was Eleanor's Uncle Ted and a cousin to Franklin.[3] ER and FDR chose St. Patrick's Day as their marriage date in New York City because Uncle Ted, who was to escort the bride, would be in town for the Irish holiday's parade.[4] The incumbent president performed the ritual of accompanying the bride because her father, whom she had adored, died of alcoholism when she was nine, leaving her an orphan. Her mother had passed away just two years previously, and ER's four-year-old brother had died shortly after their mother. Although Eleanor admired her mother's beauty, she always felt "a curious barrier" between them. Put off by the little girl's solemnity and "old-fashioned" appearance, her mother called her "Granny," even in front of visitors, which made Eleanor want "to sink through the floor in shame."[5]

After her mother's death, Eleanor's maternal grandmother raised her among aunts and uncles, who paid more attention to the young girl than her own parents had, although her uncles were quite unsettling in their raucous, alcohol-fueled behavior. Her grandmother imposed strict discipline on the child, and Eleanor became an introverted and insecure adolescent, prone to phobias. "I was usually shy and frightened because I lived an entirely lonely life."[6]

A turning point in the teenager's social and educational development came during her years in England, from 1899 to 1902, at Allenswood Academy under headmistress Marie Souvestre's mentorship. The French educator recognized leadership qualities in her protégé and kindled in her an intellectual spark that never dimmed. ER became what twenty-first-century Americans call a lifelong learner—in love with books, travel, languages, meeting new people, and developing a social conscience. Even after just one semester at Allenswood, Eleanor couldn't believe how much her "confidence and independence" had flourished. "I was totally without fear in this new phase of my life," she later recalled.[7]

Only about one-fifth of American bachelor's degrees awarded in the first years of the twentieth century went to women.[8] Like most of her female contemporaries, therefore, Eleanor didn't attend college, much to her lasting regret.[9] Instead, her grandmother insisted that she depart England to participate in the elaborate social rituals of an elite New York debutante. Just as Allenswood began expanding her horizons, high society's stultifying traditions narrowed them. Never an extrovert, even after her confidence infusion from Mlle. Souvestre, Eleanor dreaded the social whirl of "coming out." In addition to her innate shyness, she always knew that her mother's beauty had bypassed her in the genetic lottery. At nearly six feet tall, ER towered over her female cohort, whose average height was just a bit over five feet, and less than 5 percent of American men at the turn of the twentieth century measured six feet in height.[10]

Much to her relief, dashing, charismatic, and extroverted Cousin Franklin, a Harvard undergraduate, swept Eleanor off her feet. His formidable mother, Sara Delano Roosevelt, scolded that they were too young to court so ardently, but she wouldn't have deemed any woman worthy of her cherished only child. Love conquered Sara's objections, however, and the couple married in 1905. They made a striking young duo on their European honeymoon. At six-foot-two, FDR seemed the perfect mate for the statuesque Mrs. Franklin D. Roosevelt. While he studied law at Columbia, the couple settled in Manhattan, with Sara nearby. By age twenty, ER had taken on an ambitious husband, his intrusive mother, and responsibility for her teenaged brother at prep school; soon the rigors of childbearing would consume her for the next eleven years.[11]

FDR wanted to follow in his Cousin Ted's footsteps, and he did so by producing six children, becoming assistant secretary of the Navy, serving in the New York legislature, running for vice president, being elected the Empire State's governor, and then using that office as a springboard to the presidency.[12] In the first eleven years of marriage to Franklin, Eleanor gave birth to six babies. One died in infancy, but the surviving quintet included Anna, James, Elliott, Franklin Jr., and John. After the first two offspring arrived, Sara Roosevelt decided her son, daughter-in-law, and grandchildren needed more space. She built two adjacent townhomes in Manhattan and connected them by unlocked doors, which she used to come and go at will, until Eleanor ultimately installed locks.[13]

In addition to the 1909 death of her infant son, the first Franklin Jr., Eleanor faced the heartache of her husband's affair with Lucy Mercer, which she discovered in 1918. Increasing her pain and mortification

Franklin and Eleanor Roosevelt with children Anna, James, Elliot, Franklin Jr., John, and FDR's mother, Sara Delano Roosevelt, 1919. (Courtesy FDRL)

was the fact that Eleanor had brought the beautiful, charming young lady into the Roosevelts' Washington household as her social secretary while Franklin served as Woodrow Wilson's assistant secretary of the Navy. Eventually, Mercer went to work for FDR, and the two began a torrid romance while Eleanor and the children took refuge from the capital's summer heat in the family's northern homes at Hyde Park and Campobello Island, off Canada's New Brunswick province. Devastated by her husband's betrayal, ER proposed divorce, but her mother-in-law threatened to disown Franklin, which would have destroyed his finances and budding political career. In addition, Mercer was Catholic, and it is unclear whether she would have married a divorced suitor.[14]

Eleanor reinvented her marriage from a romantic to a pragmatic partnership. Her childbearing over (some speculate because she spurned marital relations as a means of birth control after delivering six babies and then as FDR's punishment for the Mercer affair), she began to contemplate how she might enhance her life beyond hearth and home as the 1920s dawned. Just when she started in this more independent direction, polio felled FDR in the summer of 1921 during the family's Campobello vacation. Now Eleanor and her husband's loyal aide, Louis Howe, devoted themselves to saving Franklin from his mother's wish that he spend the rest of his life as an invalid Hyde Park squire. Instead, ER and Howe supported his unwavering efforts to rehabilitate his paralyzed legs while they kept his name viable in New York politics.[15]

In addition to sharing Roosevelt genes and a similar career path, Theodore Roosevelt (a Republican) and FDR (a Democrat) both embraced a commitment to progressive social policy. As a young woman, Eleanor, who revered her uncle, felt somewhat torn between the two parties. It mattered little for voting, however, because women didn't achieve federal suffrage until 1920, when she was thirty-six years old. Uncle Ted's unsuccessful third-party run for president in 1912 included women's suffrage in his platform, but his niece had not yet undergone consciousness-raising and remained on the sidelines in the suffragist movement. Holding the view that politics should remain a strictly male domain, she lagged behind her husband, who'd voted for female suffrage while a New York state legislator in 1912. Their native state finally enacted women's suffrage in 1917, but Eleanor didn't cast her first ballot until she voted for the unsuccessful 1920 Democratic presidential ticket headed by James Cox, who had chosen Franklin as his vice-presidential running mate.[16]

Mentored in public speaking and press relations by Howe and women's movement leaders, Eleanor began advocating protective legislation for female workers in the '20s. In part, she based her progressive reformism on the Christian call to help those less fortunate.[17] Her work in the nascent League of Women Voters led to increasingly responsible duties in the New York Democratic Party's women's division. She labored for Al Smith's 1924 gubernatorial campaign, thus antagonizing the Oyster Bay Roosevelts, who were supporting the late TR's son Ted Jr., the GOP candidate for governor. By the time Franklin was elected to two terms as the Empire State's governor, in 1928 and 1930, Eleanor was not only ready to serve as the First Lady in Albany but had worked in national party circles and assisted Al Smith in his unsuccessful run for president in 1928. In that latter capacity, she saw firsthand the handicap that Smith's Roman Catholicism posed for his presidential campaign. She read with disgust the anti-Catholic hate mail that poured into his New York headquarters.[18]

Meanwhile, John F. Kennedy, born in Brookline, Massachusetts, in 1917, the year after Eleanor and Franklin had their last child, also carried political DNA. His maternal grandfather and namesake, John F. (Honey Fitz) Fitzgerald, held a seat in the Massachusetts legislature, became a member of the US House of Representatives in the 1890s, and was elected the first American-born Irish-Catholic mayor of Boston in 1906.[19]

All Jack Kennedy's great-grandparents had fled the mid-nineteenth-century Irish potato blight and landed in Boston with no education and no prospects for gainful employment. Yet they survived with hard work and ingenuity.[20] Like many immigrants in America's urban centers, Boston's Irish population, which continued to expand, thrived in the ethnic machine politics of New England's largest city. Rising through the ranks of local Democratic Party structures, they represented a powerful voting bloc that could place their fellow Irishmen in political and governmental offices. In turn, officials earned votes by handing out Christmas turkeys and offering patronage jobs to their constituents.

JFK's paternal grandfather, Patrick J. (P.J.) Kennedy, moved into East Boston's middle class through his tavern business and the founding of a community bank. A much more subdued personality than the ebullient Mayor Fitzgerald, P.J. preferred working as a ward heeler in local Democratic politics, although he served in the Massachusetts legislature.

Occasionally, Honey Fitz and P.J. crossed swords in the rough and tumble of Boston politics, but their eldest children, Rose Fitzgerald and Joseph P. Kennedy, met when the families vacationed together in Maine. By the time they were teenagers, they had fallen in love and would marry in 1914. Their union produced nine children between 1915 and 1932: Joseph Jr., John, Rosemary, Kathleen, Eunice, Patricia, Robert, Jean, and Edward.[21]

Joe Kennedy Sr., a Harvard graduate who'd enrolled in the university five years after FDR graduated, first encountered Franklin in 1917. Kennedy was the assistant general manager of the Fore River Shipbuilding

Joseph and Rose Kennedy with children John, Rosemary, Kathleen, Eunice, Patricia, Robert, Jean, and Edward at the Vatican for Pope Pius's 1939 installation. (President's Collection Photographs, John F. Kennedy Presidential Library and Museum)

Corporation in Quincy, Massachusetts, and Franklin was the assistant secretary of the Navy when the shipbuilders struck that November during World War I. Roosevelt sent an official dispatch to the corporation urging management and labor to come to an agreement "at the earliest possible moment" that would allow "immediate resumption of work" because "there probably is no one plant in the country whose continuous operation is more important to the success of this country in the war than that at Fore River." FDR suggested that the wages paid the shipbuilders at the Boston Navy Yard would be a fair offer for the laborers in Quincy.[22] Franklin's intervention succeeded, and the strike ended several days later.

Young Jack Kennedy endured hardships throughout his life—primarily from poor health. As a toddler, he contracted scarlet fever, a severe and potentially fatal illness in the days before antibiotics. He had to be separated from his mother, who had just given birth to Kathleen.

Although Rose Kennedy cared deeply about her children, like Eleanor's mother she applied Victorian mores to childrearing and could be somewhat distant. In fact, she would leave her children for weeks at a time to travel the country or go abroad. At boarding school, Jack frequently fell ill with hives, fainting spells, mysterious digestive ailments, low blood counts, and appendicitis. Busy managing a growing brood, his mother kept tabs on his health from afar but rarely visited. Still, the family remained close with letters, and Jack asked his mother if he could become the next baby's godfather. His parents complied; JFK would serve that role for the ninth and last child, Edward. Ongoing digestive upsets landed teenaged Jack in the Mayo Clinic, where he endured painful and unsettling tests that resulted in a colitis diagnosis.[23]

A C student, on average, who only applied effort in courses whose subjects he embraced, such as history and English, Jack consumed books, newspapers, and magazines to stay abreast of public affairs. When a visitor stopped by the young teen's Boston hospital room where he was receiving treatment for a blood disorder in 1932, she noted, "He was so surrounded by books I could hardly see him. I was very impressed because at that point this very young child was reading *The World Crisis,* by Sir Winston Churchill."[24]

Although the ringleader of juvenile hijinks that prompted both the Choate headmaster and Joe Kennedy to warn him that he faced expulsion, Jack's peers named him the graduate "most likely to succeed." He attempted a gap year between prep school and college, enrolling in the London School of Economics to study with socialist professor Harold Laski. Joe Jr. had thrived during his year in London, but illness truncated Jack's study abroad. Enrolling at Princeton, he lasted barely a half semester before landing in the hospital with a low blood count and then traveling to Arizona with hope that the climate might restore his health. Returning East, he followed his dad and Joe Jr. by entering Harvard. His long struggle with back pain began when the slightly built collegiate tried to equal his heartier older brother Joe's athletic exploits on Harvard's playing fields.[25] If not in the infirmary with myriad illnesses, however, Jack participated on the Crimson swimming and sailing teams.

JFK's World War II combat injury, suffered when a Japanese destroyer sliced his PT boat in two, only exacerbated his health problems, as did pharmaceuticals for his digestive ailments that may have caused his spine to deteriorate.[26] While visiting postwar Britain, he nearly died from what physicians ultimately diagnosed as Addison's disease. Until the development of synthetic cortisone to treat the illness, Jack was prone to dangerous infections, which almost took his life after surgery in 1954 to stabilize his debilitating back condition.[27]

JFK also faced the Kennedy family's catastrophic tragedies, starting with Rosemary's diagnosis of "mental retardation" and a lobotomy in 1941 that permanently incapacitated her, followed by Joe Jr.'s and Kathleen's husband's deaths in World War II, after which Kathleen herself perished in a plane crash.[28] Yet Jack's family seemed to grow stronger and more determined to succeed with each calamity, much as Eleanor and Franklin united to promote his political career after polio struck.

Like Eleanor, JFK relished reading, travel, and public affairs. As a boy, he saw firsthand his Grandfather Fitzgerald's skill as a grassroots politician, although by college Jack thought his namesake rather corny. His dad's ultimate career choice, however, would bring national and international policy into sharp focus for JFK. Joe Kennedy Sr. had moved his family to a tony New York City suburb in 1927 to be closer to his new work in film booking. He had grown weary of Boston's anti–Irish Catholic prejudices. No sooner had the Kennedys decamped to New York than the patriarch headed to Hollywood to produce films. There he would begin a passionate romance with screen temptress Gloria Swanson. As his fortunes rose, the family established their summer home on Cape Cod and eventually created a winter retreat in Palm Beach. Once the patriarch secured his family's multimillion-dollar fortune in stock trading and movies, he turned to politics to make his next mark.[29]

During Joe's Hollywood diversion, FDR wrote to the elder Kennedy regarding the 1928 presidential campaign. Franklin had served as Al Smith's floor manager at the Democratic convention and given a rousing nominating speech for the "Happy Warrior." Now he was asking for Joe's support to elect the first Catholic president. Although Kennedy hoped to attain that unprecedented achievement himself someday, word had reached FDR (mistakenly) that Joe would vote for Smith. Franklin, who was running to succeed him as New York governor, asked Kennedy to let him know "frankly and confidentially where you stand" on the presidential race. In this "personal letter," Mr. Roosevelt assured Joe that he was not writing in his official capacity as a member of the Democratic National Executive Committee, nor was he soliciting "a campaign contribution."[30]

Smith represented all the Irish politico stereotypes that Joe disliked about his father-in-law and that his son Jack would eschew for WASPish urbanity. In addition, the Republicans' "return to normalcy" in postwar America, combined with their laissez-faire economic policies of the Roaring Twenties, had expanded Joe's wealth. Hoover's free-market capitalism suited Kennedy's personal finances; thus, the new movie mogul refrained from supporting Smith and may have voted for the Republican candidate for president.[31]

In 1930, FDR's friend Henry Morgenthau Sr. invited Kennedy to Albany for lunch to discuss Governor Roosevelt's plans for a presidential run. Joe later reported, "I knew that big, drastic changes had to be made in our economic system, and I felt Roosevelt was the one who could make those changes. I wanted him in the White House for my own security and for the security of our kids—and I was ready to do anything to help elect him." After a spring 1932 meeting with the candidate in Warm Springs, Georgia, Kennedy publicly promised his support for Franklin at the upcoming Democratic Convention. The successful financier thus became part of a group called WRBC (With Roosevelt Before Chicago [where the convention would be held that summer]). Joe helped persuade his friend, powerful newspaper tycoon William Randolph Hearst, to switch his endorsement from House Speaker John Nance Garner to FDR, which left Garner's delegates free to swing their votes to Roosevelt. In turn, FDR chose Garner as his vice-presidential running mate.[32]

Despite doubts about the influence that Louis Howe, with whom Joe Sr. had developed a mutual dislike, and campaign manager Jim Farley would have on Roosevelt, Joe flattered FDR with a phone call not long after the convention. Unless incumbent president Hoover could "put two-and-one-half million men back to work and get wheat up to twenty or twenty-five cents a bushel," Joe declared, "the result will be overwhelming for Roosevelt." In September, at FDR's invitation, Joe joined the campaign for a coast-to-coast whistle-stop tour and secured a coveted spot in the rail cars carrying the Roosevelt team and family. Although a presidential race novice, Kennedy's political genes, gift for strategy, financial acumen, and contacts on the West Coast proved helpful to the candidate.[33] On these journeys, Joe also became friends with Eleanor and Franklin's eldest adult children, Anna and James, who campaigned with their father. Always a shrewd observer of human nature, Joe could see that twenty-four-year-old Jimmy, then in the insurance business, would appreciate a financial mentor. Moreover, taking him under his tutelage would give Kennedy another conduit to FDR. For his part, Jimmy found Kennedy's charisma irresistible.[34]

A month later, Governor Roosevelt, on another whistle-stop tour, wired that he was "having a great trip" and invited Kennedy to join the train as it passed through the Washington area.[35] Although not the most generous contributor, Kennedy attracted an estimated $150,000 (nearly $3.5 million today) in contributions to Roosevelt's campaign, including $25,000 each from Hearst and himself, and loaned $50,000 to the Democratic Party. FDR appreciated that Kennedy was one of his rare supporters among financiers, whom Roosevelt had disparaged as part of America's "economic oligarchy."[36] Despite sharing good humor, bon vivant personalities, and penchants for womanizing or at least flirtations, FDR's and Kennedy's hard-edged ambitions contributed to a mutual wariness for the rest of their association. Their superlative skills—one in business and one in politics—wouldn't always mesh.[37]

Just prior to Governor Roosevelt's last rally before election day—at Boston Garden—Joe gathered with FDR, Jimmy and his wife Betsey, Anna, campaign staffers, and the governor's so-called brain trust, including future Supreme Court justice Felix Frankfurter, at FDR's Ritz Carlton Hotel suite. Journalist Kay Halle asked to be introduced to the handsome Irishman, who had arrived with Frankfurter, a Harvard law professor. Joe told her, "Though I've been interested in all sorts of businesses in Boston and California—in films and banking and though [the] mayor of Boston, is my father-in-law, I've never had the thrill of being a part of a presidential campaign. So I've put some money into

Mr. Roosevelt's campaign, and [told him] I'd like to go along with you all and take part in the fun."[38]

Joe's victory prediction to FDR materialized when the Roosevelt-Garner ticket won in a landslide, with 57.4 percent of the popular vote. Kennedy linked up with Jimmy in the wee hours of the morning after election day to plan a small celebratory party and trip to the theater for that evening to include the president-elect's oldest children and their spouses. Joe tried to invite Elliott, Eleanor and Franklin's second son, but couldn't reach him. When Kennedy heard that Elliott expressed upset at missing the celebration, Joe wrote an apologetic letter: "I may be rated sometimes as not particularly thoughtful, but never unappreciative, and I am sure you know that I would not have had knowledge of the folks who were to be there and considered for a minute not inviting you, or whomever you might have liked to have brought along."[39]

Kennedy certainly didn't want to upset any Roosevelts, as he hoped the new president would reward him with a position in the administration. Passed over for the inaugural invitation list, Joe tried flattering FDR shortly after the festivities. He happily reported to the new president that the mother superior at his daughter's convent school had compared Roosevelt's inauguration to Jesus' resurrection! In turn, the president thanked Joe for his assistance in the campaign and issued a standing invitation for Kennedy to join him on the presidential yacht.[40] The financier hoped to become secretary of the treasury, but that post went to Roosevelt's Hudson Valley neighbor Henry Morgenthau. FDR indeed kept Joe on a list of donors to reward, but the only written evidence of the post he initially thought suitable was US treasurer, a much inferior role to a cabinet position.[41] Continuing his friendship with the younger Roosevelts, Joe invited Jimmy and Betsey to the Kennedys' Hyannis Port home in 1933 and encouraged them to rent a summer house nearby the next year.[42]

Six months after the inauguration, Joe and Rose Kennedy sailed for England with Jimmy and Betsey. In the UK, Joe and his protégé met with former chancellor of the exchequer Winston Churchill at his country estate, Chartwell, to discuss obtaining rights for Kennedy to import British liquor once the expected end to Prohibition arrived in the United

States. Jimmy's business would benefit from insuring the shipments. With his usual impeccable business timing, Joe succeeded in winning the importation rights to popular brands of British gin and scotch just as the US ban on alcohol ended in December 1933. When Kennedy sold his liquor business during World War II, he added another $8 million to his fortune.[43]

Joe waited anxiously throughout 1933 for a presidential offer that never came. Although he attended the Roosevelts' first White House New Year's party on January 1, 1934,[44] he feared that FDR might have bypassed him for an administration post because of Irish stereotypes. Would the Hyde Park aristocrat see him the way Boston Brahmins had—as an aggressive Irish Catholic on the make? Roosevelt only exacerbated Joe's concern when he offered him the US ambassadorship to Ireland. Kennedy declined, hoping for an office that would boost him beyond his immigrant heritage.[45] Joe had already rejected the president's invitation, sent through Jimmy, to accept a post as minister to Uruguay, where he would negotiate new trade deals. "I told him I was not at all interested in this position," Kennedy wrote.[46]

At least President Roosevelt stopped in Palm Beach on his way home from Miami in spring 1934 and invited Joe to board his train for a "most cordial" catch-up meeting. The two men hadn't seen each other since New Year's, and Kennedy was thrilled that FDR invited him and Rose to visit at the White House on their way north that weekend. Jimmy and Joe attended the Gridiron Dinner with the presidential party, while Rose dined with Anna and Betsey Roosevelt.[47]

Back at the Executive Mansion, the president, Joe, Jimmy, and Louis Howe, whom Kennedy now believed had blackballed him from a position in the administration, talked until well into the night about monetary and fiscal policies. The next morning FDR summoned Joe to his bedroom to discuss whether he might be interested in taking a post with the Securities and Exchange Commission (SEC), if Congress approved its creation to reform the stock market excesses that had led to its 1929 crash. Joe remained noncommittal, telling the president that his only goals were to help FDR and to come to Washington if "it really meant some prestige to my family." Joe was anxious for him and Rose to catch the train to

New York for a reunion with the children, who would be thrilled about their parents' White House adventure. Yet FDR protested, "I have had no chance to talk with Rose," and invited the couple to join him and the First Lady for Sunday lunch. No record reveals how Eleanor and Joe got along at the meal. She was already deeply immersed in her advocacy for women and those suffering the ill effects of the Great Depression. In later years, she and her husband would develop severe differences with Joe over his isolationist views. The job Franklin proposed on that visit couldn't match Joe's coveted treasury secretary position, but it suited his background and represented a foot in the door of New Deal officialdom. The president expressed his preference that Joe would serve as the commission's chairman, but the commissioners would have to select Kennedy for that role.[48]

Spring gave way to summer, and still Joe heard nothing from the president. Because Kennedy had been a Wall Street wheeler-dealer who'd timed the market perfectly and cashed out before the 1929 crash, some of the president's advisors feared (quite correctly) that naming him to the SEC would prompt criticism that FDR had selected a fox to guard the chickens. Finally, toward the end of June, Jimmy passed along his father's invitation for Joe to come to Washington. After a swim in the new White House pool, a pleasant round of cocktails, and dinner, FDR still hadn't made any official offers. As Eleanor left the dinner table, she queried, "Franklin, when are you going to talk to Joe?" "About two o'clock tomorrow morning," the president quipped and departed to give a radio address. Afterward, Franklin and Joe discussed the SEC position and the dustup sure to arise from naming Kennedy. The financier admitted that critics would undoubtedly find fault with some aspects of his quarter-century in business, but he vowed to "be a credit to the country, the president, himself, and his family—clear down to the ninth child."[49] Some people swear on a Bible or their mother's grave, but when Joe felt passionate about giving his word, he swore an oath to his pride and joy—the Kennedy children. "If you are happy, it is perfectly satisfactory to me," FDR responded. After much maneuvering among the commissioners, they ultimately selected Joe chairman, and he took his position in July 1934.[50]

Kennedy now not only had an official perch in the New Deal, he created a retreat for himself, the president, Brain Trusters, and FDR's secretaries, one of whom, Marguerite (Missy) LeHand,[51] also served as the chief executive's faithful hostess when the First Lady was away. Knowing of her long association with FDR, which began with his vice-presidential run in 1920, Joe developed a friendly relationship with Missy, to whom he would send missives for the president. Kennedy leased a 125-acre Maryland estate on the Potomac River just outside Washington. The property included a thirty-three-room mansion with a hundred-seat movie theater and large pool, around which FDR and various guests enjoyed mint juleps, shared amusing anecdotes, and broke into song as the bourbon libation took hold. Rose Kennedy and the children not away at school remained in New York because their mother didn't want to uproot them from their classes, doctors, and orthodontists, who were creating those famous Kennedy smiles.[52] And, like Eleanor Roosevelt, she had suffered through her husband's dalliances and ended marital relations, particularly as a form of birth control after nine children. While she and Joe continued to express their love for each other in letters, and apparently enjoyed the brief interludes they spent together, distance offered them opportunity to live the separate lives they had fashioned for themselves, much as Eleanor and Franklin had.

Joe relished his relationship with the president—having dinner at the White House, sometimes accompanied by Rose when she came to town, and relaying information by phone directly to FDR about the Supreme Court's approval of his Emergency Banking Act and his 1933 decoupling of US currency from the gold standard. The Supreme Court's decisions caused the stock market to rise, which Joe celebrated with a brief vacation. He made a written record of his role in informing the president of the good news "because I feel the occasion is a historical one, and I feel that the opportunity of being the person to relay this information to the president would be of value historically to my family."[53]

FDR obliged Joe's intense feelings for his brood. When the SEC chairman called home from the White House to express felicitations to his youngest daughter, Jean, on making her First Holy Communion, the president came to the phone and spoke to the seven-year-old. He related that "her father was helping him tremendously but was sorry he could not be home." Rose thought the president's "voice [sounded] fascinating on the phone—so deep—so full, so resonant—Children all excited," she recorded in her diary.[54]

Young Jean Kennedy was not the only member of the family who received the favor of presidential attention. To Joe's seventh child, nine-year-old Bobby, FDR wrote that his dad "told me that you are a stamp collector, and I thought you might like to have these stamps to add to your collection." The president enclosed "a little album which you may find useful" and added, "Perhaps when you are in Washington you will come in and let me show you my collection."[55] Franklin so loved stamps that he worked with Postmaster General Jim Farley to design and issue new stamps featuring New Deal policies and historic landmarks.[56]

Rose always encouraged etiquette among her children, so back came an immediate thank-you note from Bobby to the president: "I liked the stamps you sent me very much and the little book is very useful. I am just starting my collection, and it would be great fun to see yours, which Mother says you have had for a long time. I am going to frame your letter, and I am going to keep it always in my room. Daddy, Mother, and all my brothers and sisters want to be remembered to you."[57] Rose had started her own collection of autographs as a teenager, acquiring Theodore Roosevelt's signature as a prized possession.[58] The last line of Bobby's note, with its mature formality, indicated that the Kennedy matriarch probably helped the nine-year-old, who was prone to misspellings and syntactical barbarisms.

The SEC chairman had been completely open with the president about wanting only a short tenure in the position. Always restless and anxious to move on to the next challenge, Joe never wanted to stay long in one place, especially when he found bureaucratic administration boring.[59] He submitted his resignation in September 1935, telling the president, "To discontinue my official relations with you is not an easy task. Rather it is one involving genuine regret assuaged only by the privilege of your friendship. As a chief you have been unfailingly considerate and stimulating. In the pioneer work of the Commission, my colleagues and I have had your wholehearted and enthusiastic support. Without your backing, our accomplishments for the protection of the investors would not have been possible." Kennedy reminded the president of "how deeply devoted I am to you personally and to the success of your administration." Even after leaving the SEC post, he would "still deem myself a part of your administration."[60]

Joe wanted the freedom to accompany Rose, Jack, and daughter Kathleen (Kick) to Europe. They would enroll JFK in the London School of Economics to follow in Joe Jr.'s footsteps, and Kick would attend a French convent school for a year outside Paris. After leaving the SEC, Joe received only kudos from the press for launching it toward investment reforms. The Kennedy patriarch would announce, not for the last time, that he was now leaving politics for good.[61] But that declaration by no means removed him from Roosevelt's orbit. Joe cabled the chief executive from London, "Don't worry about election in America. You could be elected anything in England. If the papers and businessmen of America gave you ten percent of the deal that they give you here, you would be president for the rest of your life. I am seeing everybody, and it is amazing your personal popularity, and I don't mean particularly in government circles."[62]

Returning from Europe, Joe headed for California and financial consultancy opportunities with RCA, Paramount Pictures, and the Hearst media business. Yet the siren song of politics seduced him as the 1936 campaign moved closer. He and the president had discussed a publication that Joe could produce about why businessmen should support the New Deal and a second Roosevelt term. Initially, its first draft appeared as a pamphlet ghostwritten by an SEC colleague, but Kennedy turned to his friend, *New York Times* columnist and Washington bureau chief Arthur Krock, to expand the length. The final version constituted a slim book, *I'm for Roosevelt,* listing Joe as the author. He sent a copy to the president, via Missy LeHand, and asked for the president's reaction. Kennedy continued to offer his services to FDR. *I'm for Roosevelt* became the foundation for spinoff articles in the popular press and fundraising dinners for the FDR campaign.[63] The secretary of commerce constructed a list of fifty businessmen who might be inclined to support the president's reelection effort, and the president forwarded it to Joe.

He was unimpressed and struggled with a way to be most productive in assisting FDR in his upcoming fight for a second term.[64]

Many conservative businessmen and their families, who saw Roosevelt as a socialist, couldn't even utter his name, labeling him "that man." In addition, FDR and his administration had earned the enmity of fascist "radio priest" Father Charles Coughlin, an anti-Semite who stoked fears among conservative Roman Catholics that Roosevelt's New Deal represented a "communist" foothold in American.[65] Perhaps because of their denominational kinship, Coughlin had described Joe as "a shining star among the dim 'knights'" of FDR's roundtable. Kennedy responded, "Wish you were with us," in a brief note to the demagogic cleric,[66] but Joe countered Coughlin's anticommunist screeds against FDR in a national radio broadcast. Eventually working full time for Roosevelt's campaign in fall 1936, Kennedy applied his Hollywood talents to assisting with production of a short film of the president and his family at Hyde Park and swimming with other polio survivors at Warm Springs, Georgia. "Despite inherited wealth and privileged position, he has somehow acquired the common touch that endears him to the common man," the narrator declared.[67]

FDR's landslide victory, with two-thirds of the popular vote over Alf Landan, proved that he had attracted more than enough support to garner a second term, despite Coughlin's attacks and the wrath of conservative business interests. Two days after the election, the president hosted Eugenio Cardinal Pacelli, the Vatican's secretary of state, at Hyde Park. FDR rewarded Joe for his support with an invitation to him and Rose to accompany the cardinal on a private railcar for the visit to the Roosevelt estate. After a luncheon at Springwood, the Kennedys welcomed Pacelli to their suburban New York City home for tea.[68]

Joe continued his close association with Jimmy Roosevelt, who sent him Brooks Brothers studs for Christmas in 1936. In his thank-you note, Kennedy asserted that he considered himself Jimmy's "foster-father."[69] Indeed, the two families were growing closer, as Joe and Rose's seven youngest children traveled to Washington for the president's 1937 inauguration, the first to be held in January as a result of the Constitution's Twentieth Amendment. The Kennedy clan attended a luncheon at the

White House and met Mrs. Roosevelt in the receiving line. Jimmy singled them out among the three thousand guests and took them for a chat with his father. FDR loved youngsters and always enjoyed bantering with them: "It is about time you came," he exclaimed. "How can I put my arm around any of you? Which is the oldest? You're all so big."[70]

Joe still longed for the treasury secretary slot, and his "foster-son" Jimmy thought he deserved a reward for supporting FDR. Louis Howe had died in 1936, and Franklin's eldest son tried to replace him the next year as a confidante in the role of secretary to his dad. Eleanor was "appalled," predicting (correctly) that the move would provoke charges of nepotism and corruption against her husband and son if critics thought Jimmy profited from the arrangement. "I protested vehemently to Franklin," ER wrote in her memoir, "and told him he was selfish to bring James down [to Washington]. I talked to James and tried to persuade him not to come, but he could see no objections." FDR "silenced" his wife's objections with the question cum proclamation, "Why should I be deprived of my eldest's son's help and of the pleasure of having him with me just because I am the president?"[71]

Franklin offered Joe another regulatory chair, this time at the new Maritime Commission, created under the 1936 Merchant Marine Act, to oversee US merchant shipping and the shipbuilding industry. The appointment, once the Senate was convinced that Kennedy's investments didn't constitute conflicts of interest, kept Joe cooling his heels for a more prestigious appointment.[72] Like his SEC tenure, however, this role also suited his business acumen. His background in management of the Fore River shipyard during World War I added a bonus credential. His tenure at the helm of the new Maritime Commission revealed his bureaucratic acumen in administering the merchant marine industry and government contracts. Even more impressive to President Roosevelt was Kennedy's support for FDR's ill-conceived court-packing scheme to counter the conservative justices' opposition to New Deal policies.[73] The plan, which most Americans never supported, despite their overwhelming vote for Roosevelt's second term, proved how far the president had moved beyond the vox populi.[74]

The president and Jimmy discussed the next role for Kennedy after his successful year as chair of the Maritime Commission. "We've got to do something for old Joe, but I don't know what," the president confided to his son. "He wants what he can't have [treasury], but there must be something we can give him he'll be happy with."[75] Jimmy recalled, "Father was not going to remove Henry Morgenthau from office. Father did not tell Joe in so many words, but in time it became clear to him." Aside from loyalty to a Hyde Park neighbor, FDR believed that "Joe would want to run the treasury in his own way, contrary to my plans and views."[76]

FDR deputed his son to discuss Kennedy's wishes if the cabinet wasn't to be his destination. Joe surprised the president's assistant with the declaration, "I'd like to be ambassador to England." "I really liked Joe," Jimmy remembered, "but he was a crusty old cuss, and I couldn't picture him as an ambassador, especially to England." The president's response to Joe's request? He "laughed so hard he almost toppled out of this wheelchair," Jimmy recorded.[77]

Although Joe seemed an unlikely candidate for such a prestigious and crucial assignment, given that he was neither a diplomat by experience nor personality, Franklin saw the potentially helpful qualities that Joe did possess as Europe careened toward war. What better person to understand the economic factors at play and their impact on the geopolitical and military variables? Jimmy told Kennedy in early December 1937 that the president would name him to the ambassadorship he so craved.[78]

One more hurdle remained prior to the actual nomination. Jimmy arrived at Kennedy's rented Maryland estate to inform Joe that the president had changed his mind and now wanted him to be secretary of commerce. Kennedy was enraged and told the president's son that the London post was "the only one" he would accept. Despite pushback from presidential advisors who mistrusted Joe and abhorred his arrogance, FDR moved forward with the appointment of Kennedy to be the US ambassador to the Court of St. James's.[79]

Just before Christmas, Joe began to alert friends that "under the law of inherent probability," FDR would appoint him ambassador to Great

Britain. He wanted to live up to the progress made by "the Irish lads in America"; Joe wrote "that only by giving my best efforts can I keep faith with my dear father and mother." He began using the phrase "hostage to fortune" to describe his children and how he might have an impact on history that would shape their future. "My only personal satisfaction is that I will leave the heritage to them that I did the best I could for a great nation."[80] He couldn't have known that always putting his family first (out of concern for their financial and physical well-being) would warp his vision of foreign policy by reinforcing his embrace of isolationism and would eventually place him at odds with the president. Upon Senate confirmation, his wire to FDR, expressing gratitude, was all too prophetic on its first point: "I don't know what kind of diplomat I shall be, probably rotten, but I promise to get done for you those things that you want done."[81] It was Kennedy's "rotten" tenure that would color Eleanor's view of him and Jack for the next two decades.

On February 18, 1938, in FDR's private White House office, Supreme Court Associate Justice Stanley Reed swore Joseph P. Kennedy Sr. in for the most consequential ambassadorial post in the US diplomatic corps. Four days later, just before sailing for London, he joined Franklin, Eleanor, Sara, and Betsey Roosevelt for a farewell lunch at Hyde Park, where the president and Ambassador Kennedy discussed foreign policy, British politics, and the Anglo-American alliance.[82]

Jimmy came to Joe's shipboard cabin to bid farewell.[83] The ambassador wrote one his first letters to him from London, marked "Personal and Confidential," about his initial impressions of England. He remarked that the English economy was "as dangerous as ours was in 1929," and he made a prediction ("We're headed for the ashcan") that would haunt him for the rest of his life when the press published a similar statement he would utter in 1940. His political and economic prognostications about the United States never came to pass, but his conclusion to Jimmy would color Joe's entire tenure in England: "Tell the boss that, leaving aside the Kennedy family, there are two things I am for—the USA and FDR, and you can put that last paragraph on the last letter I write when I leave here."[84] Prioritizing his family over the country meant that he would run afoul of the president's eventual policy toward the brewing world war.

The Kennedy patriarch had sailed alone for England while Rose recovered from an emergency appendectomy, but she arrived in London with five of their children (Kick, Pat, Bobby, Jean, and Teddy), appropriately on St. Patrick's Day. Joe Jr. and Jack remained at Harvard to complete the spring term, and their father would accompany them to England after his summer trip to the United States. Rosemary, who needed special supervision because of her intellectual challenges, arrived in April with sister Eunice. The Kennedys never wanted to draw attention to Rosemary's special needs, and they would do their best to "mainstream" her when feasible. She, Kick, and Rose were formally presented to King George VI and Queen Elizabeth, the Queen Mother, in May 1938, at Buckingham Palace. Dowager Duchess of Devonshire Deborah Mitford remarked that the family made a sensation when they all gathered in London "because no diplomat had ever arrived with nine children attached." As *Life* magazine enthused about the handsome brood, they were "the most politically ingratiating family since Theodore Roosevelt's."[85]

The two youngest of Franklin and Eleanor's five offspring, Franklin Jr. and John, captured headlines and newsreels with their respective marriages in the summers of 1937 and 1938. They were the hit of the Northeastern establishment's social seasons. Their older siblings had made less joyous headlines with marital breakups early in the Roosevelt presidency. Elliott divorced his first wife after only one year in 1933, abandoning her and their infant son to find his future out West. Anna left her first husband, with whom she had two children, and lived in the White House until 1935, when she married a reporter whom she had met on her father's 1932 campaign train. The towheaded children, Anna and Curtis, nicknamed Sistie and Buzzie, were media stars and appeared in photos with child actress Shirley Temple, who visited them at Val-Kill.[86]

While the photogenic Kennedy family dominated newspaper society columns, magazine photo spreads, and newsreels at home and abroad with admiring stories, many Brits were less enamored of Joe's early diplomatic efforts. With FDR's approval, his secretary of state Cordell Hull had warned Ambassador Kennedy to "avoid the extremes of isolationism and internationalism."[87] But strong-willed Joe veered toward noninterventionism in his first public speech. Kennedy the businessman saw everything through the lens of a financier and stock trader. He wanted to make the world safe for American capitalism, which he had mastered with demonstrable success, and he tried to will the United States away from a lengthy world war that might put his three oldest sons' lives at risk. He also had designs on becoming the first Catholic president and preparing his sons to carry on his legacy not in business but in a powerful political dynasty. Isolationism not only reflected Kennedy's *Weltanschauung* but his accurate understanding of American public opinion that opposed US involvement in another global war. Thus, if he harbored presidential ambitions for the 1940 Democratic nomination, when FDR faced the traditional two-term limit, aligning with the electorate made strategic sense. "The [March 1938] speech was intended primarily for home consumption," he confided to his diary, "as I am very anxious that my friends there should not think I have gone over to the British."[88]

Kennedy and Prime Minister Neville Chamberlain, whose name would become synonymous with appeasement when he acceded to Hitler's demands for the Sudetenland in September 1938's Munich Pact, developed a mutual admiration through their common goal of avoiding war. It was one thing to speak theoretically about nonintervention in Europe's dilemma over the rise of Hitler's, Mussolini's, and Franco's fascism, but quite another to make Kennedy's pronouncement in a public speech that fall. The ambassador provoked a major uproar when he revealed that "it has long been a theory of mine that it is unproductive for both the democratic and dictator countries to widen the divisions now existing between them by emphasizing their differences, which are now self-apparent. . . . After all, we have to live in the same world." Joe was simply asserting that democracies had no obligation to thwart dictatorships and that free societies shouldn't let "these differences [with authoritarian regimes] grow into unrelenting antagonisms."[89]

American isolationists agreed, and they formed a potent, if unlikely, faction of conservative businessmen, left-wing pacifists, Midwestern farmers, and Northeastern intellectuals.[90] They knew that the Japanese Empire had invaded Manchuria in 1931; Mussolini conquered Ethiopia in 1935; Germany reoccupied the Rhineland in 1936 and perpetrated war crimes with indiscriminate bombing of Guernica, Spain, on behalf of

Franco's fascists in 1937; and Hitler seized Austria that same year. The Fuhrer's deprivation of civil rights for Jews, Catholics, Jehovah's Witnesses, Romani, communists, gays, the disabled, single and childless women, and anyone else he deemed "abnormal" alarmed internationalists and human rights advocates. How would the world respond if he began expanding the Third Reich into western Europe, with his military sights set on the British Isles? Still two years away from becoming British prime minister, Winston Churchill's response to the disastrous Munich Pact made the case for intervention: "The whole equilibrium of Europe has been deranged. . . . This is only the beginning."[91]

As an internationalist promoting peace after World War I, Eleanor was far ahead of Franklin in encouraging collective security among free nations against totalitarians. Yet just as race issues would find them on different paths because FDR had to placate Southerners, foreign policy disputes meant that he had to consider strong isolationist sentiments in Congress and across the country. This political fact had prompted Secretary of State Hull to caution Kennedy about extremes of either isolationism or interventionism. ER had been pleased when her husband made a speech in October 1937 calling for a "quarantine" to protect nations from the war "contagion." She wanted more and bolstered his speech by advocating diplomatic opposition to aggressor nations. Her husband's appointment of Kennedy to the UK ambassadorship perplexed Eleanor. She just didn't trust Joe, who she believed was duplicitous—sycophantic toward FDR only to achieve the financier's own ambitions. When she inquired about her husband's decision to appoint "that awful Joe Kennedy," FDR reportedly laughed about the joke he had perpetrated by naming "an Irishman to the Court of St. James's."[92]

ER surely found nothing amusing about Kennedy's public statements once he landed in England. They only confirmed her fears about his isolationism. Moreover, he allied with pro-German Nancy Astor's Clivedon Set. Astor's and Kennedy's shared anti-Semitism and belief that Hitler's fascism would counter communism's spread fostered their friendship, despite her well-known anti-Catholicism.[93]

Joe's association with isolationist Charles Lindbergh, who courted Hitler and accepted an honor for assisting the Reich, especially repelled

Eleanor.[94] Just before Chamberlain infamously declared that he had achieved "peace in our time" by appeasing Hitler at Munich, Lindbergh and his wife, Anne, paid a visit to Joe and Rose at the embassy. Charles declared over lunch that "Germany could turn out dozens of planes to England's one."[95]

Eleanor also disagreed with her husband and his ambassador to England on US policy surrounding the Spanish Civil War. Like other progressives in the Democratic Party and the leftist youth leaders whom ER had befriended, she abhorred Franco's designs to establish a fascist dictatorship. She supported the Loyalist freedom fighters and International Brigades who opposed him.[96] "While I often felt strongly on various subjects," she wrote in 1949, "Franklin frequently refrained from supporting causes in which he believed, because of political realities. There were times when this annoyed me very much. In the case of the Spanish Civil War, for instance, we had to remain neutral, though Franklin knew quite well he wanted the democratic government [in Spain] to be successful. But he knew he could not get Congress to go along with him."[97] The 1937 Neutrality Act, which FDR had signed—"reluctantly," according to his wife—precluded sending arms to the freedom fighters in Spain.[98]

Joe Kennedy assisted Sacred Heart nuns, from the same religious order that taught his wife and daughters, to escape Spain after air raids by Gen. Francisco Franco's Nationalist forces killed six of the sisters.[99] But Kennedy's religion and anticommunist ideology wouldn't allow him to counter the fascist pro-Catholic perpetrators of the Spanish Civil War. ER's fellow internationalist, Secretary of the Interior Harold Ickes, encountered religion's political role in FDR's calculus regarding that war. The president told him "frankly that to raise the embargo would mean the loss of every Catholic vote next fall and that the Democratic members of Congress were jittery about it and didn't want it done." Ickes observed that "the Catholic minorities in Great Britain and America have been dictating the international policy with respect to Spain."[100] FDR's fears about the 1938 midterm elections were valid. His attempt to purge the Democratic Party of its more conservative members, particularly from the South, backfired. Although the president's party still held a majority in Congress, it lost eight seats in the Senate and eighty-two in the House.[101]

The same Catholic-centric force that would drive Joe Kennedy's support of Sen. Joe McCarthy's "Red Scare" tactics in the 1950s had its roots in his view of Franco's anticommunist regime fifteen years earlier. As ER warned after observing that opponents of labor unions and Black and Jewish Americans labelled all of them communists, "People have reached a point where anything which will save them from communism is a godsend; and, if fascism or Nazism promises more security than our own democracy, we may even turn to them."[102]

It's a wonder that Eleanor could abide Ambassador Kennedy's visit to Hyde Park in June 1938 for a consultation with her husband. She found Joe's descriptions of Rose's friendship with the queen amusing,[103] but, appropriately, the First Lady wouldn't have discussed details of foreign policy with the president and his envoy. Their meeting seemed cordial enough, so press rumors that a rift had opened between the two puzzled Joe, particularly when he heard that the White House had planted the rumor. After returning to London on July 4, with Joe Jr. and Jack in tow, the ambassador believed that "deep within me I knew something had happened" to his relationship with the president.[104] He was right.

Jack's arrival in London during Harvard's 1938 summer break, and the opportunity to serve as his father's secretary over the next few months, would prove a turning point in his intellectual maturation, allowing him to develop his own public policy views and eventually the confidence to depart from his father's perspectives. JFK absorbed international debates as the world moved closer to war, traveled through Europe, and gathered research for his senior thesis on England's unpreparedness to fight Hitler. Although it could reflect Jack's attempt to defend his father's position that Britain would fail to withstand Germany's inevitable onslaught, the thesis argued that democracies, subject to popular will, often respond too slowly to outside threats. Harvard's Pulitzer Prize–winning Kennedy biographer Fredrik Logevall asserts, "Not every undergraduate thesis can truly be called an original contribution to knowledge, but Jack's fit the bill."[105] When it was published in 1940, after stylistic edits from Arthur Krock, who also suggested its title,

Why England Slept,[106] Jack sent an inscribed copy to FDR. "To President Roosevelt, With sincere regards, Jack Kennedy," he wrote on the flyleaf, to which the president added his name.[107]

ER's friend Marion Dickerman returned from England with firsthand reports of Joe's unconcerned attitude toward the privations European Jews were suffering. His expression of admiration for Hitler appalled Eleanor's friend, as did his view that US Jews would have to provide funds for their coreligionists to emigrate to Africa and America. Dickerman's visit with the ambassador "left a very unpleasant feeling in my mind in regard to Mr. Kennedy."[108] Unfortunately, his views about Jews attempting to flee Hitler's grasp squared with the State Department's, as well as with a majority in Congress. ER's efforts, along with those of her cohorts in the American Friends Service Committee, to move the Roosevelt administration toward a pro-refugee policy proved ineffective.[109] Emboldened by the democratic nations' unresponsiveness to Britain's appeasement policy or Germany's reign of terror against Jews on Kristallnacht in November 1938, Hitler increased persecution and inched closer to what would develop into the "final solution" during World War II, a genocide against Jews throughout Germany and the territories he had conquered.[110]

As tensions rose over Hitler's next move after Munich, Joe lost one of his conduits to the president when a medical crisis forced Jimmy Roosevelt's departure from the White House. Eleanor, who had thought the strains of working for his father would overwhelm her eldest son, saw her fear materialize when Jimmy underwent serious abdominal surgery for bleeding ulcers at the Mayo Clinic in September 1938. Jimmy's physicians and family believed that the heavy workload of a presidential secretary and the conflicts with other advisers (who called him the "crown prince" and "assistant president") had pushed young Roosevelt to the breaking point. He had to leave the White House, regain his health, and try to restore (unsuccessfully) his marriage to Betsey, which had also suffered from his unrelenting schedule.[111]

Following the Kennedys' 1938 visit with Cardinal Pacelli, FDR named Joe the president's personal representative to the prelate's coronation as Pope Pius XII in March 1939. All the Kennedys except Joe Jr., who was observing the Spanish Civil War, convened in Rome for the joyous occasion, and young Teddy became the first child to receive his First Holy Communion from the new pope. Yet President Roosevelt's State Department excluded his ambassador to Britain from participating in the triumphant royal visit of King George VI and Queen Elizabeth when they traveled to the United States in summer 1939. It was the ultimate ceremonial slight for Joe and revealed his lowered status via-à-vis FDR. Eleanor invited Rose, enjoying a summer break at Hyannis Port, to join events for the royals, but she declined, saying that her parents would find her early departure from Cape Cod disappointing. Perhaps Mrs. Kennedy's real reason for sending regrets to the First Lady involved sensitivity to her husband's snub by the administration. If he couldn't participate in welcoming the king and queen to the United States, neither would his spouse. FDR's demotion of Joe Kennedy in ceremonial affairs reflected the president's increasing lack of confidence in the ambassador, evidenced by Roosevelt's bypassing him at every opportunity.[112]

Later that summer, the entire Kennedy clan assembled on the French Riviera for what would be their last prewar holiday, but their vacation ended abruptly with news that Germany and the Soviet Union had signed a nonaggression treaty on August 23, 1939. It appeared that Hitler's next target would be Poland. Joe hurried back to London and prepared to send his family packing for home. On September 3, 1939, two days after Hitler invaded Poland, Prime Minister Chamberlain announced that Britain was now at war. "I almost cried," the usually stoic Joe confided to his diary. "I had participated very closely in this struggle, and I saw my hopes crash, too."[113] Not only had his and Chamberlain's appeasement strategy failed to keep the peace, but it also fed the Hitlerian beast.

Yet Ambassador Kennedy continued to maintain his position that fascism and communism would be the dynamic and, therefore, triumphant forces in Europe. The United States couldn't prop up the crumbling British Empire, but it could accept "leadership of the

English-speaking world," he wrote to FDR in late September 1939. Our "vital interests" didn't lie in Europe but rather in the Western Hemisphere, Joe concluded.[114]

When Churchill replaced Chamberlain as prime minister in May 1940 and became Britain's inspirational wartime leader, Joe now had no ally at 10 Downing Street. He threatened to resign.[115] The Dunkirk debacle seemed to prove Joe's point that the British couldn't match the Third Reich's Wehrmacht. When the Luftwaffe launched the Battle of Britain in June 1940, it initially appeared that Lindbergh's prediction about England's air inferiority might come to pass. While dodging German bombs raining down on London and the English countryside, Ambassador Kennedy found himself a diplomatic outcast at home and abroad. He was grateful that his family was safe in the United States, but he missed them in this troubling and uncertain time. While most American ambassadors to European countries had headed home, Joe hung on. "I don't want to do anything that that would reflect [poorly] on the family," he reasoned. "After all that is why we went into this [ambassadorship], and I don't want to spoil it."[116]

But he was spoiling it with his insistence that the United States remain on the sidelines, while FDR moved as far toward helping Britain as domestic politics would allow. To Clare Boothe Luce, *Life* magazine editor Henry Luce's wife and Joe Kennedy's occasional paramour, the ambassador expressed a threat to turn "25 million Catholic voters" toward the Republican candidate, Wendell Willkie, in the 1940 presidential race.[117] Rose wrote to Joe that his former legal counsel at the SEC and Maritime Commission, John Burns, thought that the president "does not want you home before the election due to your explosive—defeatist, point of view, as you might so easily throw a bomb, which would explode sufficiently to upset his chances."[118]

Yet the shrewd president knew exactly how to handle the volatile Kennedy. Summoning him to the United States for "some relief" from the Blitz and to learn his "last reactions with regard to the war in England," the president specifically asked Joe "not to make any statement to the press on your way over nor when you arrive in New York until you and I have had a chance to agree upon what should be said." He ordered his ambassador to "come straight through to Washington . . . since I will want to talk to you as soon as you get here."[119]

To diffuse a potentially strained visit, FDR invited Joe and Rose to spend the night at the White House.[120] Joe joined the president for cocktails in his study. The Kennedys, Sen. Jimmy Byrnes of South Carolina, and his wife then gathered for an informal dinner with FDR. Byrnes lobbied Joe to deliver a radio address supporting the president's bid for an unprecedented third term, while Roosevelt turned on the charm for Rose, reminiscing about her beloved father, Honey Fitz. After Joe vented over being supplanted by the president's surrogates in London, the Kennedys both agreed to endorse FDR with radio addresses just before election day.[121] Eleanor, never surprised at the impact of her husband's charm, pondered what deal he forged with Kennedy to earn his endorsement. Claire Luce maintained that Kennedy exacted a promise from the president to support an eventual run by Joe Jr. for the Massachusetts governorship.[122] If true, the promise would have required FDR to overlook the fact that young Joe, as a delegate to the 1940 Democratic Convention, had supported Postmaster General Farley over Roosevelt for the nomination.[123]

Joe's radio endorsement explained his case against war hinged on the welfare of his family, but he now tied his "nine hostages to fortune" to a victory for Roosevelt. Rose picked up the theme with reference to her four boys. "Like all of you American mothers," she implored, "I want to vote for a president, who will keep your boys and mine out of war and will make this country so strong in its defense, that never again will I have to see gas masks on my children, as I did in London. . . . Therefore, on next Tuesday I feel I have a solemn duty to my sons and to all the sons of all the mothers of America to vote for Franklin Roosevelt and the road to peace." It appears that Rose deleted a sexist passage from her statement, which began, "It is impossible for me to understand all of the issues of the campaign." Although it is unclear who drafted her endorsement, she obviously felt uncomfortable with the deprecating reference to herself. She was no Eleanor Roosevelt, deeply immersed in public policy, but she understood issues, and she certainly possessed an intuitive feel for politics.[124]

The president not only neutered Joe's potential public criticism, but FDR also won two important endorsements that resonated with Catholic men and women alike. And the coup de grace? Joe used his family's money to pay for radio time on 114 CBS radio affiliates. The president embraced the Kennedys' "family values" theme, announcing at his Boston Garden rally, attended by Jack and Honey Fitz, "Your boys will not be sent into any foreign wars."[125] Prior to Pearl Harbor, isolationism still required explicit deference, at least right before an election.

Yet the war that Kennedy so hoped to elude for his family, fortune, and country crept closer with Joe Jr.'s report from Harvard Law School that he would like to enlist in the Navy Air Corps. With his dad's controversial "stand on the war" and Jack not yet in the service, the eldest Kennedy offspring, now twenty-five, thought "people will wonder what the devil I'm doing back at school with everyone else working for national defense." He assured his father that "as far as danger is concerned, it doesn't bother me very much. . . . As far as the family is concerned, it seems that Jack is perfectly capable to do everything, if by chance anything happened to me."[126]

A day after FDR defeated Willkie, with 73 percent of the Catholic vote in the North, Joe submitted his resignation as ambassador to England. He cited "personal affairs" as reason for wanting to relinquish his title and thanked the president for the opportunity to serve him, "our country and the cause of world peace."[127] On December 1, Joe met with Franklin, who asked him to remain in the United States but keep the ambassadorial title until he named a successor. Kennedy's press release declared that he would "devote his efforts to . . . help the president keep the United States out of the war," which Kennedy believed was the best way to preserve "the American form of democracy."[128] A few days later, while visiting Boston, Kennedy dropped a bombshell—not on the president but on himself. The media explosion he unleashed destroyed his political career. He would have to fulfill his ambitions through his sons.

Thinking that an interview for the *Boston Daily Globe* was off the record, Joe expounded on his views regarding the war and its impact. He admitted that he was viewed as a "pessimist," but he wondered what could justify optimism. "Democracy is all done," he declared. When the reporter asked if he meant in England or the United States, the ambassador initially responded, "Well, I don't know." But then he opined, "If we get into war it will be in this country, too. A bureaucracy would take over right off. Everything we hold dear would be gone. They tell me that after 1918 we got it all back again. But this is different. There's a different patter in the world." He thought the rise of British labor signaled a movement toward "national socialism," which to him meant that "democracy is finished in England. It may be here [in the United States]. Because it comes to a question of feeding people. It's all an economic question. I told the president in the White House last Sunday, 'Don't send me fifty admirals and generals. Send me a dozen real economists.' It's the loss of foreign trade that's going to threaten to change our form of government. We haven't felt the pinch of it yet. It's ahead of us."[129] Kennedy the businessman once again overtook Kennedy the ambassador.

As if Joe's lack of diplomacy about America's future wasn't damaging enough, the reporter baited him by asking his opinion of Eleanor Roosevelt. Knowing that many conservatives, like Kennedy himself, found her politics unacceptable and her role in the administration beyond the normal bounds of an unaccountable First Lady, the journalist might have been surprised at what should have remained Joe's complete answer: "She's another wonderful woman. And marvelously helpful and full of sympathy." But then Harvard Law School Dean James Landis entered the room to meet with Kennedy. "Jim will tell you," remarked Joe, "that she bothered us more on our jobs in Washington to take care of the poor little nobodies who hadn't any influence, than all the rest of the people down there together. She's always sending me a note to have some little 'Susie Glotz' to tea at the embassy."[130] Note the Jewish surname, Glotz, that Kennedy assigned to his fictional character—not "Suzy Q," or "Suzy Smith or Jones,"—as if he wanted to link Eleanor to her support for European Jews.

To Joe's surprise—and everlasting regret—the interview appeared on the *Globe*'s front page and then ran in newspapers around the country and in Britain to withering criticism. The president took the high road, choosing not to excoriate Kennedy in public, but he told his cabinet that Joe clearly wanted to inflict "damage" on the administration. Eleanor, too, confined criticism of her detractor to private correspondence with a friend, to whom she wrote that Kennedy "has always been a pessimist and always wrong, so I do not worry very much. I do, however, hate to see any American want to make peace with Hitler by being short-sighted enough to think Hitler would ever keep his word."[131]

Even in his circumscribed role as an ambassador just waiting for the president to nominate his successor, Kennedy took every opportunity to fire his parting shots. He began by sending regrets to an invitation to attend the 1941 inauguration luncheon at the White House. How a mere four years had changed the Kennedys' relationship to the Roosevelts, when the president's family had welcomed the Irish American clan to the 1937 festivities. Joe's January 1941 trip to Washington was triggered by a request to appear before the House of Representatives Foreign Relations Committee. Hamilton Fish, a Republican isolationist who represented FDR's home congressional district in New York, wanted Kennedy to oppose the president's Lend-Lease legislation that would allow the commander in chief to disperse "any defense article" to any country the president deemed crucial to the United States' own defense.[132]

FDR asked Kennedy to meet with him before testifying on Capitol Hill, and the usual playacting between the two forceful personalities resumed in the unlikely venue of the president's bathroom, while he shaved. The symbolism of Joe being assigned to perch on the toilet seat while he complained to the chief executive of mistreatment by the press and his administration surely wasn't lost on the president, who relished bringing self-important figures down a peg. Under no circumstances would FDR apologize to Kennedy, but he did commiserate, saying that "no one had received worse treatment than he had in the last years" and that his son Elliott had taken considerable flak from the press over his marital escapades and his recent Army Air Corp Reserve captain's commission, despite his abysmal eyesight and dearth of flying experience. Joe responded that attacks on him came from "both sides"—the media and the president's own advisors. According to Kennedy's diary, FDR agreed both with that assessment and with Joe's desire to make a farewell radio speech. On policy, the ambassador told his boss that he "was all for aid to Britain short of going to war," but he thought the

Lend-Lease bill, if rammed through Congress by presidential force, "would leave a very bad taste."[133]

Jack, between his Harvard graduation and enlisting in the Navy, had enrolled in business courses at Stanford and travelled to South America, but he also served as an advisor to his father. He cautioned him against making an embittered attack on the press and urged him to counter "appeaser" charges but not use the "a-word," so frequently associated with his dad. As biographer David Nasaw has observed, however, Joe "was too stubborn, too proud, and too loyal to the master appeaser Neville Chamberlain, to do this. Instead, he tried to deflect criticism by redefining the term" in his radio speech to the nation on January 18, 1941.[134] Paradoxically, young Jack's discernment in counselling his father couldn't convince the obstinate parent to retreat from his increasingly unpopular views or absolve the son of his father's sins when JFK entered politics.

Joe's position on Lend-Lease, both in his speech and in his testimony before the House committee, was inscrutable. He rambled, he dissembled, he self-contradicted, he avoided unequivocal support of the president, and he treated congressmen with disdain.[135] Kennedy only confirmed the stereotype he always feared elites applied to him: that of the aggressive and arrogant Irish American from immigrant roots, on the make but rising to the level of his own incompetence.

Joe appreciated the supportive letter Anna Roosevelt Boettiger and her husband John sent him. Yet he undoubtedly stepped on toes with his response that the "hatchet men" who worked for Anna's father "were great contributors toward my difficulty." His self-pity oozed from the page:

> I didn't think it was fair to wind up seven years in service to his administration with a bad record, and I had gone in for everything he wanted, and this time I had to do something for the Kennedy family. . . . Now if my statements and my position mean that, outside of the ever-loyal Boettigers, I am to be a social outcast by the administration, well so be it. I will be sorry, but, if that's the way it is, it's just too bad. I will, at least, have the satisfaction of having fulfilled my obligations.[136]

He could never accept that, as he predicted to FDR at the outset of his ambassadorship, he had been a "rotten" diplomat. He had pledged to accomplish the president's goals, but he failed in that attempt as well.

With the appointment of his successor, John Winant, Kennedy's tenure at the Court of St. James's officially ended in February 1941. The First Lady and her New Deal colleagues, especially labor supporters like Frances Perkins, promoted Winant's candidacy. Although a Republican, Winant, while New Hampshire's governor, had been such a staunch advocate of the New Deal's Civilian Conservation Corps that FDR named him the first director of the Social Security Board. Before his ambassadorship, he had served as the head of the International Labor Organization in Geneva. Unlike Kennedy's steely noninterventionist demeanor in the face of Britain's war efforts, Ambassador Winant's empathetic humanity proved a tonic for Anglo-American relations.[137] "He was an extraordinary human being," ER commented two decades later.[138]

What began for the entire Kennedy family as a fairy-tale journey to England in 1938 ended with the onset of World War II and created a deep schism between FDR and Joe Kennedy that would taint Eleanor's view of Jack for two more decades. Ambassador Kennedy's isolationism, pessimism toward the viability of British and American democracy, and lack of sympathy for Europe's Jewish refugees soured the First Lady on the Kennedy patriarch and ultimately his son. Her social anti-Semitism, so common among Gentiles and revealed in her 1918 letters to Sara Delano Roosevelt, remained in the distant past.[139]

Joe Kennedy, who proudly used the ambassador title for the rest of his life, had returned to the position he'd always despised from his earliest days as an upstart businessman; he was again on the outside looking in. His public remarks consisted primarily of commencement speeches, where he diluted his anti-interventionist rhetoric that had cost him his future political career. Just after the Japanese attack on Pearl Harbor, he wired FDR: "Name the battle post. I'm yours to command," but the president didn't respond.[140] When he hadn't heard from the commander in chief by March 1942, Kennedy sent him a copy of his December 7, 1941, telegram. Joe felt even more sidelined with Joe Jr. and

Jack in uniform, but the president never offered a position that appealed to Joe's interest or vanity, even after he pleaded his case personally at the White House in April 1942.[141] By the summer of '43, Kennedy told Lord Beaverbrook that he had no more "desire for public office," and his only concern was Joe's and Jack's political careers, if they chose to pursue them after the war.[142]

Meanwhile, both Joe and Rose spent time and psychic energy on Kick's determination to marry a British nobleman, Billy Hartington, heir to the Cavendish dukedom. His deep roots in the Anglican Church meant that he and Kick couldn't marry in a Roman Catholic ceremony. Joe pledged his support, but his more devout wife virtually disowned their daughter when Kick and Billy married in a London registry civil ceremony. Joe Jr., who was stationed in England, accompanied his sister to the nuptials in May 1944. Meanwhile, Rose landed in a Boston hospital with nervous exhaustion. The Roman Catholic Church didn't recognize such mixed marriages. Therefore, under Catholic dogma, Billy and Kick were living in sin, and the new bride could no longer receive the church's sacraments, including communion.[143]

Yet fate would make these concerns pale in contrast to what the war wrought upon the Kennedy family from August 1943 to September 1944. Jack went missing in action when the PT boat he skippered took a direct collision from a Japanese destroyer while patrolling one moonless night in the Solomon Islands. Miraculously, the lieutenant (j.g.) saved all but two of his crew and led them to rescue after a week of dodging the Japanese from island to island. The joyous news of Jack's survival and heroism, which his father ensured the media trumpeted, sustained the family until one year later, when the Navy informed the Kennedys that Joe Jr. had been lost over the coast of England when his plane exploded. Although he had flown enough missions to return home, he volunteered for a secret mission to pilot a bomber packed with explosives toward Nazi V-2 rocket launchers on the French coast. He was to bail out, and then remote control would guide the pilotless plane, now a missile, to the target. Before Joe could exit, the plane blew up, leaving no trace of the twenty-nine-year-old pilot.[144]

The president sent a brief condolence message to the devastated Kennedy patriarch: "Dear Joe: On my way back to Washington, I heard of your great sorrow and wish it were in my power to say a word that would lighten your burden of grief. I do want you to know that I am thinking of you and offer you and all the members of your family this assurance of heartfelt sympathy in which Mrs. Roosevelt joins. Always sincerely, Franklin D. Roosevelt."[145]

Barely a month later, word arrived at Ambassador Kennedy's New York office that his new son-in-law, Billy, had died instantly from a Nazi sniper's bullet to the heart, suffered while leading his Coldstream Guards in fierce fighting through Belgium. FDR wired Joe asking him to tell Kick, a widow at twenty-five, that he was "thinking of her in her crushing sorrow" and that he and Mrs. Roosevelt conveyed their "heartfelt sympathy."[146] Although Ambassador Kennedy's foreign policy proved out of step with the eventual US strategy to defeat fascism, his desire to avoid war at all costs to elude his family's ultimate sacrifice attested to his prophetic insight.

Joe Jr.'s death would have been hard enough to accept without his father's belief that it hadn't been "for a great cause," but as "a result of the stupidity of our generation. The one thing he did die a martyr to was his own conscience. He wanted to do the right thing because it was his idea of the thing to do, and for that—and that alone—he died. That is the satisfaction . . . I will always have," Joe Sr. explained.[147] But it was little consolation for losing his cherished first-born child, in whom he had placed all his hopes and dreams for the family's legacy. "I find it very difficult to get over Joe's death," he mused. "It does seem ironical that somebody who opposed the war as bitterly as I did should lose his oldest son, his son-in-law, and have his second son badly banged up."[148]

The Kennedy-Roosevelt rift didn't preclude the president's reaching out to his former ambassador in the runup to 1944's election. Grace Tully, who had replaced Missy LeHand, phoned Kennedy in October to inquire how the family was coping with its tragedies. She told Joe that the president wanted to meet with him. As bitter as ever, especially now that the war had taken such a disastrous toll on his family and its future, he had no confidence in the Roosevelt administration, which he believed had treated him so poorly, or the president, whose health had declined precipitously. Having heard from others about how dreadful the president looked in person, Joe nevertheless found him in a worse condition than he had imagined. At age sixty-three, FDR, always so robust, despite his paralysis, now suffered from congestive heart failure, unbeknownst to the public, and he displayed every symptom of the disease: gray skin tone, palsied hands, shortness of breath, gaunt appearance, and difficulty speaking.[149] Of course, Eleanor had seen these worrisome signs of Franklin's decline but simply couldn't believe he would fail to overcome this illness as he had polio.[150]

Joe took his opportunity of meeting with the president to complain that Jack had been denied a medal that was "two degrees higher than what he finally received. He was reduced by [Admiral William] Halsey's group for reasons unknown to me, but which I suspect were because I was persona non grata to the powers that be in Washington—the result being that he received only the same honor that members of his [PT 109] crew received." Once again, FDR tried to deflect Joe's complaints by commiseration, noting his son Elliott had been denied the Medal of Honor and a promotion to general because of his father.[151]

Ambassador Kennedy took one more parting shot, expressing yet again his bitterness toward the president's "group" and how they had failed to accept his offer of service over the last four years. In telling Joe that he would be concluding his fourth presidential election campaign in Boston, was the president hinting that Kennedy could agree to stand with him there to show support? That's what Joe presumed, and he took vengeful delight in not responding to the president's implicit request. Franklin told the next visitor about his disappointment at not receiving a commitment from the prickly Kennedy. Joe reported that he "couldn't come out for Roosevelt, when I have so little confidence in what they do." According to the former ambassador, vice-presidential candidate Harry Truman "begged" him to make a speech advocating a fourth FDR term, though Kennedy recorded that the Missouri senator believed the president wouldn't live much longer. At their meeting, Joe claimed, Truman also told him that he "disliked Mrs. Roosevelt very much and that she had snubbed him when she was out West."[152]

In Truman's version of the encounter, related some fifteen years later in a controversial oral history, Kennedy railed at him, "Harry, what the hell are you doing campaigning for that crippled son of a bitch that killed my son Joe." Truman claimed that he responded, "If you say another word about Roosevelt, I'm going to throw you out that window." When an aide took him aside to say they needed $10,000 from Kennedy for the campaign and to keep him from badmouthing the president publicly, Truman calmed himself.[153] They achieved both of their goals and succeeded in making Joe think a future Truman administration might call him back to service.

Truman's prognostication about FDR's longevity proved accurate. He assumed the presidency upon Roosevelt's death from a cerebral hemorrhage on April 12, 1945, barely three months after the inauguration. Joe wrote to Kick that the president's demise came as "a great shock to the masses" because they hadn't understood the state of his health. The Kennedy patriarch couldn't resist taking another swipe at the deceased president:

> There is no doubt that there was real sorrow on the announcement of his death and for two or three days after. Now [May 1, 1945] you rarely, if ever, hear his name mentioned, and there is no doubt that it was a great thing for the country. He had stirred up a hatred in the minds of at least half of the country, and no matter whether he proposed anything good or bad, half the country would be against it and half for it. He had lost control of Congress, as I wrote you he would and had been licked on almost every suggestion he had made.[154]

On what basis Kennedy determined that half the nation would oppose FDR is unclear. Although he garnered 53 percent of the 1944 popular vote against GOP challenger Thomas Dewey, who won 46 percent, FDR's approval ratings were in the 70 percent range as he led the country to victory in World War II.[155]

Kennedy admired President Truman's "common sense," his desire to choose the "best people as advisors," and his "advocating Americanism as the Midwest knows it and not as the elements in New York want it." He hoped to assist Truman but preferred that a job offer go to Jack. Joe Kennedy thought Jack would be a solid candidate for "minister to some country or assistant secretary of state or assistant secretary of the Navy."[156] But by Thanksgiving 1944, JFK had set his sights on a postwar run for a Massachusetts congressional seat, which he captured in 1946. His father couldn't have known that JFK would do battle with another Roosevelt—Eleanor—as his political trajectory moved ever upward.

2

DIVERGENT PATHS TO POWER

ON THE SECOND ANNIVERSARY OF Franklin Roosevelt's death, his widow told a reporter that people often remarked about her late husband, "We miss hearing his voice in our living room."[1] How incongruous that Franklin's patrician Hudson Valley accent had such a comforting impact on average citizens during the dual crises of the Great Depression and World War II. The first president to make wide use of radio, his broadcasts met Americans where they were—in their homes, taverns, cars, and on front porches. Wherever families, neighbors, friends, and even strangers gathered, the president's confident tenor tone resonated with them for more than twelve years. Those who were children when he assumed the presidency were now young adults and had never known another occupant of the White House. His messages—informative and accessible—made most Americans feel a part of his crusades to address economic hardships and then to vanquish fascism. His appearances in silver screen newsreels never portrayed him in a wheelchair or being carried because of his paralysis; instead, they depicted him as larger than life to movie audiences who flocked to theaters, desperate for escapist entertainment in such unsettling times.

Following this first truly "personal" president, who had forged such an intimate bond with so many Americans, would have been a challenge for any vice president. For Harry Truman, a little-known Missouri senator when the 1944 Democratic convention chose him to run with FDR, the task proved formidable. Whereas Roosevelt had already earned an iconic position among history's three greatest presidents (with Washington and Lincoln), Truman wouldn't be celebrated for his down-home demeanor, common sense, plain speaking, and autodidactic background until the nadir of the Nixon era, some two decades later, when the poplar band Chicago sang, "America needs you, Harry Truman; Harry, could you please come home?" Quite the contrary, he prompted the dubious aphorism "To err is Truman" during his presidency, and he departed the White House in 1953 with an approval rating that would rival only Nixon's depths, in the 20-percent range. As one writer observed about how people responded to the thirty-third president, "The public deemed him . . . unfit for the mantle worn by the greats."[2]

Difficulties abound for presidents who serve after wars. The American people demand diminution of the power that accrues to the commander in chief during military campaigns.[3] Thus, his ability to meet policy challenges shrinks just when he needs to win the peace. Wars' aftermaths often include employment disruptions and housing shortages as service members muster out; industrial restructuring as manufacturing retools for a peacetime economy; foreign policy crises in new world orders; baby booms; and demands for financial and health benefits from veterans who devoted their lives to the war effort.

No wonder Truman, once a "Show Me State" farmer, later described hearing the news of Roosevelt's death from Eleanor as worse than having a load of hay collapse on him. He elaborated, "I felt like the moon, the stars, and all the planets had fallen on me."[4] When he asked the First Lady what he could do for her, she replied, "Is there anything we can do for you? For you are the one in trouble now."[5]

Some of that trouble would arise from Eleanor herself. Democratic Party leaders, who could see FDR's health declining in 1944, had engineered Truman's selection as a moderate replacement for Vice President Henry Wallace, thought to be too liberal for the ticket and for possible assumption of the presidency. However, Eleanor's progressive ideology more closely matched Wallace's than Truman's, and she had been "a known champion" of her husband's vice president during FDR's third term.[6] Yet in the Truman presidency's initial days, Mrs. Roosevelt appreciated his kindnesses—offering her all the time she needed to pack twenty trunks and vacate the White House, her home for more than a decade. He also provided her a car and driver for the first month after she returned to Hyde Park and secretarial assistance to answer the thousands of condolence notes she received.[7]

With little firsthand knowledge of Truman, Eleanor initially thought that he had few convictions when he suddenly found himself president of the United States.[8] Or worse, she feared his Missouri conservatism and cronyism would overlook the New Deal coalition's constituencies that meant the most to her: women, Blacks, labor, and urban populations.[9] An astute politician, he knew that the former First Lady's favor with those blocs made her an invaluable asset to him, and he genuinely admired her.[10] His label for Mrs. Roosevelt, "First Lady of the World," became a lasting tribute to her global reputation. No wonder the new president phoned her New York apartment with news that he wished to appoint her a US representative to the first session of the UN's General Assembly, to be held in London just after New Year's 1946.[11] "My dear Mrs. Roosevelt," he affectionately addressed her in his official letter. You "will bear the grave responsibility of demonstrating the wholehearted support which this government is pledged to give to the United Nations organization, to the end that the organization can become the means of preserving the international peace and of creating conditions of mutual trust and economic and social well-being among all peoples of the world."[12]

Although she questioned her worthiness for such a consequential post, Eleanor believed she must fulfill her duty to serve when the president called on her.[13] Ultimately, they formed an unshakable bond, sealed with frank correspondence from the former First Lady to the new president in which she revealed her positions on as many issues—foreign and domestic—that she cared enough to share.[14] In turn, the president would thank her for alerting him to her views and would explain his posture on social and international policies.[15]

Harry Truman, Adlai Stevenson, and Eleanor Roosevelt at the Democratic National Convention in Chicago, 1956. (Courtesy Harry S. Truman Presidential Library)

Without Franklin to lead the party, Eleanor vaulted into the national Democrats' upper echelon, and she continued to participate in New York State's political machinations. (ER would top polls of the most admired women from 1948 to 1962, until First Lady Jacqueline Kennedy overtook her.)[16] What a difference twenty years made. In the 1920s, all-male, smoke-filled caucuses refused to listen to her and other women leaders. Now supplicants encouraged her to run for office. "I heard that I was being offered the nomination for governor or for the United States Senate in my own state, and even for the vice president. And some particularly humorous souls wrote in and suggested that I run as the first women president of the United States!" she reported. But Eleanor preferred an appointed position in the UN delegation, where she thought she could prove her belief "that women might have a better chance to bring about the understanding necessary to prevent future wars if they could serve in sufficient number in these international bodies." As a self-described "elderly woman," though she was only sixty-one and brimming with the energy of someone half her age, she wrote that she didn't have time to achieve seniority in elective politics. "There is freedom in being responsible only to yourself which I would now find it hard to surrender in taking a party office," the former First Lady observed.[17] She also avoided conflict in the public arena with her sons James, Elliott, and Franklin Jr., who were interested in pursuing their own elective political careers, as well as John Roosevelt, who became a Republican.

Just as voters had turned out of office Prime Minister Churchill in 1945, despite his leading the British Empire to victory in World War II, the 1946 midterm elections proved disastrous for FDR's party. Republicans scored majorities in both the House of Representatives and Senate. Jack Kennedy, however, survived the GOP onslaught. After a brief stint as a journalist for Hearst newspapers, during which he covered the 1945 United Nations founding conference in San Francisco,[18] he decided that he would rather *make* news than report it. Following in his Grandfather Fitzgerald's footsteps, he focused on Massachusetts's Eleventh Congressional District. "I had in politics, to begin with," he commented years later, "a great advantage of having a well-known name, and that served me in good stead." With his mother and sisters drawing record crowds to Kennedy tea parties (as women were consigned to such feminine duties at that time) and his father behind the scenes providing strategy, unlimited funds, and public relations resources (including disseminating stories of Jack's wartime heroism), the young veteran swept to victory in the Democratic primary and won the general election with 73 percent of the vote. The cornerstone of the Kennedy dynasty was now in place.[19]

As for the Hyde Park Roosevelt dynasty that would interact with Jack Kennedy throughout his political rise, Eleanor's oldest son James—after distinguished service in the Marine Corps, where, like JFK, he had been decorated for combat service in the South Pacific—began serving as chairman of the California State Democratic Central Committee in 1946.[20] Elliott, Eleanor's favorite of her five children and named for her beloved father, also served in the war, but he had a more controversial tenure in the Army Air Corps, owing to a scandal involving his role in purchasing aircraft. As an aviator-photographer, he claimed to have witnessed the explosion of Joe Kennedy Jr.'s Liberator bomber over the English coastline in August 1944, but no evidence exists for that assertion. After the war, he moved to Top Cottage, his father's getaway up the hill from Val-Kill, and formed a farming partnership with ER, but the venture proved unsuccessful and caused rifts with his siblings, as his failed business ventures led to increased financial dependence on his sympathetic mother.[21]

Prospects looked bleak for Truman in the approaching 1948 presidential contest when he would have to run at the top of the ticket. Eleanor advised him to appeal to labor and women and remember that the latter often supplied the most dedicated campaign workers. Franklin Jr., after earning a degree at the University of Virginia School of Law and service awards in the war, entered law practice in New York City. Truman appointed him to the President's Commission on Civil Rights in 1946, but he became so disenchanted with his father's successor that he and his brothers James and Elliott supported what they hoped would be a 1948 Democratic Party run for president by Gen. Dwight Eisenhower, whose ideology remained unclear. FDR Jr. had joined his mother in the Americans for Democratic Action (ADA), which she and other prominent liberal, but anticommunist, Democrats (John Kenneth Galbraith, Walter Reuther, Arthur Schlesinger, and Reinhold Niebuhr) founded in 1947 to perpetuate the New Deal. The ADA, with Franklin Jr. leading the cheers, tried to engineer a ticket headed by Eisenhower, with Supreme Court Associate Justice William O. Douglas, a Roosevelt appointee, in the vice-presidential slot. FDR Jr. represented a reincarnation of his late father's bearish physique and garrulous persona. His chutzpa, however, annoyed more senior members of the party's leadership. ER begged off joining the draft-Ike movement on the grounds that her UN role required a hiatus from partisan politics. Yet Truman knew that he needed the exceedingly popular former First Lady's endorsement, as JFK would in 1960.[22]

Like FDR, Truman complained about having to fight conservative Southern Democrats in Congress in addition to Republican opponents. That rationale for moderation, accurate though it might have been for FDR and eventually for Kennedy, rarely convinced ER.[23] She frequently pushed presidents—from her husband to his vice president turned chief executive to "my dear boy" JFK—to lead rather than capitulate on principle.

FDR, with Eleanor's contributions, had molded the New Deal Coalition that united labor, Blacks, women, Catholics, Jews, farmers, and

Southerners into a potent, if sometimes fractious, mix, especially over civil rights. Racial policy, social class, gender, and religion constituted the major fault lines among these loosely coalesced groups. In the American tradition of two major parties that boasted "big tents" encompassing divergent views, the Democrats included progressives from the Northeast and Midwest, along with conservative Southerners.

Accepting the possibility of Southern retaliation, Truman established by executive order the Civil Rights Commission in 1946. The commission's 1947 report, "To Secure These Rights," included recommendations to desegregate the military and the federal workforce; pass a federal antilynching law; create a permanent fair employment commission; and abolish the poll tax, a Southern tactic to suppress Black votes (along with literacy tests, "grandfather" clauses, and more violent measures). He sent a special message to Congress in early 1948, urging passage of the commission's legislative proposals.[24]

Although Eleanor would later criticize Kennedy for his tepid support of civil rights, as a member of the House of Representatives, he had voted for legislation to abolish the poll tax in 1947. It would take until 1964, two months after his assassination, for the Twenty-Fourth Amendment, which eliminated the tax in federal elections, to be ratified. His youngest brother, Edward Kennedy, who had garnered JFK's Senate seat in 1962, was instrumental in passage of the 1965 Voting Rights Act, which banned the tax in state elections, thus removing one obstacle to Black voters in the South.[25]

The 1948 Democratic Convention adopted a platform entitled "A Program of Progressive Liberalism," with a preface dedicated to FDR's Four Freedoms: of speech and religion and from want and fear. Minneapolis Mayor Hubert Humphrey, running for the Senate as a member of the Democrats' younger generation, declared, "The time has arrived in America for the Democratic Party to get out of the shadows of states' rights and to walk forthrightly into the bright sunshine of human rights." Just after emerging from the fraught platform committee meeting, Humphrey, sans suit coat, tie askew, and collar open, sat in front of FDR's portrait and TV cameras (new to the political process) to describe his faction's position on race: "We have always believed in, and we continue to express our belief in, the right of every individual, regardless of race, color, or creed, the right to live, to work, to vote, and full and equal protection of the laws, on the basis of equality for all people, as under the rights of our constitution."[26] The platform plank that he and other Northern liberals supported included a federal antilynching law, which Mrs. Roosevelt had advocated for more than a decade. Other progressive policies the Democratic platform demanded included abolishing public school segregation, outlawing Jim Crow laws banning Blacks from public facilities or relegating them to separate areas in them, ending employment discrimination, and desegregating the military.[27] The so-called Dixiecrat wing of the party, led by Mississippi and Alabama delegates, stormed out of the convention in a long-planned protest of these civil rights proposals, both in the party platform and in Truman's recommendations to Congress.[28] White supremacists nominated segregationist Strom Thurmond, a senator from South Carolina, as a third-party candidate for the White House.[29] Unable to budge Congress on his civil rights agenda, Truman issued executive orders desegregating the military and the federal workforce just after the convention.[30] Intractable Southerners now had all the more reason to oppose him.

On the left, progressives launched a separate party of their own, led by Henry Wallace. Three years after his vice presidency ended, however, Eleanor's views on him had shifted. "So Henry Wallace is really going to head a third party and run for president!" she exclaimed. "What strange things the desire to be president makes men do!" She recalled that in 1945 she "believed in and admired him" but thought he would use his following among progressives to bolster the Democratic Party, not fracture it. On this point, Eleanor foreshadowed the pragmatism she would eventually apply to her relationship with Kennedy. A splinter party couldn't win the presidency, as her Uncle Ted proved in his unsuccessful 1912 Progressive Party gambit. In fact, he had only divided the Republican vote between himself and incumbent president William Howard Taft, ensuring Democrat Woodrow Wilson's victory. "As leader of a third party, [Wallace] will accomplish nothing," ER wrote. "He will merely destroy the very things he wishes to achieve." She refused to join such a centrifugal movement, especially one with "American communists" at its "nucleus."[31] Broadminded Eleanor had worked with young communist students in the 1930s, aware of how disenchanted they had become during the Depression, and she always asserted everyone's right to free thought, but she knew a left-wing party would only dilute Democrats' votes. That's why she and her friends had founded the ADA—to support progressivism *within* the party. Conversely, she warned Truman that the Democratic Party couldn't out-conservative the GOP.[32]

One progressive plank of the 1948 platform, however, constituted a bridge too far for ER. It called on Congress to pass the Equal Rights Amendment,[33] which she feared would destroy protective legislation for women in the workplace. She had fought so hard in her early public life for these protections that she couldn't bear to see an ERA void them.[34] She would bring this view into her work with the Kennedy administration on women's rights. Although the amendment was proposed in every session of Congress from 1923 onward, JFK never had an opportunity to vote on it while in the House or Senate, where the bill met frequent legislative bottlenecks.[35] Both Eleanor and Jack may also have feared angering their labor allies, who were typically opposed to opening their ranks to women and minorities. After all, men had only recently retaken their jobs from the women who'd replaced them during World War II.

Imagine how the 1948 election appeared to Eleanor. Ever since she had voted in her first presidential election in 1920, her husband had been on the ticket in five out of the seven contests, and her friend Al Smith was the nominee in 1928. New York corporate lawyer John W. Davis headed the Democratic ticket in 1924. National elections must have seemed like family affairs or at least close to her Empire State roots. Now a rough-around-the-edges Missourian topped the ticket. From the UN meeting in Paris, ER wrote to Truman in early October with assurances that, newspaper reports to the contrary, she didn't "prefer the election of the Republican candidate. I am unqualifiedly for you as the Democratic candidate for the presidency." She hoped for "the election of as many liberal Democrats to Congress as possible," especially for the sake of "labor and farm groups who have perhaps the greatest stake in the preservation of liberal leadership."[36]

Ultimately, FDR's widow gave her public imprimatur to Truman and declared on a radio broadcast from Paris that Truman had "shown courage." She then stated a simple but compelling fact: Truman "needs the people's mandate to help him if he's going to be our president." Indeed, the accidental president required the voters' legitimization.[37] Nevertheless, she believed, as did pollsters and the media, that Harry was headed for defeat against Thomas Dewey, despite the Republican candidate's stiff mien. Eleanor's acerbic cousin Alice Roosevelt Longworth had famously dismissed the stilted New York governor with the pencil mustache as "the groom on the wedding cake."[38] ER's only hope for the Democrats was at least to hold liberal seats in Congress and try to increase their number.[39]

The recalcitrant Republican House and Senate generated a Truman battle cry against the "do-nothing Congress." As he excoriated Capitol Hill opponents out on the hustings, supporters exhorted, "Give 'em Hell, Harry!" Now he had a slogan that would follow him into history by leading the pugnacious politician to an upset victory over Dewey. Despite Truman's 40 percent approval rating the summer before the election and opinion polls showing the GOP candidate ahead two weeks prior to voting, Dewey "snatched defeat from the jaws of victory," allowing a beaming Truman to hold aloft the *Chicago Tribune*'s embarrassingly premature front-page banner headline, "Dewey Defeats Truman." Telephone polling had missed pro-Truman Democrats who didn't own phones. Moreover, the president's indefatigable whistle-stop campaign throughout the country, his fiery stump style, and the rural and Black votes that broke for him in the final days of the race all led to his unpredicted win.[40] Thurmond and Wallace each won 1.1 million votes as splinter-party candidates, but the Dixiecrat amassed thirty-nine electoral votes (all in the South), while the Progressive totaled zero ballots in the Electoral College.[41]

Abroad in England, Geneva, and Paris on UN business during most of the campaign, Eleanor had a valid reason for misjudging the election environment at home. She admitted privately that she had shown too little faith in the American voter's independence to evaluate the "Man from Independence." She bestowed a left-handed compliment on Truman:

"I think they felt more sincerity if not ability from Truman." She always thought her husband's success flowed from his talent for connecting with voters, but she also believed that his intellect and leadership traits completed his portfolio for greatness, despite Justice Oliver Wendell Holmes's oft-quoted conclusion that FDR had a "second-class intellect but a first-class temperament."[42] Her hope that Democrats could increase their seats in Congress exceeded ER's expectations. Harry's coattails amassed 54–42 and 263–217 Democratic majorities in the Senate and House,[43] including the reelection of Jack Kennedy to his House seat by a landslide of more than 78,000 votes over his nearest opponent.[44]

Democrat Adlai E. Stevenson scored a 1948 victory when he captured the Illinois governorship with 570,000 more votes than the corrupt incumbent Republican. Truman had carried the state by only 34,000 ballots more than Dewey. Stevenson, part of a political dynasty that had included a vice president and would propel the governor's son into the US Senate, now appeared on the national Democratic Party radar.[45] He wrote to Mrs. Roosevelt in Paris, "It's all your fault. You told me last fall to go ahead and have a try at it, and I have profited enormously from the experience quite aside from the amazing victory."[46] A Princeton graduate with a Northwestern University law degree, Stevenson had worked in the State Department, which deputed him to the United States' first UN delegation staff. In that capacity, he had impressed Eleanor with his knowledge, wit, and charming personality.[47] Headed toward divorce in 1949 and never to remarry, Adlai always attracted an enthusiastic feminine following. The testosterone-infused Kennedy men found his mannered personality grating, but Jacqueline Kennedy appreciated his many kindnesses toward her.[48]

Franklin Jr. joined the US House of Representatives after winning a special election in 1949 against the Tammany Hall candidate, a special point of pride for Eleanor, who had fought the New York machine all her political life. Now perhaps he would follow his father into the governorship and then on to the White House. Jimmy used his base as chair of the Golden State's Democratic Party apparatus to win nomination for California governor in 1950, but he lost in a landslide to the incumbent, Earl Warren. Eleanor had campaigned for her eldest son, but much to her upset, President Truman offered no support to Jimmy (who had promoted Eisenhower as the Democratic candidate in 1948). Franklin Jr., who by all accounts was among the most neglectful of congressmen, sought the 1954 Democratic New York gubernatorial nomination, but a Tammany candidate defeated him. Instead, FDR Jr. ran for state attorney general but also failed to win that post.[49]

In addition to these losses, Eleanor had to endure the breakup of Anna's second marriage and the suicide of her ex-husband John Boettinger, one of ER's favorite in-laws.[50] Whereas Rose Kennedy never hesitated to critique her children's behavior, even as adults, in order to preserve her vision of familial perfection, Mrs. Roosevelt let her brood make their own decisions, no matter how ill-considered.[51] She recognized that their upbringing had been distorted by her mother-in-law's indulgence, Franklin's polio and his distracting political career, their marriage difficulties, and Eleanor's self-admitted failures as a Victorian disciplinarian. Like the Kennedy brothers, the Roosevelts' sons were prone to speeding, partying, drinking, and carousing. In both families, someone was always there to repair the damage. Might Eleanor have seen the irresponsibility of her sons replicated in Jack's playboy image?[52]

While serving together in the House of Representatives, Franklin Jr. and JFK had collaborated on an education funding bill authorizing $300 million annually in federal grants to states for elementary and secondary schools, with some aid to nonpublic schools (in transportation, for example). Eleanor could support this "child benefit" theory of public funding for Catholic schools. Her husband's first Supreme Court nominee, Hugo Black, as strict a church-state separationist as ER, had propounded the idea in 1947's *Everson v. Board of Education of Ewing Township.* Black's doctrine posited that Catholic children—*not* the parochial schools that they attended—benefited from government reimbursement of bus fare.[53]

Like FDR Jr., JFK found the routine of a freshman representative uninspiring and set his sights on moving up the ladder as soon as feasible. Unlike Franklin Jr., however, who trained his gaze on state office in New York, Jack believed the US Senate would be his next perch from which to launch a presidential run. With the future in mind, JFK was not nearly as neglectful as Franklin in fulfilling his legislative duties, though he found the minutiae of public policy boring. He admitted that his family was more interested "in the mechanics of the political process than in its outcomes." His dad ensured that the mechanics ran smoothly for Jack: promoting his name throughout Massachusetts, providing funds for extra staff, and prevailing on the Bay State's Democratic congressional leader John McCormick to assign JFK to the House Education and Labor Committee. There he could debate policies related to schools and unions, issues that appealed to his fellow vets.[54] How different might James's and Franklin Jr.'s political careers have been had their father survived to promote them? Eleanor was popular and could campaign for them, but she couldn't manipulate the levers of congressional power as Joe Kennedy did for his sons.

Congressman Kennedy combined his procapitalist agenda, inherited from his father, with what biographer James MacGregor Burns labeled "bread-and-butter" liberalism. Thus, JFK hewed to fiscal conservatism except when supporting social programs for housing, the minimum wage, immigration, and education that benefited his constituents.[55] This more pragmatic approach would sometimes put him on a collision course with ER's idealism.

In foreign affairs, Kennedy exhibited the cold warrior traits typical of his era and supported the containment of communism in Europe, as did Eleanor, through the Truman Doctrine, the Marshall Plan, and NATO. He criticized his own party's presidents, FDR and Truman, for the loss of China to the communists, and he spoke out against communists' and racketeers' infiltration of labor unions. Although Mrs. Roosevelt supported freedom of thought, she trumpeted "the need for labor to clean house—the AF of L [American Federation of Labor] to get rid of its racketeers, the CIO [Congress of Industrial Organizations] to get rid of its communist leaders."[56] JFK provided a vote for labor's interests against management by his opposition to the 1947 Taft-Hartley bill, which the Republican Congress repassed over Truman's veto.[57] ER, too, opposed the legislation's segments that weakened the New Deal's National Labor Relations Act (NLRA), signed by her husband in 1935. It had guaranteed workers' rights to join unions for collective bargaining with management. The next year, Eleanor, by then a newspaper columnist, joined the CIO-affiliated American Newspaper Guild and remained a proud union member for the remainder of her life. She opposed Taft-Hartley's efforts to weaken the NLRA's guarantees for labor, including allowing states to enact right-to-work policies. "This bill seems to me to strike at the fundamental rights and protection of labor."[58]

Esther Peterson, a lobbyist for the Amalgamated Clothing Workers union, met Congressman Kennedy his freshman year on the Hill and instantly liked the young military veteran: "I was assigned [to him] because we have a lot of members of the Clothing Workers in his district. I remember going in and seeing him. One of the things that really pleased me, he was brand new, and we immediately got along. . . . He was so easy to talk with, completely at ease." Some union lobbyists thought JFK too ambitious, Peterson remembered, but she appreciated that "he really listened, and I felt if you went to him with a good outline of arguments, he would use it. And that's very satisfying for a lobbyist."[59] For a woman low in the pecking order of congressional influencers, working with Kennedy, who respected her knowledge, would prepare the way for Peterson and Mrs. Roosevelt to collaborate with him on women's equity issues fifteen years later.

By 1948, Eleanor's progressivism found a more prominent stage for her to pursue workers' rights as part of her seminal role in drafting and leading approval of the Universal Declaration of Human Rights. In addition to serving as part of the US delegation to the UN for six years (1946–53), ER became a member and chairman of the UN Commission on Human Rights. The honor confirmed the former First Lady's effectiveness as part of the US delegation. As the only woman in that group of formidable American politicians and diplomats (former Secretary of State Edward Stettinius, incumbent Secretary of State Jimmy Byrnes, Senators Tom Connally and Arthur Vandenberg, and alternate John Foster Dulles), Eleanor admitted that she "walked on eggs," during the first UN session. "I was not very welcome" among her male colleagues, ER reflected. But she also knew that, like all women thrust into unprecedented roles, "if I failed to be a useful member, it would not be considered merely that I as an individual had failed but that all women had failed, and there would be little chance for others to serve in the near future."[60] She didn't fail. After the first UN session, Vandenberg and Dulles approached her: "Mrs. Roosevelt, we must tell you that we did all we could to keep you off the United Nations delegation. We begged the president not to nominate you. But now we feel we must acknowledge that we have worked with you gladly and found you good to work with. We would be happy to do so again."[61]

Now tinging her idealism with a dash of pragmatism, ER resurrected her post–World War I belief in international institutions—not to achieve the unrealistic goal of outlawing war but to promote peace through global understanding and dialogue, universal rights, and systemic enforcement. Thus, the UN Human Rights Commission's first task under her leadership was to draft a declaration that the General Assembly would adopt. While not legally binding, a proposed covenant, with the force of a treaty, would be authoritative. The commission also planned to develop procedures and institutions to enforce the covenant.[62]

Mrs. Roosevelt considered this endeavor the most meaningful of all the tasks she undertook in her six years of UN labors. After strenuous months of drafting, meetings, guidance, and heated discussions (especially with the increasingly oppositional Soviet representatives), the declaration included all traditional political and civil rights, combined with more modern social, economic, and cultural rights. It passed the General Assembly on December 10, 1948. The obstreperous Soviet Union, followed by its satellite countries, abstained, arguing that the document emphasized traditional over contemporary rights, clearly a slap at the American republic, founded on eighteenth-century Enlightenment principles. But the communists couldn't have been more wrong: the contemporary rights they had demanded were indeed included. In addition to the Madisonian guarantees embedded in the US Bill of Rights (freedom of speech, assembly, press, religion, privacy, and criminal rights), the Universal Declaration precluded discrimination based on "race, color, sex, language, religion, political or other opinion, national or social origin, property, birth, or status," and enshrined "the right to work, to free choice of employment . . . and to protection against unemployment." It advocated "equal pay for equal work," the right to

Eleanor Roosevelt holding a copy of the UN's Universal Declaration of Human Rights, which she helped to draft, 1948. (Courtesy of FDRL)

"join trade unions," to "rest and leisure," paid holidays, to travel freely to and from countries, to "food, clothing, housing, medical care," social security, childcare (including for those born out of wedlock), and free primary and secondary education as well equal university access "to all on the basis of merit."[63]

At the same time, Representative Kennedy supported many of these "bread-and-butter" issues during his freshman years in Congress, especially with his advocacy for labor rights, affordable housing, and government funding of education in the United States. He also endorsed, along with a hundred other House and Senate members, a 1949 proposal to transform the UN into a world federation "to preserve peace and prevent aggression through the enactment, interpretation, and enforcement of world law."[64]

Only the freest and most socialistic countries in western Europe, with strong majoritarian labor movements, had achieved the rights delineated in the UN declaration by the twentieth century without succumbing to Marxism's authoritarian tendencies. Eleanor knew that her own nation remained far from achieving the UN declaration's rights; in fact, it violated many of them. When she had offered to resign from the commission after receiving instructions from US authorities that she should settle for including only traditional rights and liberties,

Truman allowed her to push for inclusion of the Soviets' modern social guarantees, which she had promoted for decades. She not only swayed the president to her side but brought along his new Secretary of State George Marshall. Her indefatigable and ultimately successful struggle for the most complete Universal Declaration of Human Rights feasible in the international political context only made her more opposed to Red Scare tactics at home following World War II.[65] Here she would cross swords with President Truman.

His moderate, border-state credentials had boosted him into the vice presidency and, consequently, the White House. As president, he tried to placate his party's two wings: for progressives, he promoted civil rights and health care for the aged; and for conservatives, he signed the 1947 Loyalty Oath executive order, designed to identify communists in government.[66] Of course, that action enraged liberals, including Mrs. Roosevelt. "Such measures always are a sign of lack of confidence in ourselves," her column declared. "If we were sure that our citizens understood the value of democracy and were clear in their minds on the subject, I doubt if we would need such an investigation as the president has ordered."[67]

ER's fears about the post–World War II Red Scare's loyalty policies proved true. She understood the need for labor unions to rid themselves of communist leaders and abhorred communism for its authoritarian bent and desire for world domination. But simply having participated in a labor strike or political protests could subject an individual to investigation. The US attorney general created lists of potentially "subversive" Americans and the organizations to which they belonged. Truman's loyalty oath policy ultimately screened more than five million federal workers, of whom some 2,700 were fired and 12,000 resigned. Untold numbers of employees experienced the chilling effect of such witch-hunts.[68]

Kennedy and Roosevelt would soon clash over his tolerance for Sen. Joseph McCarthy—a communist witch-hunter extraordinaire—but later in the decade, JFK, as a senator, would introduce an amendment to the National Defense Education Act to abolish the requirement that aid recipients sign a loyalty oath and offer affidavits to confirm their fealty to the United States.[69]

Although Truman longed to return to Missouri, he could run for another full term in 1952 because the new Twenty-Second Amendment, ratified in 1951, exempted the incumbent president from its ten-year limit for service (two four-year terms plus two years after succession from the vice presidency). He remained ambivalent, especially with his approval ratings dipping to 22 percent early that year.[70] Truman allowed his name to appear on the New Hampshire primary ballot with no intention of campaigning there, still an option before such contests became de rigueur for aspirants in the 1970s. An embarrassing loss in New Hampshire to Tennessee Senator Estes Kefauver persuaded the president to announce his decision to step aside from the election.[71] The president continued to pressure Governor Stevenson, trying to convince him that he should be the nominee, but Adlai played Hamlet in this Democratic tableau. "Those who make the [Shakespearean] comparison," Kennedy speechwriter Richard Goodwin explained, "do so as a metaphor of irresolution. Hamlet is the story of a man who tries to understand and reach for certainty before he strikes."[72] Governor Stevenson coyly awaited a groundswell to run, which Truman found annoying, at best, and falsely modest, at worst.[73] One of Adlai's closest aides, Carl McGowan, remembered that the governor wasn't only waiting for the Democrats to court him. Rather, he also struggled with the decision to run for president because he worried about its impact on his three sons, for whom he took responsibility after his 1949 divorce.[74]

When Stevenson finally called to ask the president for support, just as the July convention began in Chicago, Truman erupted with a stream of his patented "vigorous words," followed by, "I have been trying since January to get you to say that."[75] It took three ballots, but Truman's choice prevailed. "The Man from Libertyville" became the Democrats' 1952 presidential candidate. His brilliance, urbanity, wry wit, and oratorical skills seemed just the mixture to contrast with the GOP standard bearer, General Eisenhower.

Franklin Jr. had supported his home state governor, Averell Harriman, for the nomination, but Mrs. Roosevelt found Adlai generally aligned with her liberal ideology. Yet she still hadn't returned to partisan campaigning because of her UN obligations. At Truman's request, however, she spoke on the United Nations at the 1952 Democratic National Convention.[76] She began by thanking the delegates for their warm welcome but acknowledged that she knew it was for her husband. The former First Lady called on FDR's memory to defend the UN and its Commission on Human Rights as means to achieve peace, which he had envisioned up to his dying day.

Eleanor spoke self-deprecatingly to the convention about the criticism she had provoked as First Lady: "I returned not long ago from parts of the world where our attitude on human rights and freedoms affect greatly our leadership. Some of you by now will probably be thinking that once upon a time the old lady speaking to you now did a tremendous amount of traveling around the United States. In that you may remember a cartoon showing two men down in a coal mine, one saying to the other, 'Gosh, here comes Eleanor.'"

Now critics asked if she was "just making more trouble" by traveling around the world. She recalled the poignancy of visiting wounded GIs in remote Pacific outposts during World War II: "I was glad I had traveled so much through my own country and could say to a lonely boy far away from home in a hospital bed, 'You come from Lovett, Texas.' The boy's face would light up. 'Yes, ma'am, I remember when you came there.' I can only hope that in the future there may be some little unexpected value which will come out of these latest travels, too." Primarily, she wished that her journeys on behalf of the UN might bring peace to the world.[77]

ER supported Stevenson but remained on the campaign's sidelines. Always drawn to cerebral policymakers, she wasn't bothered in the least by Stevenson's "egg-head" persona or his divorced status, but they appealed far less to grassroots Americans who simply liked Ike. Eleanor believed that "Governor Stevenson would probably make one of the best presidents we have ever had, but, I also believed that it was practically impossible for the Democrats to win the election because of the hero worship surrounding General Eisenhower."[78]

A fateful twist made Republican Eisenhower's 1952 presidential candidacy a victory for Democrat Kennedy. JFK had augmented his foreign policy portfolio with two trips abroad while a congressman. The first included stays in England, France, Spain, Yugoslavia, Turkey, and Italy, where he had a private meeting with Kennedy family friend Pope Pius XII. The second voyage circled the world, with stops in Israel, Iran, Pakistan, India, Singapore, Thailand, Japan, South Korea, and Indochina, and included meetings with public officials, politicians, ambassadors, reporters, and citizens in each country. In Vietnam Kennedy formed detailed impressions of France's attempts to reassert its colonial dominance over a native independence movement led by communist revolutionary Ho Chi Minh. JFK returned home determined to move up in Congress and tackle international issues that he found more interesting than local politics.[79]

By December 1951, Jack had decided to challenge incumbent Henry Cabot Lodge Jr. for his US Senate seat. Lodge was so preoccupied with Ike's campaign, having persuaded the war hero to cast his lot with the GOP, that he neglected what he thought would be an easy reelection. Instead, he faced the Kennedy family juggernaut that moved into high gear while Lodge handled his presidential campaign duties around the country. "In 1952 I worked a year and a half before Senator Lodge did," JFK recalled. Kennedy believed that most candidates start much too late in campaigns and that successful aspirants should build their "brand" and name recognition well in advance of election day.[80]

Joe Kennedy continued to remain behind the scenes, but he played a crucial role with his financing. He drafted twenty-six-year-old Bobby Kennedy as campaign manager and promoted journalistic support for Jack.[81] Rose and daughters Eunice, Jean, and Pat fanned out across the state to make speeches to women voters at large receptions and homey teas. Lodge blamed "those damn tea parties" as the reason for his defeat.[82] Jack, still a boyishly handsome bachelor in his mid-thirties, hobbled on crutches from his war-caused back injuries. Older women wanted to mother him, and younger women wanted to marry him, so the saying went. Family-oriented 1950s culture required that Jack marry and produce children to remain politically viable. In September 1953, he married Jacqueline Bouvier in high society's wedding of the year. Three thousand onlookers swarmed the newlyweds as they emerged from St. Mary's Catholic Church in Newport, Rhode Island.[83]

Despite Ike's landslide defeat of Stevenson (including in the Bay State), Kennedy achieved a stunning win over the venerable Lodge, heir to a Massachusetts Brahmin political dynasty, by a slim 70,737-vote margin.[84] It couldn't have hurt that Eleanor had published a favorable column about Jack after a brief visit with him six weeks before the election: "Mr. Kennedy has been a congressman for six years and in the state of Massachusetts I think they should know him well enough to realize that he has certain very good qualities that should recommend him for election to serve in the Senate. It is important, I think, that these young, courageous representatives who have had experience in the House, move into the Senate and bring into that body some of the influence of youth."[85] At this point, Mrs. Roosevelt was bullish on JFK, despite her differences with his father a decade earlier.

ER lauded experience but made a clarion call for change and growth in organizations. She believed that the Democratic Party had constantly evolved since her husband's first presidential election in 1932, and she always encouraged infusions of youthful creativity to reach her progressive goals. Eleanor thought JFK just the sort of senator a potential Stevenson administration could partner with in domestic and foreign policy.[86] In addition, ER and Franklin Jr. helped Jack win Jewish voters by vouching that he was pro-Israel and not an anti-Semite like his father.[87] JFK's future brother-in-law, Sargent Shriver, became a liaison to Stevenson and told him that when he campaigned with Jack in Massachusetts, he should avoid references to isolationism, presumably to bypass unfavorable comparisons to Joe Kennedy's prewar position of appeasement.[88]

Tradition required that the UN delegates named by Truman had to submit their resignations after the Eisenhower-Nixon ticket's victory. Mrs. Roosevelt did so, and Ike accepted it. Her days as an official representative to the UN ended, but now she embraced the role of supporting the organization through her work with the United Nations Association. She also returned to party politics. "I had not been much impressed by the progress of what President Eisenhower called Modern Republicanism," ER wrote. It featured New Deal elements that younger members of the GOP accepted, like Social Security, but "there were enough old-line

Republicans in powerful positions to keep the party, on the whole, a conservative, businessmen's party."[89]

Eisenhower's decision not to sign the UN Covenants to enforce the Universal Declaration of Human Rights saddened Mrs. Roosevelt, even if she was unsurprised. "We are not willing to sign anything which binds us legally in the field of human rights and freedoms," she lamented. "Yet we in the U.S. find legal decisions helpful in gaining rights for our own people."[90] Isolationist sentiment won the day in the new Republican administration.

One of the historic decisions "in gaining rights for our own people" appeared in May 1954, when the Supreme Court declared racial segregation in public schools unconstitutional. Mrs. Roosevelt particularly hailed the justices' unanimous vote. "I think it will be difficult for the states with segregated school systems to hold out against such a ruling," she wrote in her column.[91] Unfortunately, her assumption failed to anticipate the South's "massive resistance" to the decision. ER completely agreed with Chief Justice Earl Warren's assertion in *Brown v. Board of Education* that racially separate schools were inherently unequal and stamped the Black race with a "badge of inferiority," in violation of the Fourteenth Amendment's equal protection clause.[92] She recognized that "southerners always bring up the question of marriage between the races, and I realize that that is the question of real concern to people. But it seems to me a very personal question which must be settled by family environment and by the development of the cultural and social patterns within a country. One can no longer lay down rules as to what individuals will do in any area of their lives in a world that is changing as fast as ours is changing today."[93]

As prominent Black journalist Vernan Jarrett recalled,

> Eleanor Roosevelt, in the wake of *Brown v. Board of Education,* not only supported it; she was relentless. And she wanted everybody to know where she stood. She wanted it implemented. She didn't even want Black people being too cautious about the implementation of that Supreme Court decision. She made it clear to everybody that she was supporting Daisy Bates, head of the

local NAACP in Little Rock, and those youngsters [Black students attempting to attend all-white schools]. She was with them all the way. And I think shortly after that she made a statement to the effect that if you don't take a stand, you've got to leave the impression that you're cowardly. She used the word "cowardly," which meant that she had been growing firmer and firmer. She had a deep resentment, the more she heard of both southern senators and congressmen who would just blatantly use the word "nigger," who blatantly and unnecessarily wanted to segregate people.[94]

ER found herself at odds with Stevenson and Kennedy, however, over the *Brown* decision's implementation timetable. In the court's subsequent, and seemingly oxymoronic, mandate for "all deliberate speed" in desegregating schools,[95] Adlai and Jack focused on gradualness and Eleanor on rapidity. Was Stevenson looking ahead to another run for the presidency and trying to placate the Democratic Party's Southern wing?[96] Probably so, and JFK felt no need to join the party's more progressive bloc on public school desegregation.

Despite this policy difference, ER told Adlai in 1956 that she could think of no one else "who has the ability to do the job you could do in meeting the vital needs of the day."[97] He had campaigned across the country for Democratic candidates and to raise money to retire the party's debt. As is typical for presidents in midterm election, Eisenhower lost ground in Congress when the Democrats took back majorities in the House (232–203) and Senate (48–47).[98] James Roosevelt, who had served as a Democratic National Committee member from 1948 to 1952, became one of the new Democrats in the House of Representatives, winning the race from California's Twenty-Sixth Congressional District.[99] As a freshman congressman, he appeared on a public affairs television program where the host asked if he would compare criticism of First Lady Mamie Eisenhower with that aimed at his mother over the years. Jovially referring to his father, he quoted FDR's famous quip that he didn't mind attacks on himself or his family, but his "little dog Fala" should be off limits! Congressman Roosevelt suggested that politicians had to maintain a sense of humor in the face of assaults. Did he aspire to higher office in the Senate or the presidency? "Never say never," was James's cautious reply, but he added a pat response that congressmen should stay in office to achieve seniority.[100]

Stevenson broadened his experience with a trip around the world on a fact-finding mission, and Eleanor received positive reports from the leaders with whom he met. She felt that Adlai could provide the Free World's leadership necessary during the Cold War. Eleanor continued her own globe-trotting, seeking pleasure and continuing her commitment to lifelong learning, and she planned a trip to Europe with two of her grandsons in summer 1956. She saw no need to attend the Democratic Convention in Chicago—until one of her friends expressed fear that her absence might signal less enthusiasm for Stevenson the second time around. So off she flew to the Windy City.[101]

There she would not only support Stevenson's second nomination as the Democratic standard bearer but would have a direct contretemps with Senator Kennedy that added to their conflict over the next four years.

3

THE GRANDE DAME AND "MY DEAR BOY"

BEFORE EXERCISING HER POWER OVER Senator Kennedy at the 1956 Democratic convention, Mrs. Roosevelt had to go head-to-head with former president Truman, who had supported Stevenson in 1952 but switched to Gov. Averill Harriman four years later.[1] Truman bluntly identified Harriman as someone the country needed because he wanted the job. Stevenson lacked "the kind of fighting spirit we need to win," the former president declared at a Chicago press conference. At a private meeting with Stevenson, Homespun Harry had pointed out his hotel window toward a random pedestrian on Michigan Avenue: "The thing you have to do is learn how to reach that man."[2]

Now two of the party's leading celebrities, Mrs. Roosevelt and Mr. Truman, sparred over which of their preferred candidates would capture delegates' votes. Looking for common ground, ER made good on her lunch invitation to the former president and his wife Bess. Mrs. Truman sent regrets, but Harry and Eleanor chatted amiably over a meal at the Blackstone Hotel's grill. Accepting that they backed two different candidates, the former First Lady and her husband's successor agreed to disagree. As they entered the convention hall separately, both received warm ovations from the attendees. Outside the arena, Eleanor made the rounds of state delegations with Adlai, attended a reception in her honor, met with women delegates, and advocated her position on education and civil rights in the platform committee's meetings. The Democratic manifesto reflected her views on internationalism (support for the UN), labor (amend Taft-Hartley), civil rights (enforce school desegregation and employment nondiscrimination), and women in the workplace (guarantee wage equity).[3] Her appearance at the podium to deliver a brief speech produced such wild cheering that it nearly drowned out her words.[4]

Mrs. Roosevelt speculated that Truman's gambit for Harriman might be an attempt to deadlock the convention and open the way for Missouri's favorite son, Sen. Stuart Symington, to seize the nomination. Harry claimed that he wanted the delegates to "think" about their choice, but Eleanor believed that if they did so, Stevenson would be their candidate. And he was—on the first ballot. Eleanor reported that women had finally worked their way into the caucuses and that these rooms were no longer smoke-filled.[5] Observing a difference between her experience as a woman in 1920's Democratic politics, completely controlled by males, and how she saw more participation by women three decades later didn't mean that numerous females genuinely exercised power in 1956. Arguably, not until twenty years later, when caucuses and primaries became the route to presidential nominations, did women have demonstrable influence in this open system.

Although the erudite Stevenson never completed Truman's assignment to resonate with the common voter, he garnered the Democratic nomination a second time. He left the choice of vice-presidential nominee to the delegates, and Jack Kennedy decided to make a run for it. In his distinctive Irish brogue, he had effectively narrated the convention's PR film on the Democratic Party's history and had delivered an inspiring nomination speech for Stevenson. As the *New York Times* reported, "Senator Kennedy came before the convention . . . as a photogenic movie star."[6] Although FDR's widow had supported Kennedy in his 1952 Senate victory over Republican Henry Cabot Lodge,[7] she would not back JFK at this convention four years later. JFK explained their schism this way:

"She hated my father, and she can't stand it that his children turned out so much better than hers."[8]

But Eleanor's dislike for the younger Kennedy involved much more than his allegation of wounded maternal pride. In addition to civil rights, another wrenching political issue in the 1950s cast a shadow over how Mrs. Roosevelt viewed the Massachusetts senator. His family had long-standing personal and professional ties to Republican Sen. Joseph McCarthy of Wisconsin, who lent his name to the era's hunt for communists in government, Hollywood, academe, labor unions, and the armed forces. Jack and his father espoused anticommunism and knew many Massachusetts Irish Catholics admired McCarthy, prompting Joe Kennedy to contribute to the Wisconsin senator's 1952 campaign war chest. The elder Kennedy also hoped his contribution would dissuade McCarthy from campaigning in Massachusetts for the GOP ticket, and he succeeded. Two of JFK's sisters, Eunice and Pat, had dated McCarthy when visiting Jack in Washington, and he socialized with McCarthy occasionally. The family enjoyed his visits to Hyannis Port, and Robert Kennedy served as a deputy counsel on McCarthy's Senate Permanent Subcommittee on Investigations for seven months in 1953. The subcommittee formed McCarthy's platform for launching vicious attacks on communism and its alleged adherents. Bobby left the post over an intense dislike for McCarthy's henchman (and future Donald Trump mentor) Roy Cohn.[9]

Anticommunism attracted many American Catholics, who despised the ideology's atheism and its regimes' persecution of all religion, which Karl Marx labelled "the opium of the people." Soviet-aligned governments behind the so-called Iron Curtain targeted Roman Catholic leaders, clergy, and adherents in an attempt to abolish any threats to Marxism. Yet American Catholics' attraction to McCarthyism raised a troubling specter for Kennedy's eventual presidential ambitions. Non-Catholic Americans wondered why allegiance to Rome's patriarchal church also seemed to entail adherence to demagogues like McCarthy and fascist "radio priest" Father Charles Coughlin.[10] But liberal Catholics opposed McCarthy and his tactics, and they made their views known in intellectual outlets like the magazines *Commonweal* and *America*.[11]

At the time, Kennedy's Senate record on McCarthy reflected a mixture of his personal brand of liberalism that focused more on economic issues than civil rights and liberties. He voted, along with most of his colleagues, to fund the Wisconsin senator's investigations. As an anticommunist, JFK sometimes sided with security concerns rather than with civil liberties, although he voted to uphold the Fifth Amendment right against self-incrimination for witnesses before congressional committees. Kennedy opposed McCarthy's pick, Robert Lee, for the Federal Communications Commission, and JFK supported Eleanor Roosevelt's protégé, Charles Boland, as ambassador to the USSR, whose nomination McCarthy tried to block.[12]

Hospitalized and debilitated for months following near-fatal complications from back surgery in the fall of 1954, Kennedy missed the Senate's vote condemning McCarthy for his demagogic methods that defamed his targets and ruined careers.[13] Biographer James McGregor Burns described Kennedy's approach to McCarthy thus: "Always a bit detached and emotionally uncommitted, he tended to view McCarthy more as a procedural problem than a moral one."[14] Yet Eleanor described Americans' support for the Wisconsin demagogue as the most disturbing thing in her life, indicating that, in contrast to JFK, she prioritized civil liberties.[15]

This rift began to widen when Kennedy sent an emissary to Mrs. Roosevelt at the convention, asking if the senator could meet her to request her blessing of his impromptu candidacy for the vice-presidential spot on the Stevenson ticket.[16] Eleanor minced no words, simply stating that she couldn't support Jack "because he had avoided taking a position during the controversy over Senator Joseph McCarthy's methods of investigation." She recognized that Senator Kennedy had been indisposed during the censure vote, "but later, when he returned to the Senate," she argued, "reporters asked him how he would have voted, and he failed to answer directly."[17]

The emissary dismissed her concerns by claiming that the McCarthy matter was "a thing of the past," but Mrs. Roosevelt countered, "I think McCarthyism is a question on which public officials must stand up and be counted." She hadn't heard JFK express his position, and she ominously noted that she couldn't "be sure of the political future of anyone who does not willingly state where he stands on that issue."[18]

Kennedy hoped a face-to-face meeting with the party's grande dame might change her mind about his vice-presidential gambit. Yet when he arrived at her room in Chicago's Blackstone Hotel, it was filled with Roosevelt family members, ER's secretary, clattering typewriters, and ringing telephones. Amidst the commotion, Kennedy's renowned charm failed to move Eleanor, and she cut right to the heart of her concern: "Why did you not stand up against McCarthyism?"[19] The stark query reflected her expert political acumen. Suspecting that JFK would either offer the excuse of illness or resort to legalistic explanations about the Senate's censure process (or both), she broadened her demand to know why Kennedy hadn't stood firm against the entire Red Scare.

JFK repeated his emissary's explanation that the Senate's condemnation of McCarthy in 1954 "was so long ago." Not to Eleanor. She lectured the Massachusetts senator and then dismissed him from her room.[20] As Arthur Schlesinger Jr. described ER, "She was, in many ways, a tough and salty old lady. No one could deflate a person or idea more artlessly and devastatingly than Mrs. Roosevelt."[21] Defending himself after the awkward meeting in which he felt she wasn't really paying attention to him, JFK complained, "My point was that because I had never been particularly vigorous about McCarthy that it would really make me out to be a complete whore for me to be really champing and jumping [about McCarthy now]."[22] Simply put, such an about-face on the Wisconsin Red-hunter would be undignified, Kennedy thought.[23]

In part, Mrs. Roosevelt's refusal to endorse JFK led the convention delegates to choose Sen. Estes Kefauver of Tennessee as Stevenson's running mate, but the ambitious Massachusetts senator had burst on the national scene and now set his sights squarely on the White House. Toward that goal, his Chicago defeat, while stinging at the time, constituted a proverbial "blessing in disguise." Kennedy failed to capture the VP spot on the doomed Stevenson ticket, but Ambassador Kennedy, who had opposed JFK's Chicago venture to pair up with Adlai for the 1956 Democratic ticket, concluded that his son's Catholicism would have been blamed for the defeat, ending Jack's quest for the presidency before it had really begun.[24]

For the rematch between Ike and Adlai, seventy-two-year-old Eleanor hoped she could "play only a very quiet role in the presidential campaign."[25] After returning from the European trip with her grandsons, however, she accepted the Stevenson camp's request to hit the road for Adlai, proving once again her perceived role as a potential king-maker. Two solid months of campaigning, which she wedged in between her lecture tours and writing her daily column, took her from coast to coast, including appearances in Oregon, California, Wisconsin, West Virginia, Missouri, and Washington, DC.

At a rally in Charleston, West Virginia, a state where many residents revered the Roosevelts, Eleanor spoke of her admiration for Stevenson that had developed when they worked together in the UN's formative years. She reminded voters that he'd made many friends for the United States in his 1952 trip around the world. Heads of state reported to her that the former Illinois governor listened to them. "All of the trips taken by the secretary of state [for Eisenhower] have not gained friends for us," she asserted. ER called for patient progress toward "equal opportunity" for all Americans, especially to legitimize our leadership in the world. "We must bear in mind that two-thirds of the world's population is colored, and we are a minority race."[26]

In Los Angeles, Eleanor appeared at the Stevenson headquarters to bolster morale among the volunteers. One Japanese American teenager would remember for the rest of his life how the former First Lady shook his hand, saying, "Thank you, George, for helping Adlai." He and his family had suffered internment during World War II (because of FDR's Japanese removal policy), but his father never relinquished faith in American democracy. George, whose surname is Takei, would become a beloved character in the *Star Trek* television show and films. His father taught him that only by working within the American political system could its ideals reach fulfillment.[27]

Another participant in the Stevenson campaign gained perspectives that he would apply to the 1960 race. Adlai had reached out to JFK with an invitation to join the bandwagon, but Jack already had designs on the White House and wanted to create his own 1956 national speaking tour. He volunteered his brother Bobby, who ostensibly joined as an intermediary for Stevenson to Catholic officials and voters. RFK witnessed a presidential contest firsthand and up close to glean lessons for Jack's future effort. His observations centered on how Adlai's strengths morphed into deficiencies. Stevenson's capacious intellect and oratorical talents didn't translate effectively in grassroots politics or on the new medium of television. Bobby saw the same weakness as Truman had in the former Illinois governor. To a group of West Virginia coal miners, Stevenson gave a sophisticated analysis of foreign affairs that fell flat. Even when he presented populist themes at whistle-stops in small towns across America, he read from his self-styled text instead of speaking from the heart.[28] "Because of his looks and his accent and his known background, this gave the appearance of insincerity. . . . I spoke again and again to people around him [and to the candidate] to try to get him to change his technique, but he never would do it," Bobby concluded.[29]

In addition to the candidate's aloof personality, RFK focused on the Stevenson campaign's disorganization and Adlai's inability to make decisions. Meetings meandered for hours. Determinations that could have been made by lower-level staffers bubbled up to the candidate himself. Tactics such as attacking Vice President Nixon Bobby found ridiculous because voters who disliked Ike's running mate were already Stevenson devotees. Thus, the pool of potential Democratic supporters never expanded. Bobby bluntly observed, "Stevenson was just not a man of action at all."[30] Not even Eleanor, who proudly wore "Adlai" buttons, was surprised at her friend's second defeat, by a larger margin than his 1952 drubbing, winning only 42 percent of the popular vote against Eisenhower. No matter that Ike had suffered a massive heart attack in 1955, which confined him to a Denver hospital for seven weeks, or that he underwent major abdominal surgery the summer before the reelection campaign. The then oldest American president, who was noted for his meandering syntax, Eisenhower earned another four-year term. So disheartened by Stevenson and his campaign was Robert Kennedy that he voted for the Republican ticket.[31]

Now the Democratic Party looked ahead to the 1960 campaign, with hopes of regaining the White House. During a 1957 interview, CBS's Mike Wallace asked if Mrs. Roosevelt saw the makings of a great president among the Democrats' younger generation, including Jack Kennedy, Stuart Symington, and Michigan Governor G. Mennen (Soapy) Williams. She replied that she couldn't predict what would happen in the next two years, but the only person in whom she saw the "beginnings" of greatness was Adlai Stevenson, who had vowed not to run again. As did Truman and RFK, she believed that his losses resulted from "an inability to quite put the things he believes in the language or in the emotional way that will come home to the average human being."[32] Undeterred by his unsuccessful vice-presidential gambit, in March 1957, Kennedy made the case for new leadership to unite the Democratic Party and win back the presidency. "Without a singular titular leader, with prestige and publicity divided among congressional leaders, governors, and the national committee and the party's elder statesmen (such as Messrs. Truman and Stevenson and Mrs. Roosevelt), the Democratic Party appears at times to speak with many voices and in many accents," JFK wrote in *Life* magazine, which featured the smiling, youthful senator on its cover.[33] He obviously hoped his own thick Boston accent would overcome Harry's border-state "plain speaking," Stevenson's Midwestern "egghead" speeches, and Eleanor's refined Hudson Valley trill.

Kennedy may have wanted to move on from McCarthy and the communist witch-hunt to dilute the inconvenient truth that he had been missing in action on *the* civil liberties issue of the 1950s, but Democratic liberal lions couldn't be so easily placated. Mrs. Roosevelt took the opportunity in publishing volume three of her autobiography, *On My Own*, in 1958, to include the story of how she had refused to support Senator Kennedy's attempt to capture the vice-presidential nomination because of his failure to oppose McCarthyism during or after the mayhem it wrought.[34]

When the *Saturday Evening Post* serialized Eleanor's book and highlighted the story of her feud with JFK, the press pounced, quizzing Kennedy on CBS's *Face the Nation* about her statement that "you had dodged the McCarthy issue in 1954, and then in 1956. Do you think she is beating a dead horse, or is that still a live issue?" JFK cited his medical absence from the Senate for most of 1954 but noted that he had answered this question "before the [1956] convention that while I regretted having missed it, I consider the censure action a reasonable action and a proper one, and one that I approve of. I have said it on other television programs, and I am glad to say it again." When asked why ER insisted on resurrecting this issue, Kennedy responded that she had included the 1956 story and opinion in her new memoir and added, "I admire her and what she has done"—a gracious and diplomatic answer. He hoped that his response was now "clear to her" and, without specifying his "civil liberties or due process" record over twelve years in Congress, he claimed that it stood "up very well in comparison with that of any man."[35]

That conclusion would depend on the men to whom Kennedy was compared. Perhaps trying to erase his connection to Joe Kennedy's reputation as a Nazi appeaser in the pre–World War II era, JFK, as a consummate cold warrior, would never be viewed as soft on communism. He blamed Truman's State Department for the 1949 loss of China to the Reds, and he voted for the McCarran-Walter Act, which required communists to register with the government and for the Justice Department to investigate them. He was no rabble-rouser in the McCarthy mold, but liberal Democrats like Eleanor Roosevelt took little comfort from his more civilized method of fighting communism or even from his effort to remove the loyalty oath from the National Defense Education Act.[36] They correctly viewed guilt by association and banning membership in certain political parties as gross violations of basic constitutional liberties. In turn, such liberties constituted the "honor roll of fundamental rights," as Supreme Court Justice Benjamin Cardozo had labeled them in 1937. First Amendment freedoms of speech, press, religion, and association represent the foundation of our democratic-republic.[37] "There are moments when I listen to Senator McCarthy and hear about an un-American activities committee when I wonder where our freedoms are going and hope that the academic tradition, which is perhaps one of the strongest in this country, will save us from the kind of complete conformity which kills originality and truth," ER had written in 1952.[38]

Moreover, this Red Scare represented the third of its kind in Eleanor Roosevelt's lifetime. During World War I, the United States had prosecuted pacifists, anarchists, socialists, and communists via the 1917 Espionage Act and 1918 Sedition Act. These dissenters from America's policy to enter the Great War encouraged draftees to ignore their induction notices and clamored for men already in military service to desert. When the war ended, fears arising from the Soviet Bolshevik revolution and American progressivism stoked so-called Palmer Raids, named for the aggressive US attorney general who ordered disruption of labor union meetings and political gatherings. These raids resulted in arrests and the brutalizing of attendees. In 1924, a reorganized Federal Bureau of Investigation and its new director J. Edgar Hoover began compiling files on nearly anyone who advocated progressive social, political, and economic change, including Eleanor Roosevelt.[39] Thus, as early as the Roaring Twenties, she had been the victim of guilt by association.

Threats posed by the most extreme antigovernment advocates were not a figment of Hoover's vivid imagination. In June 1919, Eleanor and Franklin Roosevelt returned to their Washington home after a dinner party to discover that their neighbor's house across the street, where Attorney General A. Mitchell Palmer and his family resided, had been the site of an anarchist bombing. The attorney general escaped unharmed, but the anarchist didn't. The blast blew him to bits, some of which the Roosevelts discovered, along with broken glass and other fragments, strewn over their front porch. Eleanor, reporting on the morbid scene to her mother-in-law, exclaimed that son James, age twelve, "glories in every new bone found!"[40]

Jack Kennedy, only a toddler at the time, would have had no personal memories of this violence, but like the Roosevelts, his father had experienced an anarchist bomb blast, this one on Wall Street in front of J. P. Morgan & Co. The September 16, 1920, terrorist act killed forty and injured scores. Joe Kennedy, shaken by the brush with terrorism, considered joining the law-and-order Republican Party, but his wife Rose convinced her husband to maintain the family's long ties to the Democrats.[41]

A second wave of anticommunism swept the nation as World War II approached. To bolster the antifascism movement—against Hitler,

Mussolini, and Franco in Europe and the German American Bund, Father Coughlin, Charles Lindbergh, and other right-wingers at home—liberals and communists made common cause to support democracy and peace. First Lady Eleanor Roosevelt never espoused communism. In the depths of the Great Depression, however, she worried that capitalism's excesses and its economic inequities might lead some members of the American proletariat to embrace Marxist tenets. As a liberal, she felt comfortable with parts of the left's agenda and its organizations, including the American Youth Congress (AYC), the National Association for the Advancement of Colored People (NAACP), the League of Women Shoppers, and labor unions—all accused by the right as being communist fronts. She asked the AYC leaders about accusations regarding their communist ties because she wanted to know the basis of their views and where she might differ with them. ER accepted their denials of links to the Reds.[42]

When Congressman Martin Dies's House Un-American Activities Committee began investigating such groups for communist sympathies, Eleanor spoke out against fear-mongering. "Because I dislike Gestapo methods in this country, I have never liked that kind of congressional committee. I do not think such methods are necessary. I doubt they harm the really powerful, but they do harm many innocent people who are unable to defend themselves," she wrote in her 1949 memoir.[43] She even accompanied her young friends in the AYC and the American Student Union (ASU) to the Dies committee's hearings where they testified.[44]

The ASU's former executive secretary Joseph Lash so impressed the First Lady that they developed an abiding friendship. When the antiwar AYC refused to support the United States' attempts to assist countries fighting Hitler's aggression, Mrs. Roosevelt parted company with the young radicals. Nevertheless, the FBI's massive ER file tracked her relations with alleged communists (including Lash), her criticism of JFK in the late 1950s for not condemning McCarthy, and her positive comments about a 1957 visit she made to the Soviet Union.[45]

As Jack Kennedy's 1960 presidential run grew closer, Gridiron Club reporters lampooned him by singing to the tune of the Western folksong *Oh My Darling, Clementine,* "Where were you, John; where were you,

John? When the Senate censured Joe?"[46] Kennedy's characteristic wit usually allowed him to take humorous jabs in stride, but he remained unamused by the persistent questions about his stand on McCarthy. Nothing would cause his painful spine to stiffen more than a press or public audience challenge on the issue. He testily replied to one such query, "I am not ready to accept any indictment from you or Mrs. Roosevelt on that score."[47]

McCarthy succumbed to the ravages of alcoholism in 1957. Robert Kennedy attended his funeral mass in Washington and flew to Wisconsin for the burial service.[48] But the Red-baiter's demise failed to remove him or his movement from the political agenda. The editorial board chair of ER's publisher, Harper's Cass Canfield (whose son Michael was JFK's brother-in-law), entered the fray. Given Kennedy's *Face the Nation* statement, Canfield asked Mrs. Roosevelt to consider revising her book manuscript or adding a footnote, which a Harper editor took the liberty of drafting, to respond to JFK.[49]

Eleanor remained firm in her recollection of the 1956 convention meeting with Kennedy and his response to her queries about his position on McCarthy. She told Canfield, "I usually understand people or at least am able to gather what they mean," but she was willing to acknowledge that she might "have misunderstood the senator" in Chicago. ER accepted that he supported the Senate's condemnation of McCarthy. Yet she believed "that a public servant must clearly indicate that he understands the harm that McCarthyism did to our country and that he opposes it actively, so that one would feel sure he would always do so in the future."[50]

Despite this ongoing, and increasingly public, clash, Kennedy reached out to Mrs. Roosevelt about meeting with him in the spring of 1958. Their calendars didn't square for the times they were both in Washington, so JFK offered to visit her in New York. She replied rather curtly that she had no plans to be in DC in the near future but that she would "be happy to arrange to see" him when he was in New York City if he could let her know his plans in advance.[51] They apparently did meet but to no avail: ER reported to a friend that Kennedy failed to persuade her that he comprehended the true danger of McCarthyism.[52]

Mrs. Roosevelt then took a swipe at him in a December 1958 televised statement, a month after his landslide Senate reelection. She would "hesitate to place the difficult questions that the next president will have to make with someone who understands what courage is and admires it but has not quite the independence to have it."[53] Here again was the "salty" Mrs. Roosevelt, as described by Arthur Schlesinger. This sarcastic reference to Kennedy's 1957 Pulitzer Prize–winning book *Profiles in Courage,* about legislators who had supported righteous causes despite their political costs, understandably rankled JFK. So did her charge that his father was spending "oodles of money all over the country" and "probably has paid representatives in every state by now."[54]

Many of Kennedy's critics also accused him of taking credit for a book ghost written by his masterful wordsmith and speechwriter Ted Sorensen. Kennedy's definitive biographer, Harvard historian Fredrik Logevall, himself a 2013 Pulitzer winner and a jurist for the prestigious award, asserts that the charge is "largely baseless. For one thing, Kennedy had a bigger role in the writing, and certainly in the conception and framing of the book, than many of these [critics] suggested; the book's broad themes and overarching structure were his."[55]

Kennedy's flurry of letters to ER in late 1958 challenged her assertions about his father's role in the forthcoming presidential campaign. He marked the letters "Personal" but blind-copied his friend and *Washington Post* publisher Philip Graham. In a thinly veiled reference to McCarthyism, Senator Kennedy recognized Eleanor's "long fight against the injudicious use of false statements, rumor, or innuendo as a means of injuring the reputation of an individual" and asked for evidence of her accusations about his father. He concluded gently, "Whatever other differences we may have had, I'm certain that we both regret this kind of political practice."[56]

Undaunted, Mrs. Roosevelt responded that if her comment was untrue, she would "gladly so state," but she had been told that Ambassador Kennedy had "openly" declared that "he would spend any money to make his son the first Catholic president of this country."[57] Senator Kennedy rejoined that her letter "disappointed" him because she seemed to "accept the view that simply because a rumor or allegation is repeated" it becomes "a fact." "My father has not spent any money around the country," JFK asserted, "and has *no* 'paid representatives' for this purpose in *any* state of the union—nor has my father *ever* made the statement you attributed to him" about making his son the first Catholic president. If her "informants" had no "concrete evidence" to support these claims, he again asked that, in the spirit of "fairness," she "correct the record."[58]

Former President Truman likewise harbored suspicions about Ambassador Kennedy's largesse. "Old Joe Kennedy is as big a crook as we've got anywhere in this country, and I don't like it that he bought his son the nomination for the presidency," Truman exclaimed in his early 1960s oral history. He accused JFK's father of buying the West Virginia primary. "And it wasn't only there," Truman continued in his tirade. "All over the country old man Kennedy spent what he had to to buy the nomination."[59]

An NBC correspondent asked Mrs. Roosevelt about a new generation of American leaders in 1958. She offered no names but noted that they would require "maturity" to address problems at home and view them in the context of global challenges now that the country led the Free World. She took another swing at McCarthyism, saying that its fomenter had perpetrated "harm." "It hasn't dawned upon people that we are actually strong enough to allow the communists to come, and to show what we have of value."[60]

An ardent peace advocate since World War I, Eleanor also held a different view of the Soviet Union's nuclear strategy that conflicted with the JFK's Cold War posture. "I think they've [the USSR] ruled out a nuclear war for the simple reason that they realize that they couldn't with one blow wipe out the possibility of retaliation," she reasoned, "and they know if there was retaliation they would be as much hurt as we would be. And they want a world that is a going concern. It doesn't mean anything to them to have a world in ruins." Khrushchev had told her that "the future is communism, and we are to have a communist world." Why would he destroy it?[61]

As 1959 dawned, Eleanor included JFK's retorts about his father in her "My Day" column, sent it to the senator, and hoped he would believe that she had "handled the matter fairly." She added, however, in her letter to Kennedy that she could not reveal the names of those who had told her about Joe Kennedy's activities on his son's behalf because it would open the informants to "liability."[62]

Neither Mrs. Roosevelt's column nor her letter to JFK placated the senator. He appreciated her "courtesy" in publishing his "denial of the false rumors about my father and me," but he wanted her "to state that you had been unable to find evidence to justify the rumors." Admitting that his antagonist "may feel that I am being overly sensitive about this issue," Kennedy explained that merely printing his denials would prove inadequate for Eleanor's followers who didn't have the benefit of reading the Kennedy-Roosevelt correspondence. Once more he turned the criticism of his inaction on McCarthyism back on her by invoking her "long fight against the use of unsubstantiated charges and the notion that merely because they are repeated, they attain a certain degree of credibility." Yet he offered an olive branch in concluding that if she felt "the matter was disposed of by your column, I certainly am prepared to let it rest on the basis of our correspondence."[63]

ER clarified for the senator that her "informants were just casual people in casual conversation. It would be impossible to get their names because for the most part I didn't even know them." She thought that perhaps the Kennedys suffered from the same public rumors as the Roosevelts had in relation to their fame and fortune. Publishing his "categorical denial," she believed, constituted JFK's strongest case against the reports about his father's influence in the campaign. And she assured him that her "opposition" to him was never "based on these rumors or that I believed them." "From now on," she offered, "I will say, when asked, that I have your assurance that the rumors are not true. If you want another column, I will write it—just tell me."[64]

Kennedy expressed "many, many thanks for your very gracious letter," and he appreciated the former First Lady's "assurance that [she] did not believe in these rumors." "I would not want to ask you to write another column on this," Jack conceded, "and I believe we can let stand for the present." Thanking Eleanor for her "consideration and courtesy," he once more suggested that he would like to meet with her "sometime in the future to discuss other matters."[65]

The war of letters seemed to have de-escalated, even if the correspondents had not reached a genuine truce and certainly not a reconciliation. Yet Mrs. Roosevelt apparently needed to have the last word in the missive competition with Kennedy. Her final comment on this spat over Jack's father could hardly have been more condescending or patronizing. Just a week after JFK's conciliatory letter, ER wired him with the salutation, "My dear boy." She had signed a 1940 letter to her surrogate son and political soulmate, Joe Lash, with "Much love, dear boy."[66] He was thirty at the time, a quarter-century her junior. JFK was forty-one when Eleanor referred to him as a "boy." But their age difference was thirty-three years, and Kennedy was nearly the same age as Eleanor's youngest child, John. Whereas Eleanor's reference to Lash as a boy reflected endearment, she followed her disdainful opening of the 1959 telegram to JFK with yet another sarcastic reference to his Pulitzer Prize–winning book. "I only say these things for your own good," she cabled. "I have found in a lifetime of adversity that when blows are rained on one, it is advisable to turn the other profile."[67]

Kennedy did. Or at least he turned the other cheek, with his tongue firmly in it. He publicly tried to diffuse the issue of his father's political expenditures with satiric humor. Following reporters' rendition of "Send the Bill to Daddy," sung to the tune of *My Heart Belongs to Daddy*, at the 1959 Gridiron Club dinner, Kennedy brought down the house when he read a mock "message from my generous daddy": "Dear Jack—Don't buy one more vote than is necessary—I'm damned if I'm going to pay for a landslide!"[68]

Yet satire, no matter how witty, wouldn't sway Eleanor. Why did JFK care so much about countering her attacks? In light of her influence in the Democratic Party, her public megaphone via TV appearances and daily newspaper column, and the germs of truth about his approach to McCarthyism and Joe Kennedy's deep pockets, Jack couldn't let ER's critiques go unanswered. If he was going to win the 1960 Democratic presidential nomination and general election, Kennedy believed he had to have Mrs. Roosevelt's support. As the party's matriarch, she influenced both public policy and the political leaders who made it.[69] But another obstacle—their differing views on civil rights—faced the senator in his attempt to win over the former First Lady.

4

CLASHING OVER RACE

JACK KENNEDY COULD ALWAYS ENGAGE in self-deprecating humor as a foil for his critics, especially those who pointed to his father's deep coffers. But as Eleanor Roosevelt had written to JFK, his father's influence wasn't the key source of her opposition to young Jack. In addition to his failure to fight McCarthyism, his civil rights record also troubled her. Kennedy's life story illuminates his relation to race. Despite the Irish immigrant roots that made him sympathetic to Black Americans' fight against discrimination, he came late to the modern civil rights movement.[1] Personal experience and politics contributed to his tardiness. He spent the first ten years of his life in Boston, which in the 1920s had only about a 3 percent Black population.[2] Although his parents had always employed servants, they were usually drawn from "shanty Irish" (a derogatory term for poor or working-class immigrants from Ireland), except perhaps at their Palm Beach estate, which the family acquired when Jack was sixteen. Yet the Kennedys brought their Irish governess when they decamped to Florida each Christmas and Easter. Tony New York City suburbs, where the family settled in 1926; elite prep schools; Harvard and London aristocracy in the 1930s; and the US Navy officer corps during World War II had not exposed JFK directly to the plight of African Americans.

Jack, Joe Jr., and their Harvard roommates hired a Black valet, George Taylor, to help arrange their clothing and perform odd jobs.[3] Jack and Taylor occasionally had a drink together and talked politics. George worked for Kennedy after the war, as both a valet and chauffeur, and introduced JFK to Black voters when he ran for Congress in 1946. But the valet grew discouraged when Kennedy refused to increase his weekly pay from $45 to $100. Taylor also thought that Kennedy's campaign, via his sister Eunice, treated Black and white volunteers differently: white women were invited to restaurants at mealtime, while Black women had food brought to them. Taylor confronted JFK with the discrepancy in treatment, saying, "They're all giving their time. They're all human beings. Why segregate in this way, that you can't take the colored girls down, with the white girls. . . . They're giving their time freely and I don't think it's fair." Kennedy told Taylor he was "thin-skinned" about "the things of the time." The assistant insisted that "a color line" didn't exist in Cambridge and that JFK's Black staff was upset over the disparate treatment. When the candidate refused to change, Taylor left the campaign.[4]

About the time Jack took his US House of Representatives seat in 1947, he hired George Thomas, a Black Virginian, as his new valet. Joe Kennedy's friend, columnist Arthur Krock, paid the former ambassador a debt by offering Thomas's services to Jack, who had just moved to Washington.[5] An experienced Black "gentleman's gentleman," he would serve JFK for sixteen years, including as a live-in valet at the Kennedy White House. Jack's painful spinal condition required Thomas to assume responsibilities beyond supervising the congressman's wardrobe. He also drew therapeutic hot baths, assisted Kennedy on stairs, and helped him into his back brace, trousers, and shoes.[6] Addison's disease rendered the congressman prone to periodic illnesses, and he required even more assistance after his spinal surgeries. Once in the White House, Kennedy traveled the globe with Thomas at his side, including the fateful trip to Dallas in November 1963. JFK's second valet never uttered a negative word about his boss.[7]

John F. Kennedy and his valet, George Thomas, at the president's 1963 birthday party. (Cecil Stoughton, White House Photographs/ JFKL)

As a member of the House of Representatives, Kennedy supported civil rights for African Americans in the District of Columbia. He also voted against the poll tax and for antilynching laws.[8] Yet in planning a run for the White House, Senator Kennedy tried to find a midpoint between the Democratic Party's Northern and Midwestern pro–civil rights wing and its powerful Southern segregationist bloc.[9] His comments and votes on the 1957 Civil Rights Act reflected a purely pragmatic (some might say opportunistic) mix of conservatism and liberalism.[10]

In 1961, biographer James MacGregor Burns wrote that JFK "has dealt so long with intractable problems that he resists sweeping judgments and doctrinaire solutions. . . . To him, politics is the art of the possible. Kennedy is a pragmatist." Burns asked whether JFK on civil rights was "a profile in cowardice," but he noted that the moderate 1957 civil rights bill reflected "a tangle of conflicting ideologies, sectional strife, party maneuvering, and presidential ambitions."[11] In the wake of the US Supreme Court's 1954–55 *Brown I* and *II* decisions, voiding law-based racial segregation in public schools and ordering compliance "with all deliberate speed,"[12] the 1956 presidential campaign included civil rights agendas in both the Stevenson and Eisenhower campaigns.

As historian Robert Dallek concluded, "Unlike Hubert Humphrey, another rival for the White House, who had a long-standing, visceral commitment to ending segregation, or even LBJ, whose political actions masked a sincere opposition to segregation, Jack Kennedy's response to the great civil rights debates of 1957–60 was largely motivated by self-serving political considerations."[13] Mrs. Roosevelt thought likewise about Kennedy's opportunism and believed only Humphrey exhibited the courage to warrant a ticket to the Oval Office.[14]

On both procedure and substance, Senator Kennedy made the choices of an ambitious legislator trying not to inflame constituencies. In the procedural realm, liberals wanted to bypass the Senate Judiciary Committee and its rabid segregationist chair James Eastland (a Democrat from Mississippi) to bring the House's civil rights bill directly to the Senate floor for consideration. JFK opposed the rare tactic, fearing that conservatives could abuse it in the future. Southern delegates had supported his VP run at the 1956 Chicago convention, and he knew he needed them for his presidential bid in 1960. His more liberal colleagues narrowly won a vote to discharge the bill from committee. An affronted Black voter in New York wrote to Kennedy to express his disappointment over JFK's procedural stance and promised that "Negroes" would long remember his decision.[15] In forthcoming speeches, Kennedy cited a poem allegedly discovered in the files of a deceased parliamentarian:

> Among life's dying embers
> These are my regrets:
> When I'm "right" no one remembers,
> When I'm "wrong" no one forgets.[16]

Certainly, Mrs. Roosevelt wouldn't. The congressional battle over civil rights turned to the merits of two particularly contentious debates on the 1957 bill. Title III would give the attorney general power to enjoin violators of school desegregation orders. Southerners complained such increased federal power would resurrect despised Reconstruction policies perpetrated on the former Confederacy by the victorious Union after the Civil War. Knowing the title would fail, JFK felt free to court liberals by voting for it.[17]

The next controversy arose over an amendment to the bill that would have required jury trials for election officials accused of criminal contempt for denying Black Americans' voting rights. All the pro–civil rights constituencies supported by Eleanor—labor, the NAACP, and Americans for Democratic Action—opposed the requirement, presuming that local juries would never convict voting rights violators. Southern senators planned a filibuster of the entire legislation if the jury mandate wasn't added. Governors in the South amplified the pressure Kennedy felt by cabling him to support the amendment, and one linked it to his political "future."[18] JFK's contorted straddle of civil rights advocates, Black voters, and Southern segregationists boded ill for his presidential aspirations.

Looking down the road three years to the 1960 campaign, Kennedy understood that Southern Baptists and other Protestants in the Bible Belt already viewed his Catholicism as one strike against him. He didn't want to add strike two by taking a liberal stand on civil rights.[19] After consulting two renowned Harvard Law School professors, Mark DeWolfe Howe and Paul Freund, who counseled that he should support the jury trial provision because its importance had been exaggerated by both sides, the Massachusetts senator followed their advice. With Southern backing, the provision prevailed by one vote. Ultimately, the 1957 Civil Rights Act, the first such legislation since the immediate post–Civil War era, passed.[20] Just after Eisenhower signed the bill into law, he had to dispatch the Army's 101st Airborne Division to Little Rock, Arkansas, to keep order when nine African American students attempted to enroll in the city's all-white high school, as the *Brown* decisions mandated.[21] The 1957 act left unaddressed discrimination in employment and public accommodations; those third rails of American politics would await Ike's successor.

Burns concluded that JFK hadn't displayed a "profile in cowardice" on civil rights, but rather a "profile in caution and moderation."[22] Although Eleanor Roosevelt could embrace moderation when political circumstances required it, she preferred to address issues from a position of moral principle and ideological purity. Never having to run for elective public office afforded her that luxury, and she deliberately eschewed electoral politics to maintain that privilege. She admitted in her 1956 oral history that she would have made a poor politician, as her husband observed, because she wasn't "patient."[23] Yet Joe Lash, who witnessed her principled stands, also praised her ability to "[temper] idealism with practicality" when necessary.[24] As Allida Black, founder of the Eleanor Roosevelt Papers Project, concluded, "She embraced coalitions and championed compromise, but she always tried to 'compromise up.'"[25]

ER's grandson David B. Roosevelt wrote that her idealism demanded to know

> why were the laws and traditions that reinforced social injustice and economic imbalance perpetuated? In asking such questions and demanding answers, she would challenge other leaders about society's accepted norms. She sought to strip those institutions and laws of the elements that separated people. There was a purity, some would say a naïveté, in her vision and course. She held the single belief that all people *are* equal, and that no law or institution can place conditions on equality. These attributes lent all the more power to her positions, for she would not hesitate to ask questions that others should ask but wouldn't.[26]

Yet even Eleanor Roosevelt's worldview had to evolve toward progressivism, especially in civil rights. "I quite understand the [white] southern point of view," she explained in 1935, "because my grandmother was a southerner from Georgia, and her sister had a great deal to do with bringing us up when we were small children, therefore, I am familiar with the old plantation life."[27]

A generation older than JFK, descended from a longer line of socioeconomic elites raised in segregated enclaves, and limited by her gender in professional opportunities, she, like Kennedy, had minimal direct experience with African Americans in her early years. At the turn of the twentieth century, when Eleanor was sixteen, Black residents constituted less than 2 percent of New York City's population.[28] And she was unlikely to encounter them at her family's Hudson River estates. Also like the Kennedys, the Roosevelts employed white household staff in their Northeastern homes. When Eleanor accompanied her husband to Raleigh, North Carolina, in 1913, she seemed to comprehend her parochial upbringing, commenting to her aunt, "There seems so much to see and know and to learn to understand in this big country of ours, and so few of us ever try to even realize that we ought to try when we've lived in the environment that you and I grew up in."[29] Yet biographer Blanche Wiesen Cook explains that ER, trying to ingratiate herself with her formidable mother-in-law, Sara Delano Roosevelt, parroted her racist observations in letters: "One is continually surprised to read sentences in this correspondence [between Eleanor and FDR's mother] of flip, class-bound arrogance and egregious racism."[30] As late as 1937, through a letter from her secretary Malvina (Tommy) Thompson, ER defended her use of the term "darky," which her "Georgia great aunt" had used "as a term of affection."[31] The First Lady had "always considered it in that light." She apologized to a young Black woman who had written to complain of Mrs. Roosevelt's usage of this "hated" and "humiliating" label. "What [term] do you prefer?" she asked the complainant.[32]

Eleanor's more independent streak in public policy began to appear when her husband entered politics in 1910 with a successful run for the New York state senate. After his election, she discovered that learning about social issues in Albany appealed to her. Her previous interest in antipoverty programs, dating from her work in the Rivington Street Settlement House and her visits to New York City tenements, had been discouraged by her family, especially after her children were born, for fear that she would expose them to disease.[33]

When her husband was appointed assistant secretary of the Navy in 1913 during the administration of Woodrow Wilson, she and FDR moved to Washington. For the first time, she lived in a city with a large African American population—nearly 30 percent of Washington's residents.[34] Legally mandated racial segregation in housing, schools, and public accommodations, however, would have made Eleanor's interaction with them unlikely. She sent her children to elite private schools in the nation's capital. The federal government also followed strict segregation policies mandated by President Wilson, who was born and reared in the South.[35] In her memoir, Eleanor made a point to note that "two old colored servants" cared for her aunt's home, where she and Franklin lived initially. With three surviving children and two more who would survive infancy, her life centered on family and the social obligations of a political wife, which primarily included making formal calls on the wives of government officials or being visited at her home. In retrospect, she regretted not learning more about national government and public policy during those years.[36]

The nascent civil rights movement of the early twentieth century, including the establishment of the NAACP—founded in 1910 on a platform of ending segregation, discrimination, disenfranchisement, and racial violence (especially lynching)—failed to attract her attention. Neither did she join First Lady Ellen Wilson's crusade to improve housing for Washington's Black community. Eleanor unwittingly prompted a racial tiff with her husband's boss, Secretary of the Navy Josephus Daniels, a white supremacist newspaper publisher from Raleigh, North Carolina, when she brought her family's white household staff to DC. Daniels believed that such menial laborers should be Black people.

As the United States came closer to entering the war that raged in Europe, ER found herself moving from a completely family-centric life to broader thoughts about the nation. Franklin's work focused on implications for the US Navy should America's entry into the war become a reality, as it did on April 6, 1917, with Congress's declaration (six weeks prior to John Kennedy's birth).[37] Now Eleanor's volunteerism and public consciousness expanded markedly. In addition to the usual female contribution of knitting socks, sweaters, and scarves for servicemen, she donned a Red Cross uniform and attended soldiers who passed through Washington's rail depots. Through bitter cold conditions in winter and oppressively hot DC summers, she labored to ease the burdens of men headed to the trenches of French battlefields—sometimes serving as many as 3,700 soldiers a day. When they returned, she toured hospitals for the wounded and "shell-shocked" and began her habit of assisting individuals with their personal needs and collecting funds to help improve conditions for those confined to institutions.[38]

Following World War I, Eleanor's progression on race and gender traced (if slowly) her own personal and marital evolution. After discovering Franklin's affair with Lucy Mercer in 1918, ER asserted herself in both her private and public lives. The next year, she terminated her white household servants, except for a British nurse, and hired a Black cook, kitchen maid, butler, and house maid. Using the vernacular of the time, she wrote to Sara, "Well, all my servants are gone, and all the darkies are here, and heaven knows how it will all turn out!" She found the cook more than capable in producing meals for numerous guests, but she was skeptical of the butler when he missed serving at an important luncheon because of pleurisy. "With darkies, one is always suspicious, even of a death in the family." On the other hand, she thought them "pleasanter to deal with" and uncomplaining about division of labor in the household. Still, Lash writes, "There was a long journey ahead before she freed herself of racial stereotypes and bias." When the nation's segregated capital erupted in race riots and harsh police crackdowns during the summer of 1919, in part because of Black military veterans returning to second-class citizenship, Eleanor, who had gone north with the children, worried more about her husband's safety than racial harmony in Washington.[39]

Franklin's dogged attempts to recover full mobility after his 1921 polio-inflicted paralysis included purchasing the dilapidated Warm Springs resort in Georgia in 1927, where he found that the spring water's buoyancy allowed him to "walk around in water 4 [feet] deep without brace or crutches almost as well as if I had nothing the matter with my legs." The rural Georgia enclave, which he revitalized with a new cottage for him and facilities for other polio survivors, would become his home away from home when he was not in New York.[40] Although the philanthropic project and FDR's personal therapeutic progress pleased Eleanor, she never embraced the Georgia venue wholeheartedly as a place where she wanted to spend considerable time. As Lash put it, "The atmosphere of the rural South, with its poverty and the degradation of Negro and poor whites, depressed her."[41] She wouldn't have encountered Black patients at Warm Springs, which banned their admission because FDR refused to counter local segregation laws and customs.[42]

Even by the late 1920s, race still had not moved to a prominent place on ER's personal policy agenda, as had women's rights and child labor issues, along with urban-rural disparities in her home state. Racial inequality began to concern her, however. When she purchased, with her friend Marion Dickerman, Todhunter, a private Manhattan girls' school, Eleanor taught American history and included this question on an exam: "How are Negroes excluded from voting in the South?"[43]

Remarkably, Mrs. Roosevelt's increased awareness about Black Americans and how she might contribute to their advancement began at about the same age (mid-forties) as it would for Jack Kennedy. Unfortunately for him, his life would end just after this awakening, but Eleanor would have another three decades to advocate expanded civil rights for African Americans, which is among the reasons, including the blessing of longevity, that her record in this area is much more extensive than the thirty-fifth president's.

ER's and JFK's respective associations with Black individuals may have sparked their epiphanies about the need for equality between the races. Just prior to her husband's election to the New York governorship in 1928, Eleanor met Mary McLeod Bethune, president of the National Association of Colored Women. Born to formerly enslaved parents in South Carolina only a decade after the Civil War ended, Bethune believed education would provide the necessary ticket to upward mobility and self-sustainability, especially for Black women. She founded what would become Bethune-Cookman University in Daytona Beach, Florida, and was its precursor's president when she met Mrs. Roosevelt, who would eventually call her the closest friend among her peer group.[44] ER's habit of greeting and bidding farewell to friends with a kiss finally extended to Bethune, and Eleanor told her daughter that when she embraced her Black friend without thinking about it, she knew she had taken another step on her enlightenment journey. She had also felt comfortable with a racially integrated household staff at the New York governor's mansion in Albany.[45]

The closer Franklin came to the 1932 presidential nominating convention, the vaguer his positions became on policies that mattered to his wife.[46] Like Kennedy nearly three decades later, FDR understood that he had to placate constituencies across the ideological and geographical spectrum to win the Democratic Party's nomination. And, as she would with JFK, Eleanor remained impatient with her husband to accomplish her policy goals.

After her husband's 1932 presidential victory, ER worried that she might be relegated to White House hostess status. But her earliest days as First Lady of the United States found her touring Washington's back-alley slums, inhabited by 12,000 African Americans who remained trapped in disease-ridden squalor, long after First Lady Edith Wilson had attempted to ameliorate such wretched conditions. From her new White House position, Mrs. Roosevelt called for running water, sanitation facilities, and regular trash collection to make the fetid tenements in the nation's capital at least minimally habitable.[47] She took her requests to FDR and the press and called on Congress to legislate needed upgrades, not only in DC's slums but also in its hospitals, jails, and nursing homes, all substandard in serving Black residents.[48]

Mrs. Bethune's role in the New Deal expanded to include her appointment as director of the National Youth Association's Division of Negro Affairs. In that capacity, she encouraged historically Black colleges and universities (HBCUs) to develop civilian aviation courses, which trained the nation's first Black pilots.[49] Bethune also would form the Federal Council on Negro Affairs. Meeting in her home, the council came to be known as FDR's "Black Cabinet." The only female among its two dozen members, who served as administrators in New Deal agencies and cabinet departments, Bethune also stood out because of her dark complexion, of which her mother had taught her to be proud. The mere fact that she collaborated with the First Lady and appeared with her in public represented symbolic victories in interracial relations. More substantively, Bethune's political partnership with ER "sensitized" the First Lady "to African American issues."[50]

Mrs. Roosevelt's first encounter with a policy dispute over racial segregation occurred after her husband placed her in charge of Arthurdale, a federally funded planned community for the impoverished in West Virginia during the Depression. White residents voted down the inclusion of Black residents in this New Deal homesteading and subsistence farming experiment. The First Lady invited African American leaders to the White House to discuss the matter and other issues related to policies toward Black Southerners. Her sympathy for their causes impressed the visitors, as did the president's brief exchange with them. Yet the Roosevelts recognized that it made more sense to push for African American participation in New Deal programs rather than dismantling Jim Crow. Even Eleanor's high ideals had to give way to the reality that her husband simply couldn't lose Southern legislators' support for his efforts to mitigate the Depression's ravages by pressing for racial equality. Likewise, John Kennedy would accept in the 1950s and 1960s that the Democratic Party's powerful Southern wing, with its seniority in Congress and votes at the ballot box, shaped the contours of public policy.

Nevertheless, the First Lady, continually importuned by NAACP leader Walter White, lobbied FDR for congressional passage of an antilynching law. As African Americans pressed for equal rights after World War I, white supremacists responded with violent reprisals, including torture and lynching. Between 1920 and 1934, 358 lynchings of Black Americans occurred in the United States. After a particularly heinous murder and mutilation of a Black victim in Florida in 1934, ER and the NAACP redoubled their efforts. The threat of a filibuster by Southern senators pressured FDR to retreat from advocating the bill. Eleanor had to accept her husband's judgment, although she reported to his Southern press secretary, Steve Early, who complained about White's lobbying of the president, that "if I were colored, I think I should have about the same obsession that he has [with the antilynching bill]."[51]

Mrs. Roosevelt reminisced in 1958 about the controversy:

> I remember very well on the anti-lynching bill, which was up at that time, when Walter White came down and asked [the president] once. [FDR] explained that he could not make that bill a must because he had to have the southern vote for what he considered a priority—rearmament—in case you had to meet war. So I said, "Well, I feel very strongly about the anti-lynching bill. You're not sure it's constitutional. Perhaps it isn't. But I feel it should pass if the public could talk about it." He said, "I didn't say you had to take any special stand. You do what you think is right."

> [She smiles.] On one other occasion, when I asked him about something, he said, "Well, I can always say I can't do anything with my wife!"[52]

When an issue involving racial segregation in the US Navy came to Eleanor's attention, she inquired of the branch's secretary, a former Virginia senator, whether Black sailors could only hold the position of messmen. Yes, came the answer, because in any other position they could advance in rank and potentially supervise white sailors, "which would result in a lack of teamwork, would create dissatisfaction, and would handicap ship efficiency." Revealing some tolerance for the status quo, one based on political realities, Mrs. Roosevelt admitted, "These things come slowly, and patience is required in all great changes."[53]

Foreshadowing the very same political dilemma that Sen. John Kennedy would face in the 1950s, between radical change and evolutionary progress on race, the First Lady wrote in a 1938 letter to a young African American woman, future civil rights leader and ER friend Pauli Murray, who complained about the University of North Carolina's ban on admitting Black students: "Sometimes it is better to fight hard with conciliatory methods. The South is changing, but don't push too hard. There is a great change in youth," she encouraged the disappointed correspondent, "and that is a hopeful sign."[54] Yet in the same year, when the federal minimum wage went into effect and some employers wanted to offer it only to white employees, Eleanor responded, "This is a question of the right to work, and the right to work knows no color lines."[55]

The most publicized racial controversy involving Eleanor Roosevelt centered on Marian Anderson's 1939 appearance in Washington.[56] The world-renowned contralto became the first African American to perform at the White House when the Roosevelts hosted her in 1936. The First Lady intended to invite her to return in June 1939 to entertain Britain's King George VI and Queen Elizabeth. Each year Anderson appeared at a Howard University benefit concert in the nation's capital, but her rising popularity necessitated larger venues. For the spring 1939 performance, the university requested use of Constitution Hall, the largest auditorium in DC. The national headquarters of the Daughters of

Eleanor Roosevelt with contralto Marian Anderson in Japan, 1953. (Courtesy of FDRL)

the American Revolution could accommodate four thousand attendees. Although it had a whites-only membership policy, the DAR had, nevertheless, allowed Black patrons to sit with whites at a 1932 performance of an African American artist—in violation of Washington's segregation laws (though they were not strictly enforced). Reaction among DAR members proved so negative that the organization promulgated a rule against hosting Black performers and stamped contracts with the phrase, "Concerts By White Artists Only." The DAR first denied Howard University a booking for Anderson based on that policy but later claimed the hall was already reserved for the requested date. For weeks, Howard University and Anderson's agent, with the support of civil rights groups, pursued efforts to find a suitably large venue.[57]

The DAR had made Eleanor Roosevelt a member when her husband won the presidency in 1932. She hadn't been active in the organization, but should she now attempt to fight its racist policy from the inside? Initially, she balked, fearing that her "radical" reputation would only inflame the controversy, aggravate the DC community, and rile Southern Democrats whose support FDR needed in Congress. Moreover, she anticipated that other DAR members would oppose such a blatantly unjust policy. Meanwhile, she worked behind the scenes.[58]

When she realized that other members failed to take up the cause of the acclaimed operatic star, Eleanor resigned from the conservative institution with a letter to the DAR's president-general. ER confessed that she had not been "a very useful member," so she doubted if it meant much whether she remained on its rolls or departed—quite a comment from a famed First Lady. Obviously, the organization thought it noteworthy to claim the president's wife as a member. But she had to admit that she "was in complete disagreement with the attitude taken in refusing Constitution Hall to a great artist. You have set an example which I believe is unfortunate." She further chastised the institution: "You had an opportunity to lead in an enlightened way, and it seems to me that your organization has failed." She knew that "many people" would not agree with her decision to resign, but it seemed to her that resignation was "the only proper procedure to follow." The DAR president-general regretted the First Lady's decision because she thought the organization shared Eleanor's goals in "citizenship education and humanitarian issues." If only she could have presented the institution's "attitude" to Mrs. Roosevelt in person, she believed the "misunderstanding" could have been avoided.[59]

Eleanor refused to buy that tepid explanation. Without mentioning the DAR, her "My Day" column described how she usually addressed principled differences with organizations to which she belonged. She would fight the good fight, but, if unsuccessful, she might then resign, realizing that perhaps she was wrong or at least ahead of her time on an issue. Because she was inactive in the unnamed organization, her column indicated, she had no choice but to depart.[60]

Given the global reputations of both Mrs. Roosevelt and Marian Anderson, Walter White accurately claimed that the First Lady's decision had "focused world-wide attention on the episode." At home, two-thirds of Americans in a Gallup poll supported her resignation from the DAR,[61] the same percentage of voters who had supported her husband in his 1936 landslide reelection victory. As author Allida Black observed, ER's "masterful political strategy resounded with long-range political and public policy implications."[62]

After the First Lady's insistent pressure, and with FDR's approval, Secretary of the Interior Harold Ickes, a former NCAAP Chicago branch leader, offered use of the Lincoln Memorial and its plaza for hosting

Anderson at an Easter Sunday concert. To avoid drawing attention away from the headliner, Eleanor sent regrets but encouraged radio networks to broadcast the event. The symbolism of the regal African American star, standing before the Great Emancipator's majestic statue, grew more explicit when Secretary Ickes introduced Anderson, and the massive crowd of 75,000 Black and white spectators cheered each line. "In this great auditorium under the sky, all of us are free. When God gave this wonderful outdoors, and the sun, the moon, and the stars, he made no distinction of race or creed or color," Ickes declared. On that Easter Sunday in 1939, the interior secretary described Abraham Lincoln as laying down his life to secure freedom for the enslaved; thus, it was appropriate that "a glorious tribute is rendered to his memory by a daughter of the race from which he struck the chains of slavery. . . . Genius draws no color lines."[63]

Anderson's stirring rendition of the patriotic hymn "America" ("My Country 'Tis of Thee"),[64] with its concluding line, "From ev'ry mountainside; let freedom ring," foreshadowed the theme of Dr. Martin Luther King Jr.'s "I Have a Dream Speech," to be delivered from nearly the same spot a quarter century later. Anderson would sing again at the Lincoln Memorial—this time to the 250,000 gathered for the 1963 March on Washington for Jobs and Freedom.

Her presentation of the African American spiritual "Nobody Knows the Trouble I've Seen," with its roots among enslaved Black people, couldn't have constituted a more poignant encore for her 1939 performance.[65] She mesmerized the masses of white and Black attendees, dressed in their Sunday best, and thousands more listening on radios across the country.

Many years later, Anderson commented with understated modesty that she wasn't "a real great fighter for anything. There are people who, if they want something, they fight, fight, fight. . . . And those people are very, very necessary. But there are some who hope that if they're doing something worthwhile that it will speak for them."[66] She may not have been a fighter in her own mind, but her steadfast courage in overcoming American racism, with fighters like Eleanor Roosevelt and Harold Ickes embracing her cause, helped her breach the barriers Jim Crow placed

John F. Kennedy with Marian Anderson and her accompanist in the Oval Office, 1962. (Robert Knudsen, White House Photographs/JFKL)

in her path to success. Just four years after the Lincoln Memorial concert, the DAR lowered its own barrier to host Anderson in concert at Constitution Hall to raise funds for the war effort. Perhaps even more significant, whites *and* Blacks attended.[67] She would perform the national anthem for the Eisenhower and Kennedy inaugurals in 1957 and 1961 and visit JFK in the White House during his presidency. Anderson met with President Kennedy, German chancellor Konrad Adenauer, South Dakota Senator George McGovern, and Mrs. Woodrow Wilson in 1961 as part of a foundation to fight world hunger. JFK inscribed a photo of the meeting to her, "With esteem and best wishes."[68]

As war grew closer in the Far East and Europe in 1939, FDR signed a law expanding the Army Air Corps and creating programs at Black colleges to train African Americans in a host of Air Corps support services beyond menial jobs in mess halls and mechanical shops. At the same time, Mrs. Roosevelt's advocacy of racial equality in the United States paralleled the fight against fascism and her plea to save Jews from Hitler's reign of terror, eventually to include "the final solution"—the extermination of non-Aryans.[69]

What an embarrassment for the United States that Nazi laws defining Jewish identity deliberately rejected America's "one drop" custom, which determined that even the smallest measure of Black blood made an individual a "Negro." Hitler's policies gave more latitude to defining the preferred Aryan caste, based on eugenics and racial science, than the United States exercised in laws that determined that an otherwise white person with only a scintilla of African heritage was Black (and therefore of the lowest caste).[70]

As the United States inched closer to war, the most prominent racial issue addressed discrimination in the armed forces and defense industries. On September 16, 1940, FDR signed the Selective Training and Service Act, marking the nation's first peacetime conscription. The law provided that "within the limits of the quota determined . . . any person, regardless of race or color, . . . shall be afforded opportunity to *volunteer* for induction. . . . In the selection and training of men under this Act, and in the interpretation and execution of the provisions of this Act, there shall be no discrimination against any person on account of race and color."[71] In other words, while Black Americans could offer their services to the military, the nation wouldn't treat them like white males, who would be drafted. Yet that new policy represented at least some progress in allowing African Americans and other minorities to serve.

After FDR signed the draft law, Howard University law professor and civil rights advocate James B. Nesbit Jr. told the First Lady, "As has usually been the past seven years, whenever Negroes are unduly disturbed, they have turned to you." He was writing to request that Black Americans be allowed to serve in all levels of the selective-service process. Eleanor agreed and urged her husband to insist that they be included on local draft boards. She also cautioned him that "there is a growing feeling amongst the colored people . . . [that] they should be allowed to participate in any training that is going on, in the aviation, Army, Navy, and have opportunities of service."[72] ER would be just as vociferous in promoting equal participation by Black and white women in the armed forces.[73]

Black leaders knew that changing military and corporate policies would form the core of their next fight, and they approached the 1940 election with pressure on the Democratic incumbent, who had tossed his trademark fedora into the ring for an unprecedented third time, and his Republican opponent, lawyer and corporate executive Wendell Willkie.[74] A native Hoosier, Willkie was more progressive than FDR on civil rights, calling for ending segregation in the federal civil service, military, and in Washington, DC. The *Pittsburgh Courier* and the *Baltimore Afro-American,* two newspapers with the largest Black readership, endorsed Willkie. Although President Roosevelt remained popular among African Americans who had joined the New Deal coalition,[75] he worried that his GOP opponent's more liberal civil rights platform might attract Black votes and return them to the party of Lincoln.[76]

Partisan identification among African American voters split evenly between Democrats and Republicans in 1940, yet Roosevelt came very close to equaling the 71 percent of Black votes that he had amassed in 1936.[77] Surely his wife's close ties to that constituency, and her untiring efforts to support it, kept Black voters in Roosevelt's corner. As Lash explained, "Eleanor was the channel through which the Negroes maintained their pressure on the president, and because she was effective in gaining consideration of Negro demands, she was also instrumental in keeping the Negro vote Democratic."[78] Notably, the First Lady didn't have to be successful in achieving all African American goals. Her sympathetic ear, transmission of the constituency's messages straight to the president, and advocacy with him often seemed good enough.

As FDR's unprecedented third term commenced, the First Lady knew that she wanted to add ending segregation to her equal economic opportunity agenda from the first two terms. She warned her husband that segregation "warps and twists" African American lives. The Navy secretary had explained to Eleanor previously that Black sailors shouldn't achieve superior rank and supervisory status over whites in military service, and it became clear that white commissioned officers would continue to command Black units. Secretary of War Henry Stimson complained that Mrs. Roosevelt supported an increase in African American officers.[79]

Black leaders grew impatient over lack of progress in providing employment opportunities for African Americans in defense industries, and some called for a protest march on Washington in the summer of 1941 to persuade the administration to address these inequities.

Knowing that such a demonstration could provoke violence in the nation's capital, still a bastion of segregation, ER's idealism yielded to pragmatism. She promised the NAACP's Walter White that she would plead the Black leaders' case to the president, who agreed to a White House meeting with them to hear their concerns and suggestions for a new policy with genuine enforcement power.[80]

In June 1941, FDR signed an executive order banning discrimination in the defense industry and establishing the Fair Employment Practice Committee to enforce the edict. Black leaders scotched the threatened march.[81] Walter White expressed his delight over the president's appointment of liberal journalist Mark Ethridge to chair the committee. Although a native Mississippian, Etheridge despised white supremacy, which he labeled "a complete denial of the democratic process and a complete humiliation of all people who profess any faith in democracy." Ethridge published editorials in the *Louisville Courier-Journal* calling for equal opportunity in business and agriculture for Black workers and abolition of the poll tax.[82]

Most HBCUs eagerly initiated programs and courses to train African Americans for wartime service. Tuskegee Institute, the Alabama college cofounded by Booker T. Washington, had established a civilian pilot training program in 1939, and two years later the War Department created the all-Black 99th Pursuit (later renamed Fighter) Squadron there. Mrs. Roosevelt's ongoing quest for racial equality and her interest in aviation pioneers (she had flown over the White House with Amelia Earhart in 1933 and earned a student pilot license) prompted her visit to the Tuskegee training center, where she accepted an invitation to fly with the African American civilian flight instructor who had founded the training program in 1939. Photos of the First Lady, smiling broadly in the passenger seat just after they landed, spoke volumes for her support of the program to train Black military aviators and, eventually, commissioned officers. They served with distinction in Europe and the Mediterranean, accompanying US bomber raids, and never lost a Tuskegee Airmen's Fighter Squadron plane to enemy fire.[83]

Black participants in the HBCU training courses thought they could achieve first-class citizenship by supporting their nation's industrial war effort following the Japanese attack on Pearl Harbor in December 1941. But many Southern companies refused to hire these well-trained, patriotic workers, fearing a backlash from white employees and undoubtedly harboring their own racist tendencies. The War Manpower Commission, established by FDR's executive order in spring of 1942, coordinated labor needs in industry, agriculture, and the armed services. Its Dallas regional office advised African Americans to head north and west if they wanted to work in defense plants and shipyards. One frustrated African American posed a riveting query: "Why should I shed my blood for Roosevelt's America, for [white supremacists] Senator [Ellison] 'Cotton Ed' Smith, and Senator [Theodore] Bilbo, for the whole Jim Crow, Negro-hating South, for the low-paid, dirty jobs for which Negroes have to fight, for the few dollars of relief and the insults, discrimination, police brutality, and perpetual poverty to which Negroes are condemned even in the more liberal North?"[84]

Mrs. Roosevelt's prewar warning to her husband about growing African American agitation proved accurate. After Pearl Harbor, she asserted in a letter to one of her white critics, "Unless we make the country worth fighting for by Negroes, we would have nothing to offer the world at the end of the war." She knew that that the United States and its allies couldn't fight Hitler's racism and then "have ten percent of our population . . . denied their rights as citizens."[85]

Led by theologian Reinhold Niebuhr, the new Union for Democratic Action asked the First Lady to arrange a meeting with President Roosevelt to present a petition calling for the abolition of the armed forces' racially discriminatory policies. Eleanor thought a delegation of distinguished citizens both white and Black should convene with her husband, but when she asked to schedule an Independence Day meeting with him, he declined.[86] Their grandson, Curtis, concluded that the war drew most of the president's attention, leaving less time for him to devote to ER's causes.[87]

As Eleanor reflected generally on her policy relationship with FDR in her 1956 oral history: "Sometimes he would like to do the easier thing, even though he was pretty well convinced that wasn't the right thing to do. And I think those were the times when he wished to goodness he didn't have to look at someone who would demand of him what he really thought was the thing to do. In a way, my conscience bothered him."[88] But wrangling FDR was good practice for how Mrs. Roosevelt would goad the conscience of a young Massachusetts senator with presidential aspirations.

Constantly on watch for denial of rights, the First Lady found another instance in summer 1942, after an all-white Virginia jury had convicted and sentenced to death a young African American sharecropper, Odell Waller, for murdering his white landlord. Waller explained in a letter to Mrs. Roosevelt that he shot him to prevent the landlord from "hurting me." The case became a cause célèbre among civil rights advocates who demanded an end to segregated juries and the poll tax, especially after the Supreme Court refused to review Waller's appeal. The Old Dominion's segregationist governor, Colgate Darden Jr., issued multiple reprieves but then denounced the campaign to commute the sentence. Black leaders pressured Mrs. Roosevelt to intervene with Darden to reduce the death penalty to life imprisonment. She contacted the governor and convinced her husband to do so, as well. They failed to convince Darden, and Virginia executed Waller by electrocution.[89]

Pauli Murray, along with many other African American civil rights activists, expressed their upset with the outcome of Waller's case. In an open letter to FDR, they demanded to know how Black Southerners could ever achieve justice when the judicial and voting systems were both rigged against them. Murray noted in a missive sent directly to the president that his 1940 GOP opponent, Wendell Willkie, had taken a more progressive stand on civil rights, and she urged FDR to do likewise if he wished to earn reelection to a fourth term. Eleanor dispatched an equally pointed reply to Murray that Willkie held no public office and could "say whatever he likes," but the president had to consider the political impact of his policies on his relations with Congress. Like Willkie, Mrs. Roosevelt had the freedom to state her mind, she observed, yet she couldn't do so "with much sense of security unless the president was willing for me to do so."[90] She wouldn't display the same acceptance of JFK's political pragmatism as an office holder.

Eleanor's public line on race, between idealistic promotion of equal opportunity and desegregation and pragmatic counseling of patience to Black Americans, reflected the realities of the country's oldest and most complex "dilemma," as Swedish sociologist Gunnar Myrdal labelled the issue of race in the United States. In 1943, ER published an article entitled "If I Were a Negro" for the *Negro Digest;* in it, she maintained that she recognized how Black people felt about injustices but warned, "I would not do too much demanding." The First Lady encouraged support for the war and acceptance of "advances" made in the armed forces but cautioned against rapid progress. This moderate approach to race pleased neither African Americans nor segregationists.[91] At least she maintained an open mind toward more radical approaches to racism, as espoused by younger civil rights leaders like Murray.[92]

Yet pivoting from one approach to another on the question of race positioned ER squarely in the sights of both sides in the civil rights debate. Southern white supremacists spread vicious rumors about her supposed activities to promote Black insurrection against the legal and cultural norms in the former Confederate states. In the North, a destination of Black Southerners' "great migration," white opponents attributed Detroit's 1943 race riot to her civil rights advocacy. For her *Negro Digest* article, however, a Black cleric chastised her, "Am I to be blamed for asking and even insisting that I be treated as a man and a full-fledged citizen in the land of my birth?"[93]

Mrs. Roosevelt defended and clarified this moderate approach in a response to the pastor, arguing that she certainly believed that "colored people" should demand what they want but should turn to "white people who believe as they do . . . to do most of the fighting and demanding." She added the truism that white Southerners were more likely to listen to advocates from their own region than from the North. The First Lady also cited "very great" advancements for the "Negro" in both the Army and Navy, in contrast to World War I, due to the executive order "against discrimination." But she noted that this progress required genuine change in "the human heart," which evolves slowly.[94] Mrs. Roosevelt's suggestions were reflected in white and Black Southern moderates' founding of the Southern Regional Council in 1944 to condemn racial violence and promote equality through Dixie's economic development.[95]

The Democratic Party hewed to the center in both the president's new choice for the vice-presidential spot on the ticket (jettisoning the left's hero and Eleanor's preference, Henry Wallace, for the party bosses' choice, Missouri Senator Harry Truman) and abjuring a civil rights plank in the 1944 party platform.[96]

Eleanor continued her drumbeat for equality in the armed forces. Whenever she visited troops overseas, at considerable risk to herself, she always made sure to see both Black and white soldiers, sailors, airmen, and marines. Whether it was her 1942 trip to the UK or her even more dangerous visit to the Pacific Theater in 1943, including a visit to Guadalcanal, she knew that photos with men and women of both races represented another symbolic push for equality. More substantively, she fought for an end to racial segregation in military recreational facilities and transportation. In 1943, the War Department issued an edict barring racial designations for any accommodations that provided welfare for troops.[97] Returning from her five-week South Pacific tour, she told the American people in a poignant radio broadcast that our men fought and died together, regardless of their race or religion, and added that "if your heart is with any man" (as hers was with all four of her sons serving in combat zones around the world), "in some ways it must be with all."[98]

In a segregated military, African Americans continued to perform menial jobs or those deemed too dangerous for white service members. The policy only began to change after a massive explosion in 1944 killed more than 250 Black sailors and nearly 70 of their white counterparts as they loaded munitions on ships at Port Chicago, a northern California base. The Navy brought mutiny charges against 250 traumatized African American survivors who refused orders to return to the same jobs that had killed their comrades and for which they were poorly trained. Courts-martial convicted fifty of the accused leaders of the supposed mutiny. NAACP lawyer Thurgood Marshall brought the injustice to Navy Secretary James Forrestal's attention, and FDR succeeded in persuading naval leaders to allow Black officers and enlisted men to serve on ships.[99] By this time, Lt. (j.g.) John F. Kennedy was a wounded war veteran of the South Pacific who had served with an all-white crew on his ill-fated PT boat and was released from active duty after returning stateside in 1944.

When FDR succumbed to a fatal cerebral hemorrhage at his cherished Warm Springs retreat in April 1945, his wife lost the First Lady's equivalent of a bully pulpit, but she gained release from her husband's political fetters. As her grandson explained, "Grandmère's freedom now provided her with an even more forceful voice on those issues of concern."[100] On the Port Chicago mutiny trials, she wrote to Forrestal, "I hope in the case of these boys, special care will be taken."[101] ER believed she and President Roosevelt had shared similar goals but different timetables on racial progress.[102] Democracy's gears grind slowly, especially when Southern leaders poured sand in the transmission. But even though FDR had to apply the brakes, Eleanor maintained that he urged her to keep an eye on the destination. One avenue to arriving there, after his death, was her acceptance of an appointment to the NAACP's board.[103] The organization's executive director, Roy Wilkins, later contrasted the Roosevelts on race, describing the president as a "friend of Negroes only insofar as he refused to exclude the Negro from his general policies that applied to the whole country, whereas Mrs. Roosevelt was the Negro's true friend. The personal touches and the personal fight against discrimination were Mrs. Roosevelt's. That attached to [Franklin] Roosevelt also—he couldn't get away from it—and he reaped the political benefit from it."[104]

Eleanor experienced the limits that office-holding can place on an official after President Truman appointed her a US delegate to the UN. He did so because of her appeal to Black voters, whom he would face for his own election to the presidency in 1948. Much as another accidental president, Lyndon Johnson, would consider naming JFK's widow Jacqueline to an ambassadorship, Truman had advised Secretary of State James Byrnes to search for a position Eleanor could fill soon after FDR's death.[105] Both domestic and international politics, however, constrained her options in dealing with racial issues. Southerners, anticommunists, and cold warriors all took issue with her positions. Yet, as previously noted, her hard-fought gains in finding common ground produced the

1948 Universal Declaration of Human Rights.[106] Still, unlike her husband and JFK, she never had to face voters or try to placate them and their representatives in passing a full public policy agenda.

Eleanor continued to expand her work incrementally, however, through organizations such as the Highlander Folk School in Tennessee, which had been founded in 1932 to teach basic skills to laborers, including how to organize unions. It attracted Mrs. Roosevelt's support in 1958, when she wrote the school a check for $100 and visited the Monteagle campus to participate in one of its workshops. The school had shifted its mission to civil rights, especially voter registration and desegregation, and had become a meeting place for leaders like Dr. King, Ralph Abernathy, and Rosa Parks to discuss strategies and tactics for the nonviolent movement's next steps after the successful 1957 Montgomery bus boycott. Highlander also joined with King's Southern Christian Leadership Council (SCLC) to form "citizenship schools" across the South, which taught literacy, civics, and nonviolent approaches to desegregation. ER's 1958 visit, despite death threats from a resurgent Ku Klux Klan (who placed a $25,000 bounty on her capture), represented another of her courageous acts in the service of equal rights. Refusing law enforcement protection, she and her hostess carried a loaded handgun, for which the former First Lady possessed a New York license, as they drove through rural Tennessee to the workshop. Her husband's former bodyguard Earl Miller had taught her to shoot when the Secret Service director gave her a handgun after the First Lady insisted on driving herself to events and appointments without security during her White House tenure.[107]

Notably, Mrs. Roosevelt included almost nothing of her views on race or civil rights advocacy in her three-volume memoir or its consolidated version. Perhaps she didn't wish to draw attention to the controversies so soon after they occurred when she published *This I Remember,* the second volume, in 1949.[108] But her work on racial issues is also conspicuously absent from the abridged compilation, published with an added update at the same time she was encouraging John Kennedy to press harder for civil rights. Foreign policy, countering Soviet influence, world peace, and training young Americans to meet these challenges occupied her thoughts and writing as the 1960s dawned. The book does, however, picture her with Martin Luther King Jr. as he receives the 1961 Distinguished Award from the Americans for Democratic Action.[109] Once more, ER said more with images than words. All civil rights advocates ran the risk of being labeled communists, none more so than Dr. King and Mrs. Roosevelt.

Yet her last testament to the world, *Tomorrow Is Now,* published posthumously in 1963, contains a chapter on the "social revolution" in race. She called for equality in employment, education, health care, and human dignity. Her description of racial intermarriage as a rarity is now as dated as the 1968 film *Guess Who's Coming to Dinner,* in which characters portrayed by Spencer Tracey and Katharine Hepburn find their liberal politics challenged when their white daughter announces she is marrying a "Negro" doctor (played by Sidney Poitier). The plot thickens when Poitier's Black father also raises objections to his son's marrying outside his race. "The immense majority of people instinctively seek their own kind," Mrs. Roosevelt wrote in her last book, to counter integration's opponents who argued that social and civil integration would lead to race mixing. "You can't change human nature. Would you like to see your daughter marry a Negro?" was the inevitable query segregationists posed to her in these debates. Eleanor argued that racial equality in education, employment, and housing had no relation to interracial marriage. Although her assertion about the social mixing of races now seems anachronistic, her support of a color-blind democracy was genuinely progressive in the early 1960s.[110]

What a journey Eleanor Roosevelt had taken on race. From the Southern prejudices imparted by her grandmother and aunt to the Hudson Valley biases of her Victorian mother-in-law, she had evolved to recognizing racial inequities as her political horizons broadened in the 1920s. By the time she arrived at the White House in 1933, with Mary McLeod Bethune and Walter White as friends and colleagues, she embraced the causes of antilynching and equal treatment of minorities in New Deal programs and their administration. Fighting murderous vigilantism, unemployment, and hunger that took such a toll on Black Americans, Eleanor perhaps deemed political rights and segregation less urgent during the depths of the Great Depression. In addition, she well understood, if not always readily accepted, her husband's need to protect his political viability in the South and among its representatives in Congress to keep him in office and effectuate the New Deal. Some congressional Southern conservatives began aligning with Republicans to oppose extension of FDR's liberal policies, and his attempt to purge the Democratic Party's right wing failed in the 1938 midterm elections. He was also losing segregationists in Sen. Harry F. Byrd's Virginia Democratic political machine because they considered the New Deal too leftist, even socialist. And they viewed Eleanor as an abomination for her racial views, association with communists, support for organized labor, and women's rights advocacy—all pursued by an unelected, and therefore unaccountable, First Lady. She gave them fodder for their attacks through her much-publicized support of Marian Anderson and her photographs with African Americans, from leaders like Mary Bethune to servicemen and -women overseas to children who welcomed her on visits to American cities. White supremacists publicized these images to reveal her breaking their Jim Crow codes of conduct.

As the social ills of hunger and unemployment eased with the start of World War II, Eleanor could turn to advocating desegregation of the armed forces and equal opportunity in defense industries. While she cautioned patience on attacking the South's racial policies during her husband's administration, Mrs. Roosevelt wouldn't grant JFK the same latitude as she did FDR, even though Kennedy faced the same problem with Southern Democrats in Congress and their constituents. As previously noted, part of her rigidity toward him at this time related to their differences in age, gender, cultural background, and family conflicts. But she was evolving more rapidly than he, owing to her longer experience as a policy advocate. Nearly a quarter century had passed between FDR's first inauguration and Eleanor's squabbles with JFK over his presidential run. Time was fleeting, along with her life, and she was more radicalized by the late 1950s. Her long-time friend Pauli Murray always tried to shift ER's moderate positions leftward. Certainly, the civil rights movement was moving forward with the NAACP's judicial successes in *Brown I* and *II*, the Montgomery bus boycott, and the 1957 founding of the SCLC and its collaboration with the Highlander School's development of citizenship schools to train civil rights leaders and workers. Mrs. Roosevelt served as an active member and fundraiser on the board of the Southern Conference Education Fund (SCEF) as it worked toward desegregation, employment opportunities, and enfranchisement for Southern Blacks in the 1950s. The SCEF also mentored young African Americans,[111] who grew impatient for faster change to integrate public accommodations and interstate travel and achieve full voting rights. In 1960, these young activists founded the Student Nonviolent Coordinating Committee (SNCC). We have seen all the reasons that JFK was slower on the uptake for racial equality than the former First Lady—from his cultural, educational, and military backgrounds that gave him far fewer interactions with people of color than ER had to his political pragmatism as a seeker of elective office, a consideration that never constrained her. Eleanor Roosevelt both foresaw and grasped the significance of the modern civil rights movement, realizing that patience and moderation were no longer viable options.

5

RIVALS TO ALLIES

ALTHOUGH THE 1956 CONVENTION CONTRETEMPS between Senator Kennedy and Mrs. Roosevelt played out in the privacy of her Chicago hotel suite, after she refused to back his impromptu run for the vice-presidential nomination, public tiffs awaited the pair as the 1960 nomination race neared. Eleanor Roosevelt was simply unwilling to accept that John Kennedy might become the new face of the Democratic Party. To her, he was too young, too inexperienced, too libertine, too ambitious, too moderate (especially on race and McCarthyism), too Catholic, and, worst of all, too close to his father, Ambassador Joseph P. Kennedy, whom she abhorred. She had tried to convert her husband to her brand of progressivism, but she made few efforts to do the same with JFK. He attempted to win Eleanor's support—or at least earn her respect—but to no avail. Instead, their mutual grievances about each other multiplied.

In mid-1959, Eleanor testified in favor of an increased minimum wage before Kennedy's Senate labor subcommittee, and JFK literally turned his back on the former First Lady, chatting with his staff during her statement.[1] Labor lobbyist Esther Peterson was taken aback. She had arranged for Eleanor to appear on the Hill at the hearing, and in

Peterson's meetings with JFK over the previous decade, she appreciated that he listened to her, unlike most of Congress's male members. But the lobbyist found his treatment of Eleanor offensive. "It was rather tense at that moment because of the relationship between the senator and Mrs. Roosevelt," she said. "I was annoyed with him the day she testified because here was this grand old lady, and he didn't come down and go through the niceties with her that one would expect, the respect, I think, that was due to her."

In addition to Kennedy's impertinence toward Eleanor, hearing-room spectators who disagreed with the former First Lady voiced their disregard for ER and her family. "I remember the dignity of this marvelous woman standing up to some of the remarks that they made about her and her children, confronting her as she was walking down an aisle," Peterson reported. "I remember her saying in answer to a 'hate' remark, '*Hate* is a strong word. Do you really want to use it?'"[2]

Perhaps Eleanor didn't hate Kennedy, yet his impudent behavior that day stiffened her opposition toward him, and ER's capacity to forgive and forget had diminished over the years. Despite her father's and brother's alcoholism, which pained her, she never stopped loving or caring for them. But Katie Louschheim, director of women's activities for the Democratic National Committee in 1960, described ER as "obdurate": "Mrs. Roosevelt, interestingly enough, I think quite late in life developed a very strong obstinate streak that you could not deal with. First of all, she had a relationship with President Kennedy's father which left its mark. And no matter what was said it could not be dislodged from her mind. . . . And she just didn't have any use for his son, and she couldn't believe that there could be any disassociation from generation to generation, which was very narrow minded of her, but was rather typical."[3]

Some politicos feared that Eleanor was just anti-Catholic enough to oppose Kennedy's White House aspirations. Yes, Mrs. Roosevelt had supported Al Smith, the first and only Roman Catholic to lead a major presidential ticket, but he had suffered a crushing defeat at the hands of Republican Herbert Hoover in 1928. JFK realized that he had to unify the Democratic Party to avoid a similar fate.

Joe Lash, Eleanor's friend, confidant, and biographer, believed that "somewhere deep in her subconscious was an anti-Catholicism which was part of her Protestant heritage" and that she wasn't immune to fears of "popery" so common among Protestants during her formative years.[4] In 1959, when JFK sent a young Jewish lawyer, Lester Hyman, to speak to Eleanor about a possible Kennedy nomination, she commented, "We wouldn't want a pope in the White House, would we?" Perhaps ER responded so frankly because she didn't know that Hyman was a JFK emissary.[5]

As Arthur Schlesinger Jr., another Eleanor ally, observed, "Old New Dealers cherished an ancient and ardent suspicion of Kennedy's father. And his candidacy touched uglier strains in the liberal syndrome, especially the susceptibility to anti-Catholicism."[6] When a brazen University of Virginia law student asked former President Truman, "What's going to happen when the pope moves into the White House?" the equally edgy Missourian responded, "It's not the pope I'm afraid of; it's the pop!"[7]

The New Deal's creator, FDR himself, may have possessed a more open mind on religion than his wife. She once mentioned to him that spiritualists frequently wrote to her about conversations they'd had with the dead, a notion she found absurd. Franklin cautioned his wife to appreciate others' spiritual beliefs, especially if unfathomable experiences couldn't be disproved: "I am interested [in] and have respect for whatever people believe, even if I cannot understand their beliefs or share their experiences."[8]

Yet Mrs. Roosevelt certainly embraced religious liberty as part of her husband's Four Freedoms and in her own contribution to the Universal Declaration of Human Rights. More likely than fears of an actual papal takeover of the presidency were Eleanor's concerns that a Catholic president might sway policy in favor of his church, particularly by diverting tax funds to parochial schools. In her liberal mind, this possibility would violate the First Amendment's ban on religious establishment. Such a deep-seated worry made her especially skeptical of Kennedy's quest for the nomination. She had already gone toe-to-toe on the issue with Francis Cardinal Spellman, who happened to be a close friend of the Kennedy family.[9] In fact, the Kennedys had turned to him for advice and as a go-between to the Vatican when JFK's sister Kathleen married an Anglican during World War II.[10]

Eleanor had drawn the ire of Catholic leaders as far back as the 1930s, when she expressed sympathy for the leftists in the Spanish Civil War, and she continued to counter Francisco Franco's victorious fascist regime. As a representative to the UN Commission on Human Rights, she successfully scuttled the normalization of relations between member countries and Spain. The Catholic hierarchy had also opposed her ties to groups like the American Youth Congress, with its communist influencers, and her support of birth control.[11]

After World War II, as the Iron Curtain descended on Eastern Europe, creating Soviet satellite nations that suppressed religious freedom, Spellman became vehemently anticommunist. It was Mrs. Roosevelt's endorsement of Congress's Barden bill, a proposed policy that would provide federal funds to public, but not parochial, schools that escalated the Roosevelt-Spellman conflict.[12] ER had already clashed with the cardinal over her opposition to the church's efforts to expunge anti-Catholic articles from New York City's public school libraries. Yet their primary battle emerged from Spellman's advocacy of federal funds to support parochial education.[13] In June 1949, Mrs. Roosevelt penned a response in her daily newspaper column calling for strict separation of church and state. Religious freedom, she argued, allowed Americans to establish private schools to promote their spiritual beliefs, but government should not fund them. Likewise, public schools should be free from religious influence.[14]

Eleanor's historically based op-ed nevertheless prompted a public salvo from Spellman, who condemned her as anti-Catholic, un-American, and unworthy of motherhood. In response, she wrote a personal letter to the fiery prelate, refuting his ad hominem attack: "I assure you that I had no sense of being 'an unworthy American mother.' The final judgment, my dear Cardinal Spellman, of the worthiness of all human beings is in the hands of God."[15]

The controversy prompted responses among religious and secular leaders as well as rank-and-file Catholics. Pope Pius XII privately ordered the cardinal to pursue a truce. The former First Lady and the cardinal exchanged public letters agreeing that government aid to religious institutions must remain within constitutional boundaries but that "auxiliary services" (like reimbursed bus fare) for parochial school *students* (not directly for schools) might fall within those lines. Soon after, Mrs. Roosevelt wrote in her column that the cardinal had made a pilgrimage to Val-Kill for a rapprochement. They chatted pleasantly, and she hoped that her peaceful country retreat provided an antidote for Spellman's toxicity toward her.[16] In addition to pressure from the Vatican for the cardinal to initiate a cease-fire with the former First Lady, he also realized that his ill-considered personal attacks on the most admired woman in the nation reflected poorly on him and his church.[17]

Eleanor found Spellman's feigned friendship completely insincere, especially because he failed to apologize for his vitriolic letter. She suspected that her opposition to sending American ambassadors back to Franco's fascist Spain constituted the real source of the prelate's attack on her.[18] On this, ER and JFK were in complete alignment about Spellman. Both despised the prelate. "He so obviously was against Jack," recalled Jacqueline Kennedy. "How could you like him? And his little mincing ways. You know, he was trying to just slit Jack's throat all the time and wouldn't be a help."[19]

Lash's conclusion that Eleanor harbored subconscious anti-Catholicism may be overstated, but no one could blame her for maintaining a suspicion of the church's misogynistic leaders who had treated her so disrespectfully. As the religious issue became more prominent in the 1960 presidential nomination race, she maintained her liberal stance, asserting that "a man should be judged on the question of his fitness for a job and not on what his religion happens to be."[20]

Even if Eleanor ultimately had no qualms about Jack's Catholicism, she still mistrusted him and much preferred another candidate. At the end of Adlai Stevenson's second unsuccessful presidential run in 1956 against incumbent Dwight Eisenhower, for which she had labored "to the point of exhaustion," Eleanor, then age seventy-two, vowed that she would never again "take a personal part in a presidential campaign."

But as a Democratic power broker in both her home state of New York and the nation, she found herself back in the maelstrom by 1960.

Eleanor Roosevelt and John F. Kennedy filming a TV program prior to Kennedy's presidential campaign announcement, 1960. (AP)

Her natural inclination to help the powerless led her to fight the Empire State's Tammany Hall political bosses at every turn, especially after they'd stymied her son Congressman Franklin Roosevelt Jr.'s 1954 bid for the New York Democratic gubernatorial nomination. As a counter to the political machine, she joined forces with Truman's former Air Force Secretary Thomas Finletter, whom Tammany had rejected for a senatorial nomination, and former New York governor and senator Herbert Lehman to establish the New York Committee for Democratic Voters. Kennedy would have to find a way to negotiate the shoals between Tammany's lead boss, Congressman Carmine DeSapio, who leaned toward Senate Majority Leader Lyndon Johnson in 1960, and the ER wing of New York Democrats, which hoped a third run by Stevenson would finally produce a presidential victory.[21]

When prominent historians Arthur Schlesinger Jr. of Harvard and Henry Steele Commager of Columbia, along with a slew of other liberals, declared in a June 1960 *New York Times* ad that they would support the most likely nominee, John Kennedy, Eleanor was livid that previous Stevenson supporters were abandoning the best man for the job. She felt certain that Adlai, and no other candidate, could defeat Vice President Richard Nixon handily in 1960. Moreover, she knew no one better than the former Illinois governor to address Cold War tensions or attract the Free World's respect.[22] Mrs. Roosevelt vowed to remain neutral until the presidential convention, to be held in Los Angeles that July, but she wrote that the "ordinary Democrat" supported Stevenson.[23] Her loyalty to Adlai pushed ER to abandon her public neutrality, endorse him (despite his exasperating vacillation), and join New York's Draft Stevenson movement.[24] Kennedy's victories in all seven of the primaries he entered, out of the sixteen held by the party, however, persuaded her by June to admit that Kennedy "had the greatest chance for the nomination."[25]

With three of her sons, Franklin Jr., James, and Elliott, supporting Kennedy, she initially decided to skip the Democratic Convention in Los Angeles so as not to draw attention to the family's schism.[26] Franklin Jr. had been instrumental in JFK's primary win over Sen. Hubert Humphrey of Minnesota in predominantly Protestant West Virginia. Appearing throughout the Mountain State, FDR Jr. resurrected warm memories of his parents' concern for the underprivileged during the Great Depression.[27]

New Deal programs had literally saved the lives of the unemployed and homeless. Eleanor had visited West Virginia coal-mining camps and even descended into an Appalachian mine, a unique feat for a woman in the 1930s. She also championed Arthurdale, intended to be a model community for poverty-stricken miners and farmers in northern West Virginia. Despite Franklin Jr.'s support for Kennedy and his regular efforts to persuade his mother to switch her allegiance, Eleanor didn't budge except on attending the Democratic convention. She arrived prepared to advocate that she was still "Madly for Adlai."[28] "I think if we really want to win in November, we will nominate a Stevenson-Kennedy ticket," she proclaimed to a cheering crowd.[29]

Such support flattered Stevenson, but his indecisiveness about whether to cast his hat into the ring a third time annoyed the Kennedys, fearful that if JFK failed to win on the first ballot, the nomination would go to Stevenson or Johnson, who had skipped the primaries. When Humphrey announced for Stevenson and the California delegation split evenly between Adlai and Jack, tensions in the Kennedy camp increased. The former Illinois governor's law partner, Newton Minow, stunned

Stevenson with news that the delegates from his home state were solidly behind JFK. Still, he wouldn't take Minow's advice to declare for Kennedy and unite the party. "I know you're right," Stevenson explained, "but what can I do with the people like Mrs. Roosevelt? Kick them in the ass?" Minow told him, "*You're* getting kicked in the ass this way."[30]

Adlai's wavering continued, giving hope to Stevenson supporters who demonstrated outside the convention venue and packed the galleries inside. His appearance in the hall sparked a nostalgic and prolonged outpouring for the party's liberal lion. Adlai's devotees snake-danced around the convention floor, shouting, "We want Stevenson!"[31] The frenzy persuaded convention organizers to invite Stevenson to the podium, offering him a last chance to plead his case for a third nomination. "If he had spoken two or three sober sentences at this point, he might almost have made himself a serious candidate," Schlesinger journaled that night. "But he chose instead to make a feeble joke." Stevenson's attempt at wit fell flat: "After going back and forth through the Biltmore [Hotel] today, I know who's going to be the nominee of this convention—the last man to survive." One observer correctly summarized, "He let all the air out with that one bad joke."[32]

Or, as Norman Mailer reported, the disappointed Stevenson bloc sounded like a home-team crowd when a potential home run soars but then drops into foul territory. Eleanor's close friend Agnes Meyer, whose family owned the *Washington Post*, recalled the scene: "Mrs. Roosevelt and I sat there. We and Finletter had worked so hard for the demonstration—we had the applause there—but then [Stevenson] went up to the platform and throws it out the window." Meyer's indignation was palpable. "I could have murdered him. . . . He should have told us he wouldn't fight."[33]

When Mrs. Roosevelt entered the arena the night of the nominating speeches, spotlights singled out the party's grande dame, everyone in the convention arena turned to face her box, and a roar of approval swelled from the crowd, lasting six minutes. She thought it rude to draw attention away from the speaker at the podium, so only reluctantly did she finally acknowledge the accolade.[34] Minnesota Senator Eugene McCarthy's nomination of Governor Stevenson, which Eleanor seconded, begged the delegates to make him the Democrats' standard-bearer a third time. "Do not leave this prophet without honor in his own party!" he pleaded.[35] Again, the Stevenson faithful erupted, but it was for naught; most of them were not voting delegates.[36]

The Kennedy camp was one step closer to the nomination, but they still had to worry about a last-minute surge by Sen. Lyndon Johnson of Texas, who tried to halt JFK's momentum.

Yet Kennedy's juggernaut couldn't be derailed, even by the party's First Lady–turned-power-broker, and JFK won the nomination on the first ballot, though it took the entire alphabetical roll-call of states for Wyoming to put him over the top. Eleanor departed the convention immediately and a day earlier than she had planned. Disappointed with the outcome, she initially refused to take a phone call from the new presidential candidate, who tracked her down at the Los Angeles airport. When she relented, Kennedy asked directly for her support. "Mr. Kennedy," she replied, "you have a son of mine on the East Coast [Franklin Jr.], a son of mine on the West Coast [James], and third son, Elliott, working for you. You do not need me."[37] She told JFK that he need not bother calling her and could send messages via his friend Franklin Jr.[38]

ER struggled to surmount her disappointment over the convention's turbulence, made all the more painful for her by the outpouring of affection and respect for Stevenson, her friend and preferred choice. In contrast to what she considered Kennedy's self-centered ambition, Eleanor interpreted Adlai's reluctance to cast his hat into the ring a third time as admirable humility.

Stevenson's ambivalence explained why he failed to secure the nomination, but ER blamed the convention process, which she claimed political bosses controlled. Although Kennedy had courted political machines where they still existed, in Mayor Richard Daily's Chicago, for instance, he also ran a grassroots campaign to attract primary election voters and thus delegates. Eleanor complained about primaries as well, arguing that the bitter intraparty contests only produced "a large amount of ammunition to the opposition party" in the general election. She proposed direct election by popular vote of all convention delegates.[39]

The Democratic Party tried a more egalitarian approach in 1972, after the disastrous 1968 Chicago convention, and selected liberal South Dakota Senator George McGovern. His lopsided loss to President Richard Nixon prompted the party to name "super delegates," officials who might balance the vox populi in choosing a presidential candidate.

At least Mrs. Roosevelt commended Kennedy's choice of Lyndon Johnson for the vice-presidential nomination. She understood that he would attract Southern Democrats to the ticket and believed LBJ "would exert great influence" in implementing the party's platform.[40] Asked to join a New York committee for JFK, she demurred, in hopes of receiving assurances from him about how he would utilize Stevenson in a Kennedy administration.[41] JFK worried that her price for support would be his explicit promise to appoint Adlai secretary of state, as she and other prominent Stevenson allies hoped. Some even wanted Kennedy to make a public promise to that effect, but Eleanor knew not to press Kennedy to do so.[42]

She was right. Jack and his brother Bobby had always found the former Illinois governor underwhelming, especially now that he was a two-time loser in races for the White House. To them, he was an effete egghead. The macho Kennedy brothers cast sexual aspersions: Bobby labeled him an "old woman"; Jack called Stevenson a "switcher," that is, bisexual. His indecisiveness, both in 1956 over the vice-presidential pick and in 1960 over whether to run again, aggravated the Kennedys. They would make their own choice for secretary of state if the time came. Ironically, JFK had offered Stevenson a quid pro quo in May 1960: If Adlai signaled that he wouldn't run for the nomination and would endorse Kennedy, the Massachusetts senator would give him the plum cabinet position as secretary of state should he win the White House.[43]

JFK's friend artist William Walton, who chaired Kennedy's New York presidential campaign, recalled one of their tactics to unite the Empire State's Democratic Party. "The main thing [is], we've got to get Mrs. Roosevelt," Walton told Kennedy, stating the obvious. In addition, Kennedy wanted Eleanor to swing her New York Committee for Democratic Voters to his camp.[44] JFK asked Walton to contact Mrs. Roosevelt's secretary about a possible meeting. He received a "warm" response and an invitation to meet with her during the senator's visit in just a few days to celebrate Social Security on August 14, 1960.[45] Eleanor was always delighted to see a new generation continue her husband's New Deal legacy, and she began to accept the fact of Kennedy's candidacy. Now she wanted to see what concessions she might extract from him.

The stage was now set for the two antagonists' dramatic Hyde Park meeting.

Thousands greeted Kennedy at the Dutchess County Airport, near Poughkeepsie, where he arrived with Walton and press aide Pierre Salinger. Mrs. Roosevelt kindly provided her driver to collect JFK at the airport and sent her longtime physician and travel companion, David Gurewitsch, and his wife Edna, to accompany the senator to the Roosevelt estate. Enthusiastic Kennedy supporters reached through the open car windows to touch the candidate. "I've never had such an experience in my life," Mrs. Gurewitsch recalled.[46]

As they drove toward the FDR National Historic Site, with crowds cheering along the roadways, JFK told Dr. Gurewitsch that he had offered to postpone his lunch with Mrs. Roosevelt because of her granddaughter's death but that Mrs. Roosevelt had insisted on keeping their date. "She knows how difficult it is for someone who is campaigning to change their plans," Kennedy added.[47] Having spent the previous day with her grieving son and daughter-in-law in Utica, where Sally died, ER had only an hour or two of sleep upon her return to Hyde Park. She'd cancelled her other public appearances, including attending the Social Security commemoration at Springwood. She insisted, however, that the Val-Kill lunch proceed.[48] Not only did the former First Lady recognize the difficulties of rescheduling a presidential candidate, she also knew the power of meeting with this young nominee on her own turf. A keen political tactician, ER planned to use the opportunity to extract a deal from JFK: her support in exchange for his willingness to embrace her policy positions.

Kennedy had already overcome one of the most bitter conflicts in his life. As a congressman visiting Japan in 1951, he asked a Japanese scholar who had studied in the United States and promoted good will between the two former enemy nations to help him locate Kohei Hanami, an Imperial Japanese Navy lieutenant commander in World War II. JFK didn't succeed in finding Hanami, who was serving as a mayor in northern Japan after the war. But the next year, Hanami wrote to Kennedy and wished him well on his campaign for the US Senate. The Japanese naval veteran had seen a *Time* magazine reference to JFK's exploits in the Solomon Islands during the Pacific war and realized that his destroyer, *Amagiri,* had collided with Kennedy's PT boat in August 1943, killing two crew members and nearly taking JFK's life. Congressman Kennedy responded graciously to Hanami's 1952 letter, which praised the young lieutenant's heroism in saving the balance of his crew. JFK's missive enclosed a photo of himself, inscribed to Hanami "late enemy and present friend."[49] Could Kennedy effect a reconciliation with Eleanor Roosevelt and apply that label to her?

Although only forty-three, Kennedy possessed a long record of meeting luminaries, from presidents to monarchs to popes to Hollywood stars, yet he had begged Walton to accompany him to Hyde Park. "You gotta come with me. I don't want to be alone on the raft at Tilsit," he said, making a typical Kennedy historical reference. At Tilsit in 1807, Emperors Napoleon I of France and Alexander I of Russia met in a pavilion atop a raft in the Neman River and carved up Europe for their respective empires. Walton assured JFK, "All right, if it's a Tilsit, I'll come." He knew that "Jack honestly didn't like her particularly," going back to FDR's falling out with JFK's father and her own issues with the Kennedy patriarch.

Walton actually liked Mrs. Roosevelt, despite thinking that Eleanor was "a little stranger than I realized . . . a little kookier," though he failed to explain that assessment, one that was especially interesting given his own artistic eccentricities. As the car arrived at Val-Kill, Mrs. Roosevelt awaited Senator Kennedy on her doorstep, where he conveyed his condolences on the passing of young Sally and thanked the former First Lady for agreeing to entertain him at such a sorrowful time. She invited him to share prelunch martinis. JFK's preternatural charm and charisma were on full display. A master of convivial conversation, he smiled and laughed easily, but his cool blue-gray eyes reflected how seriously he took this meeting. After drinks, ER showed the candidate to a corner of her book-lined living room. As lunch began, they were alone at a small table draped in a white lace cloth.[50]

Mrs. Roosevelt had invited to the Val-Kill event her daughter, Anna, and uncle, David Gray, whom FDR had appointed as US envoy to Ireland in 1940. A long table on the porch accommodated them, Walton, Salinger, and the Gurewitsches, while Eleanor and Jack dined inside on pedestrian fare of tuna casserole and salad. ER placed the senator in an armchair a bit lower than hers, so that she could hold forth from a more prominent position.

Toward the end of the one-hour lunch, a maid approached Walton and whispered in his ear, "Mrs. Roosevelt says to come on in there." She also called in Dr. Gurewitsch, a camera buff who recorded the only photos of the historic *pas de deux*. From his low perch, Kennedy looked up at Walton and urged him to join the table. Walton wondered to himself "what the hell was up," as he felt unprepared to contribute to the conversation between these two titans. JFK explained Walton's presence: "Mrs. Roosevelt, I wanted him to come in because I thought he could say some things to you that I can't say."

Walton took his cue from the senator and began to explain why he was backing the Democratic nominee. Foremost was the desire to block Vice President Richard Nixon's move to the White House. ER, who disliked Ike's VP as much as Walton did, laughed heartily at one goal they all embraced.

On this point of consent, Walton skillfully pivoted to women's rights and child labor, issues that he knew had sparked Eleanor's passion throughout her political life. He then focused on the benefits of Kennedy representing a new generation. The former First Lady smiled patiently as Walton made his case for Kennedy, but she then turned back to the candidate himself, who had gone silent. A sign that she was beginning to accept JFK's candidacy came as she advised him on how to improve his oratorical skills: "Your speaking voice leaves a lot to be desired. You must take lessons right away. Look at me. I did."

Walton thought this maternal advice ironic considering Eleanor's famously high-pitched speaking tone and aristocratic accent, but he witnessed the start of a connection between the two lunch partners based on ER's acceptance that the senator would represent their party and his willingness to listen to her critique. Each side was too shrewd to give in completely to the other's positions, but they also knew that small compromises and mutual respect were the keys to reaching their political goals.

With the lunch winding down, Kennedy explained that Walton would run his New York campaign and that JFK wanted him to be in touch with Eleanor's staff. She offered to provide the phone number of her secretary, Maureen Corr, and Mrs. Roosevelt indicated that the campaign should feel free to call on her for assistance. As they exited the sitting room, Eleanor leading the way, both she and Senator Kennedy beamed. What began as a showdown over ideological, policy, generational, familial, religious, and gender differences that could have expanded the chasm between the two political giants ended as a successful summit meeting, thanks to their eventual open-mindedness, diplomacy, political experience, and humility. Edna Gurewitsch believed that Mrs. Roosevelt had already begun to soften on Kennedy's candidacy prior to the

Eleanor Roosevelt and John F. Kennedy just after their Val-Kill lunch meeting, 1960. (Courtesy of FDRL/ Gurewitsch)

Hyde Park lunch,[51] but he couldn't have known if, or to what extent, the grande dame would explicitly endorse her "dear boy."

Kennedy once labeled himself as an "idealist without illusions." His definitive biographer, Fredrik Logevall, has described him as applying "principled pragmatism," especially in foreign policy. "I think there is a kind of realism there in terms of how he approaches pressing international issues. . . . But it's principled. . . . Take the world as it is, . . . but to do so in a way that still conforms to American institutions and to the principles upon which this country was built."[52] Kennedy had to be more pragmatic, however, on domestic issues to achieve electoral success in holding together the fractious New Deal coalition.

Flipping the equation, Mrs. Roosevelt can ultimately be viewed as a pragmatic idealist—prioritizing her first principles, derived from our nation's founding beliefs and their updates, but leavening her demands with pragmatism when necessary to reach her policy goals. Whether that meant supporting protective legislation for women rather than the ERA, diluting her policy ends to avoid damaging her husband, negotiating rights at the UN, or eventually supporting John Kennedy's candidacy, she gave herself latitude. In fact, she practiced what JFK's brother Sen. Edward Kennedy exercised in his long legislative career: Better to compromise for a half loaf than have no bread to show for a long policy battle with the opposition.[53]

The goal of compromise is for each side to feel that they've received a gain for their concession. JFK knew that he had achieved his overriding aim of convincing ER to join his quest for the White House, and he, through Walton's endorsement, had assured her that he believed in Mrs. Roosevelt's enduring concerns with women's rights and child welfare. The candidate also agreed to collaborate more with Stevenson.

Kennedy couldn't relax immediately after the lunch, however, because he still had to deliver a rousing speech in honor of her late husband that afternoon to a mass audience. Driving over to the mansion for the Social Security celebration, JFK asked Dr. Gurewitsch, "What do you think I should tell about my meeting with Mrs. Roosevelt?" Her close friend responded, "I would suggest that the statement about your meeting come from Mrs. Roosevelt," and Kennedy agreed. He opened his speech with a humble nod to the First Lady of the World: "I am grateful to you—Mrs. Roosevelt—for allowing me to be here today. For I come to Hyde Park not to instruct but to learn. And I think that we can all agree that Eleanor Roosevelt is a true teacher. Her very life teaches a love of truth and duty and courage. The wide world is her neighborhood. All its people are her daily concern. She is frank, she is outspoken, she is forthright—and I know she always will be."[54]

To cheers from the crowd, JFK declared, "Standing on this quiet lawn—this spacious and soothing scene—it is difficult to recall the furious battles which were fought by the man who lies here in honored glory. . . . Today we commemorate one of those battles—the passage of the Social Security Act of 1935—the most important single piece of social welfare legislation in the history of this country." Kennedy recalled that "it was twenty-five years ago this very day that Franklin Roosevelt could say, after a long and arduous struggle: 'Today, a hope of many years' standing is in large part fulfilled,' and with that he signed his name

John F. Kennedy speaking to a crowd at Hyde Park on the twenty-fifth anniversary of Franklin Roosevelt's signing the Social Security Act, 1960. (Courtesy of FDRL)

and social security became law." The future president concluded, "It is fitting that we celebrate this anniversary. It is essential from time to time that we pay tribute to past greatness and historic achievement. . . . We celebrate the past, to awaken the future."[55]

After the event, Kennedy revealed to Walton the real reason he'd called him into Eleanor's sitting room. JFK wanted a witness to ER's comments, which had surprised the wary senator. Mrs. Roosevelt had begun the lunch conversation by observing how interested the media were in the meeting's purpose. Instead of continuing her long advocacy for Stevenson, she admitted to Kennedy that the former Illinois governor lacked "the qualities that we need for the presidency." Accustomed to using colorful language like the sailor he was, Kennedy told Walton, "I almost peed my pants." He thought the cost of winning Mrs. Roosevelt's endorsement would be his promise to name Stevenson secretary of state. Undoubtedly, she was disappointed that Adlai had resisted her entreaties to run a third time, but she told Kennedy, "I also want you to know I don't think any man running for the presidency should commit any job in advance whatsoever, because the conditions once you have been elected are totally different. You must go in totally uncommitted in every level."

Having accompanied the Democratic presidential candidate to his Springwood speech, the Gurewitsches returned to Val-Kill with a report for Eleanor. Edna told her that she found it "curious" that the senator combed his hair twice as he reviewed his speech on the short ride to the "big house." The former First Lady responded that it made perfect sense for a youthful candidate to ensure that he didn't look "tousled" and added wistfully, "I used to carry Franklin's comb for him."[56]

Truth be known, JFK was quite vain about his thick shock of auburn hair,[57] worn noticeably fuller than flattop cuts popular in the early 1960s. He would never have used pomade to slick down his locks, as many men did in that era. And his more stylish cut certainly distinguished him from the elderly Eisenhower's nearly bald pate, with just a few wisps of white strands. In addition, most men wore hats that protected their hair from the windblown look, yet Kennedy not only found them old-fashioned but disliked how he looked in fedoras, much to haberdashers' dismay.

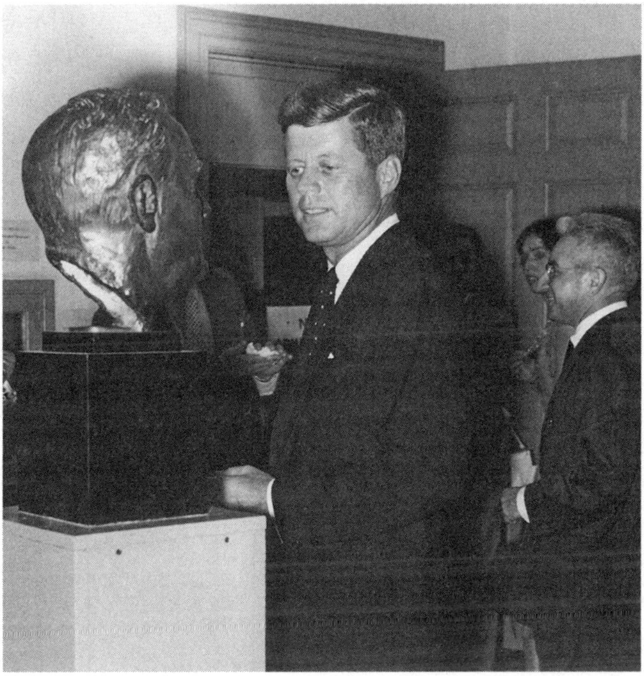

John F. Kennedy gazing at Franklin D. Roosevelt's bust, Hyde Park, 1960. (Courtesy of FDRL)

Mrs. Roosevelt was so pleased with the Val-Kill summit that she gifted Esther Peterson the photograph of her and JFK emerging from the historic lunch, "And it's a beauty," Peterson noted. "I mean his [Kennedy's] face is just so very, very pleased. Those old wounds were somewhat healed."[58]

One of Kennedy's Choate school masters observed that Jack's smile could charm the birds out of the trees, but Eleanor wasn't a schoolgirl easily wooed by a charismatic, handsome suitor, as she had been by FDR in her teens. Yet JFK's seeming flexibility and modesty at the lunch impressed Eleanor. She told her friend and public health philanthropist Mary Lasker: "I liked him better than I ever had before because he seemed so little cock-sure, and I think he has a mind that is open to new ideas." She even agreed to serve as honorary chair of the New York Citizens Committee for Kennedy. Whether she would campaign widely for him, however, would "depend on whether or not I am happy with the way he progresses as a person in the campaign." She reported to Lasker that "the enthusiasm at the big house [Hyde Park's Springwood] was tremendous, and I think he made a very good speech on the expansion of Social Security."[59] Nothing impressed Eleanor more than continued support for her husband's New Deal and the promise to expand it for a new generation.

Although she may not have insisted that a Kennedy administration select Stevenson as secretary of state, Eleanor told Lasker that she advised JFK to work hard to attract Stevenson supporters in New York and California, whose electoral votes he would need to counterbalance losses she presumed he would face among Protestants in the otherwise Democratic South. She claimed (erroneously) that the senator had not recognized how fragmented the Democrats had become since the "unity" of FDR's era. Kennedy reported to ER that Florida's new governor told him, "I want you to know that I am a conservative, I am against integration, and I am for the [antiunion] Right-to-Work Law." JFK responded, "Why don't you join the Republicans?"

While Mrs. Roosevelt's memory of her conversation with the new presidential nominee may have been accurate, it is more likely that Kennedy feigned ignorance of the Democratic Party's fragmentation and praised her husband's unifying leadership to show that he needed her knowledge of and ties to FDR. JFK had published a lengthy article in a March 1957 issue of *Life,* detailing his party's schisms and noting its lack of a uniting figure.[60] Clearly, he hoped to fill that role.

At the lunch, ER reported, the senator told her that he had met with Stevenson the previous week and asked him to establish a foreign policy research group. She responded that symbolic outreach to Adlai wasn't enough. The senator had to heal the party's divide by demonstrating substantive agreement with Stevenson liberals. Eleanor still seemed hopeful that Adlai could become secretary of state by exhibiting philosophical kinship and cooperation with Kennedy. According to ER, the senator agreed to more collaboration with Stevenson: "He also seems to realize that his own mind is so quick he may perhaps be hasty in making decisions, and he needs Adlai there."

ER asked Lasker to join her on the Kennedy bandwagon: "My final judgment is that here is a man who wants to leave a record (perhaps for ambitious personal reasons, as people say), but I rather think because he really is interested in helping the people of his own country and mankind in general. I will be surer of this as time goes on, but I think I am not mistaken in feeling that he would make a good president if elected." More important for JFK, she repeated this thought in her widely read newspaper column.[61] Now JFK had the explicit endorsement he had sought from Mrs. Roosevelt.

Even more consequential for the senator's campaign, two days after their pivotal lunch, Eleanor wrote to Kennedy, enclosing a copy of her letter to Lasker and telling him he should let Franklin Jr. know if she could assist him beyond New York. ER was interested to hear what Jack thought about their meeting, and she encouraged him to tell her son. Eleanor also advised him to call her friend, activist Anna Rosenberg, who would be more likely to support him after a personal contact.[62]

JFK responded that he had indeed called Mrs. Rosenberg, who agreed to assist his campaign, and he reassured Eleanor that he would work closely with Stevenson and Congressman Chester Bowles of Connecticut, another of Mrs. Roosevelt's favorites. He closed with appreciation for ER's hospitality, especially "at a time of personal sorrow for you."[63] He made good on the foreign affairs advisory committee, which included Stevenson, Bowles, George Ball, and Harlan Cleveland, and it would be hosted by Mary Lasker, a sign that Eleanor had successfully persuaded her to support the Democratic ticket.[64]

The senator's thank-you note for the lunch alluded to the tragic "circumstances" faced by his hostess that day. After Sally's burial at the Roosevelts' Hyde Park church, St. James Episcopal, her grandmother would visit the grave whenever in residence at Val-Kill.[65] Kennedy expressed gratitude for ER's willingness to discuss campaign issues, and he hoped to see her again in the near future. Kennedy wished "Mrs. Roosevelt," as he always addressed her, a pleasant journey on her forthcoming trip to Europe and added another respectful note by requesting that she share her observations with him on European politics.[66]

In "My Day," Eleanor described the meeting with Kennedy, saying that she found him to be "a likable man with charm" and "greater maturity" than when he started his campaign.[67] She would write in the 1961 version of her autobiography that she had "found him a brilliant man with a quick mind, anxious to learn, hospitable to new ideas, hardheaded in his approach." FDR's widow believed that JFK "was not simply ambitious to be president; he wanted, I felt convinced, to be a truly great president"—one who not only wished to help "his own countrymen but . . . humanity as well."[68]

How far they both had journeyed from Roosevelt-Kennedy family feuds of the World War II era and the resentments that ER heaped on JFK in the 1950s. However, whether they might partner effectively in the 1960 campaign following Val-Kill's successful summitry remained unclear.

6

ELEANOR BACKS JACK

THE NEWEST KENNEDY ALLY BEGAN by defending JFK in her column from attacks on his religious faith, as she fielded complaints about her support for a Catholic presidential candidate. ER cited a letter from an indignant reader: "I am amazed that you are going to back the brash, mean, and ferocious Kennedy and thereby bring the Vatican to the White House." There it was again: the ignorant view that if a Catholic moved into 1600 Pennsylvania Avenue, the pope would take up residence there, too, and run the country. Proving that she had moved beyond her great-grandmother's antipapist prejudices, Eleanor countered, "[Kennedy] is not brash, he is not mean, and he is certainly not ferocious!" Moreover, the Vatican had no influence in our country unless voters allowed Roman Catholic Americans to create public policies detrimental to religious freedom. She repeated her long-held view that the US Constitution denied no American the right to serve in government on the basis of religious affiliation. Citizens who believe an officeholder's religion is "encroaching upon our freedoms" should "fight such efforts."[1]

Kennedy preferred to avoid drawing attention to his religious affiliation. Yet when Protestant cleric and best-selling author the

Rev. Norman Vincent Peale led the National Conference of Citizens for Religious Freedom in circulating a screed that Kennedy was unfit to be president because of supposed ties to the papacy, JFK *had* to respond. He did so on September 12 in a historic speech to the Greater Houston Ministerial Association.[2]

With the help of his speechwriter and alter ego Ted Sorensen, whose Unitarian roots (on his father's side) connected him to Thomas Jefferson's theories of church-state separation, Kennedy faced the charges directly:

> I believe in an America where the separation of church and state is absolute—where no Catholic prelate would tell the president (should he be Catholic) how to act, and no Protestant minister would tell his parishioners for whom to vote—where no church or church school is granted any public funds or political preference—and where no man is denied public office merely because his religion differs from the president who might appoint him or the people who might elect him. . . . I believe in a president whose religious views are his own private affair, neither imposed by him upon the nation nor imposed by the nation upon him as a condition to holding that office.[3]

Facing an audience of male ministers, most of whom were veterans of World War II or the Korean War, Kennedy pushed an emotional button, "This is the kind of America I believe in—and this is the kind I fought for in the South Pacific, and the kind my brother died for in Europe. No one suggested then that we may have a 'divided loyalty,' that we did 'not believe in liberty,' or that we belonged to a disloyal group that threatened the 'freedoms for which our forefathers died.'"

The candidate had just visited the Alamo in San Antonio. He invoked the Texas shrine and listed several Irish surnames of defenders who lost their lives in the siege. No one knows if they were Catholics, he remarked, because "there was no religious test at the Alamo." He drew a stark conclusion: "If this election is decided on the basis that 40 million [Catholic] Americans lost their chance of being president on the day they were baptized, then it is the whole nation that will be the loser, in the eyes of Catholics and non-Catholics around the world, in the eyes of history, and in the eyes of our own people." The speech lasted only eleven minutes, but it earned rousing audience applause,[4] and Kennedy then masterfully answered questions from the ministers.

Eleanor continued to address the ongoing religious issue in her column. She recalled reading "the scurrilous literature" against Al Smith in 1928. "Nothing quite so bad is reaching me now. But some of the letters sound hysterical and purely emotional." She warned that "religious freedom cannot be just Protestant freedom. It must be freedom for all religions." Mrs. Roosevelt admitted that she had opposed Catholic attempts to procure government funding for parochial schools, which violated church-state separation, but noted that she had fought equally hard against religious discrimination at the ballot box directed at candidates of minority religions.[5]

The former First Lady and the candidate were now singing from the same hymnal regarding his Catholicism. JFK's historic Houston speech proclaimed their jointly held separationist views and dovetailed with their mutual opposition to government-funded religious schools. He could remind voters that he had sponsored a bill in 1958 to increase education funding, but when a colleague amended it to include nonpublic schools, Kennedy became the only Catholic member of the Senate to vote nay,[6] undoubtedly understanding the pragmatic wisdom of such a move leading up to the 1960 presidential race.

Equally consequential for Kennedy's candidacy, Eleanor agreed to campaign for him. She would do so in California, Illinois, Indiana, Michigan, Missouri, Maryland, Washington, DC, West Virginia, and her home state of New York, but she contracted a virus, a harbinger of her failing health, and felt less than her usually energetic self at age seventy-six. "I must slow down," she reluctantly admitted.[7] Yet her first campaign trip's schedule, in California, was anything but reduced. She flew from New York and the next morning started media appointments—press conferences, TV interviews, and radio hits—all before a quick lunch. Then she had a long drive to what seemed to her to be "a totally unimportant meeting," followed by another lengthy automobile trip to a friend's home, where she took a short break. Two meetings followed with large audiences, first at a church and then a theater, after which she downed a late dinner and caught a plane home. Sometimes she would spend only one day in New York City, attendings meetings, and then hit the road again.[8]

Especially crucial for Senator Kennedy's presidential bid, FDR's widow crusaded for him in the Protestant stronghold of West Virginia. Just three weeks before election day, Mrs. Roosevelt barnstormed the Mountain State, caravanning 250 miles through nearly a dozen tiny towns, where hundreds of people turned out to greet her.[9] The local press noted that she had served as an advisor to her late husband, was a progressive advocate on welfare, race relations, and world peace, and always scored at the top of most-admired women polls.

In Fayette County, the paper observed that FDR was beloved by the locals "as the greatest president of all time."[10] His widow rode from hamlet to hamlet in an open convertible, and well-wishers surged forward to shake her hand and have her touch their babes in arms. In Hinton, the crowds knocked over the loudspeakers, but ER calmly chatted to those closest to her until the sound system was restored. Her long experience on the hustings simply made her unflappable. "I am always happy to come back to West Virginia," Eleanor commented in Princeton, "where I have so many friends and where I worked during my husband's first administration in developing projects to relieve [un]employment." The Roosevelts were genuine heroes in the Depression-ravaged state. Eleanor mentioned that she had breakfasted with Kennedy that morning, and she reported that the poverty-stricken state was already at the top of his list for assistance. She described him as "a man with a heart, and he knows the problems and holds the answer to assist your great state."[11]

The campaign swing ended in Charleston with a speech broadcast on radio throughout the state and a late-evening press conference. When asked about concern that Nixon would try a last-minute "sneak punch," she smiled and replied that she anticipated one because she had observed his use of such devious tactics in numerous campaigns. Mrs. Roosevelt, wearing a large JFK campaign button and giant orchid corsage, speculated that Nixon's eleventh-hour attack might focus on

Kennedy's religion or his supposed lack of commitment to America's Cold War alliances.[12]

The Kennedy-Johnson ticket won West Virginia with more than 52 percent of the vote. Ironically, Joe Kennedy's distribution of funds to voters in West Virginia, per ER's early critique of Kennedy's candidacy, may have also boosted his chances there.[13]

Bill Walton didn't hesitate to involve Mrs. Roosevelt in the New York campaign: "Every time I had a rally where I could use her, I would call Miss Corr and make the date. . . . Soon as I'd get in the car, [ER] said, 'Now just tell me what this group is and what you'd like me to say.' And she gets up there and immediately she follows my outline completely but with her own twist on it. But her memory was absolutely perfect, just divine. And very powerful political stuff. Her sincerity was so great. . . . And I used her on dozens of [events], and even some emergency places."[14]

Although Catholics and Southerners had formed part of FDR's New Deal coalition, Eleanor worried that the Bible Belt's anti-Catholicism would siphon votes from Kennedy in the usually solid Democratic South. In 1928, Al Smith had lost Virginia, North Carolina, Tennessee, Texas, and Florida to Republican Herbert Hoover. The former First Lady urged Kennedy to court Black voters by emphasizing his commitment to civil rights. Although that tactic could lose Southern white votes, it would reassure liberals and possibly help him carry New York, Illinois, and California, all states where Stevenson maintained influence. The former Illinois governor campaigned hard for the Democratic ticket, delivering nearly a hundred speeches for it around the country.[15] Kennedy certainly helped his cause with Black voters by facilitating Martin Luther King Jr.'s release from a Georgia jail where he was being held on a contrived charge and by reaching out to Mrs. King to reassure her. Word of these actions spread through the Black community and swung many African American voters (70 percent), including King's father, to the Kennedy column.[16]

Bill Walton worried about the Jewish vote in New York City, fearing that Joe Kennedy's anti-Semitism would make JFK seem unfit for the presidency. The artist drafted Senator Lehman and Mrs. Roosevelt to campaign in Manhattan's Jewish neighborhoods. Converting flat-bed trucks into mobile stages, Walton stationed them on Upper West Side streets, where the senator and former First Lady advocated JFK's candidacy. "They were just troupers," Walton declared.[17]

Lehman and Roosevelt confronted the religion issue directly, declaring that JFK wasn't an anti-Semite. After his speech to the Protestant ministers in Houston, it was easier to convince non-Catholics that his religious affiliation wouldn't form the basis of his public policies. Ultimately, Kennedy would garner nearly one-third of Protestant ballots and 83 percent of Catholic votes. Cardinal Spellman was not among the latter; he made appearances with President Eisenhower and Vice President Nixon. When JFK's father heard that preelection polls showed his son with more support from Jewish and Black voters than Irish Catholics, the former ambassador blurted, "I think I'd better become a Jew. They and the Negroes are the only reliable friends we have."[18]

Walton saw no evidence of Eleanor's diminished energy and admired the former First Lady's "political vitality." He observed that she was always free to decline his invitations to campaign, but he tried never to ask her to do any events she would find onerous. ER and the artist collaborated on so many Kennedy rallies that they formed an unshakable bond. Walton "blessed her forever" because he knew how helpful her star power and political influence were in the Empire State, including at an early October fund raiser for the ticket where ER met with vice-presidential nominee Lyndon Johnson.

The next week, Jack and Eleanor gathered at her Manhattan townhome. They emerged from the meeting boasting happy smiles and with the senator carrying a gift from the former First Lady: a boxed set of FDR's speeches on vinyl records.[19] Twenty-four hours later, she sat on the platform with Senator and Mrs. Kennedy as JFK spoke at a Harlem rally, where he cited compelling statistics about disparate opportunities for white and Black children in the United States. It would take Kennedy until June 1963 to repeat that data in a nationally televised speech as the preface for his introduction of a comprehensive civil rights bill that would apply to public accommodations, employment, and education.[20]

Because of her resonance with women and Black voters, Eleanor often prompted questions about those constituencies. She rejected that women vote as a bloc, observing that they demonstrate just as many

Eleanor Roosevelt and John F. Kennedy after meeting at her New York City home. Kennedy holds a record album of FDR's speeches, a gift from Eleanor, 1960. (Courtesy of FDRL)

differences as men do. ER recalled that labor never voted monolithically, and she found it nonsensical that other groups would do so. "They're people, and if you win the people, you win the people!"[21]

Asked about Kennedy's appeal to the Black electorate, she observed that some African American leaders had been offended over his meeting with a Southern segregationist governor. She believed that he might have done so out of "ignorance" that he could influence the man but now had learned a lesson about the limits of his influence.[22] She was impressed with JFK's civil rights conference in New York and how his support for minority rights in the United States would make an impact in Africa, Asia, and South America, where discrimination flourished.[23]

Kennedy convened the National Conference on Constitutional Rights and American Freedom in Harlem one month before the election. Four hundred attendees from forty-two states, including the 60 percent of the audience who were Black, listened to stories of discrimination and ways to combat it. Chaired by civil rights advocate Sen. Hubert Humphrey, the conference presented Kennedy with recommendations, and he promised bold executive action if elected. Eleanor insisted in her column that effective presidential leadership could make the difference in bringing a peaceful end to American apartheid.[24] On UN Day,

October 24, Mrs. Roosevelt, who had played such a major role in that international institution, asserted in an Indianapolis speech that "one of the things that affects our leadership most in the world is the question of how we treat our minorities at home."[25]

In addition to campaign rallies in California, West Virginia, and New York, Mrs. Roosevelt stumped for Kennedy in the major urban areas of Chicago, Indianapolis, Detroit, St. Louis, and Washington, DC, and its suburbs. She not only delivered prepared speeches urging support for JFK, but she also used her decades of experience in press relations to answer reporters' questions. She fielded queries about her long ties to Stevenson, admitting that she would like to see him as secretary of state but noting she hadn't asked Kennedy for that favor. When prodded about his youthfulness, Eleanor replied that she believed in young people and thought that Kennedy displayed his maturity in the televised debates with Nixon.[26] She viewed them as "a milestone" in television's impact, although she still thought her husband's fireside chats on radio "almost essential" for reaching the electorate.[27]

Eleanor watched the first debate with several friends and then sent JFK a detailed letter about their reactions. Former Connecticut Senator William Benton declared the senator's performance "wonderful." Eleanor felt so prejudiced against Nixon that she dared not trust her own opinions. She reported that one of her friends thought Kennedy spoke too quickly.[28] (Jack's mother often warned him against that habit, which she believed he inherited from her.[29]) Three of Mrs. Roosevelt's closest women friends, Edna Gurewitsch, Trude Lash (Joe's wife), and Anna Rosenberg, all expressed strong emotions about the two candidates, viewing JFK as honest and Nixon as distrustful. Eleanor believed that if JFK could continue that positive projection, he would sway independent voters to his column.[30]

Mrs. Roosevelt thought that in the second debate, makeup and lighting distorted Nixon's looks, but most viewers believed it was an improvement over his disastrous decision to forgo professional cosmetics in the first debate. Eleanor assumed that JFK didn't worry about such production details because, "as I understand, he decided that it was more important that people get to know him as he is." In fact, having grown up in the spotlight, with a father who made a fortune in Hollywood movie production and a mother who valued perfect imagery, Jack always cared deeply about his appearance on the screen. His look might have been more natural because he preferred a suntan (via sunlamp, if he was not near one of the family's beach estates) to makeup. Mrs. Roosevelt, who eschewed vanity about her own appearance, concluded that the 1960 presidential race was not "a beauty contest." She was more concerned with security policy, especially as it related to the Far East, which constituted one quarter of the world's population. Managing Chinese and Soviet communist influences in that region constituted one of her priorities.[31]

Eleanor wrote directly to Senator Kennedy about his position on Fidel Castro's new communist regime in Cuba. JFK had called for support of anti-Castro forces "who offer eventual hope of overthrowing" the Marxist revolutionary government ninety miles from the coast of Florida. As a firm believer in multilateralism and the internationalism embodied in the UN and the Organization of American States, Mrs. Roosevelt urged Kennedy not to act unilaterally toward Cuba. His debate statement on Cuba, that "sanctions against Latin America" had to be multilateral and include participation by other countries in the hemisphere, reassured her.[32]

ER never hid her initial disappointment about JFK's nomination over Stevenson, but she now thought that Kennedy had "created an identification with the American people." The United States needed a leader who could tap into American exceptionalism, and she believed Kennedy might just be able to do so, reaping successes at home and abroad. When asked if she noticed any similarities between the Democratic candidate and her husband, she replied that they both drew enthusiastic responses from campaign crowds: high praise from Mrs. Roosevelt, who spoke of her late spouse in saintly terms.[33] She told reporters that the upcoming presidential election was the most important since 1932. In that year, the nation and her husband had faced an unprecedented economic crisis; now existential Cold War challenges confronted the United States and its next president.[34]

Campaigning in St. Louis, Mrs. Roosevelt was introduced as "one of the best loved women in the world today, a woman who has given so much of herself, to her country and to the world." She admitted that she originally wanted Stevenson to head the Democratic ticket, but she reiterated that she had observed Kennedy closely and now had "great faith in him." ER addressed the religion issue by recalling her memories of Al Smith's disastrous 1928 campaign. She asserted that his religion didn't defeat him. Rather, his New York characteristics made him seem foreign to the rest of the country, with which, and to whom, he was unfamiliar. She repeated her view that religion should not be given "special privileges" but argued that the country can't ask people to fight for it but not run for office[35]—exactly JFK's point in his Houston speech that more poignantly referred to his World War II service in the South Pacific and his brother's death in the European combat theater, both without regard to their Catholicism.

Warning against last-minute provocations by opponents of her party's presidential candidate, ER cited leaflets being circulated in New York City's Jewish community that attacked Joe Kennedy for his purported lack of sympathy for Jews in Hitler's Europe. Eleanor recalled how FDR had summoned the ambassador to Hyde Park to berate him over his isolationist and appeasement positions toward the Third Reich, but she insisted that the sins of the father shouldn't be visited upon the son, especially since JFK was only "a little boy" when his father was ambassador.[36] In fact, Jack was a Harvard undergraduate who had worked with his father in London one semester. Given that Eleanor still called the senator "my dear boy" as late as 1959, it seems that she couldn't quite move beyond the generation gap between them. She labelled criticism of JFK because of his father's words and deeds as a "low-down tactic." What a difference two years had made in her thinking. Only two years earlier, in 1958, Eleanor had spoken harshly about Joe Kennedy's buying votes for his son. Referring to Soviet Premier Nikita Khrushchev's recent boorish behavior, banging his shoe on the desk at the 1960 UN General Assembly, Mrs. Roosevelt called for a president who can "speak for democracy."[37]

A few days before Khrushchev's stunt, he had met with the former First Lady, and she reported on his pleasant demeanor even when discussing economic systems. She admitted, however, that because she wasn't an expert on the Soviet economy, he had no reason to attack her.[38] Whether her famous visitors simply toned down their rhetoric because of her seniority, gender, or status, she made productive use of these civil conversations to keep the lines of communication open.

As the campaign hurtled toward election day, Eleanor traveled to Chicago, key to winning Illinois. She told the press, "I hope with all my heart that Senator Kennedy will be elected on November 8." She urged Americans not to focus on religion because other countries would notice and draw negative conclusions. This assertion represented a frequent refrain during the Cold War when the United States, as leader of the Free World, worried that any stain on its civil rights and liberties record would push nonaligned Third World countries into the communist bloc. Mrs. Roosevelt urged, "Even if we haven't achieved a perfect democracy, we are trying to do so."[39]

Eleanor's constant plea to avoid the religion issue couldn't forestall efforts by some Protestant ministers on Reformation Day (which in 1960 fell on Sunday, October 30), the annual celebration of Martin Luther's break from the Roman Catholic Church in 1517. Although Norman Vincent Peale withdrew his anti-Catholic rhetoric, and some of his colleagues urged religious tolerance, many Protestant clerics preached the importance of preventing "any Catholic from being elected president of the United States—ever." ER employed her column once more to denounce any religious or racial qualification for public office and to repeat her answer to special privileges for any religious group—namely, eternal vigilance of the citizenry over public policies that might violate church-state separation.[40]

She concluded that Kennedy's personality was so different from Nixon's that it explained why the vice president drew smaller crowds and why JFK's supporters arrived in droves to see him in person and shake his hand. Jack's compelling charisma equaled FDR's, which Eleanor had witnessed firsthand. "This, I think, means a sense of identification between the people and the candidate," she concluded.[41]

ER had seen Nixon and his wife Pat try to woo voters at rallies, but Eleanor could tell that they didn't have the same electrifying impact that Kennedy did. She knew that when the electorate decides that a candidate "is their man—that he understands them and cares about them—though they may not agree with everything he says or does, they are still close to him, and they trust him and they believe in him."[42] This conclusion she knew from her own experience with audiences around the world and from observing her husband's effect on voters. Both FDR and JFK inspired crowds drawn to their magnetic personalities and genuine sense of caring.

Eleanor also recorded ads for JFK. With an announcer intoning, "Here is a message from Mrs. Roosevelt on social welfare," the camera focused on Eleanor, who sat in front of a fireplace and bookcases, a photo of her husband prominently displayed. She recalled how she met with the senator at Hyde Park. A video clip played of JFK in front of an FDR photo montage at the Roosevelt Presidential Library. ER continued to tie the candidate to her husband's New Deal, telling viewers that Kennedy would carry on Franklin's legacy. Describing the senator as a "strong and determined person," she declared that he would expand "Social Security benefits, which the social welfare of a civilized nation demands. I urge you to study Mr. Kennedy's programs, to look at his very remarkable record in Congress. And I think you will join me in voting for John F. Kennedy."[43]

Another ad, entitled "The Make-up of America: A Majority of Minorities," resonates in contemporary debates over immigration. After reciting the last stanza of the famed Emma Lazarus poem displayed at the base of the Statue of Liberty, Mrs. Roosevelt heralded our nation's "strength and vitality," which [exist] "because we are a melting pot." "You see, you need not be concerned with the color of a man's skin; it is the shade of the soul that is important in a democracy. You need not be concerned with how a man worships God, but the degree of faith." She spoke of religion in the context of immigrants, but it gave her another opportunity to advocate religious freedom. She urged everyone to read the Bill of Rights before they voted.

> If we are to be the spokesmen for the free world we must begin at home by assuring all our peoples regardless of religion, race, or national origin, equal opportunity under law and under God. When you cast your vote for the president of the United States, be sure you have studied the record. I have. I urge you to vote

> for John F. Kennedy for I have come to believe that as president he will have the strength and the moral courage to provide the leadership for human rights we need in this time of crisis. He is a man with a sense of history. That I'm well familiar with because my husband had a sense of history.[44]

Tying JFK to FDR, always listed among presidential greats alongside Washington and Lincoln, represented the most effective encomium Kennedy could earn from the First Lady of the World.

Eleanor beamed as she stood next to JFK on the stage at the New York Coliseum, waving to the crowd, just two nights before Election Day. The Empire State's forty-nine electoral votes were at stake, and what better person to rally the masses in her native city than the wife of the former governor and president, Mrs. Franklin D. Roosevelt?

On election night—Mrs. Roosevelt in her Manhattan townhome, Senator Kennedy at his family's Cape Cod compound—both had the same reaction. While those around them celebrated early returns that favored JFK, the two Democratic pros cautioned that it was too soon to call the race. When Connecticut landed in the Kennedy column, Jackie told her husband, "You're president now." He replied very quietly, "No. No."[45]

John F. Kennedy and Eleanor Roosevelt at a New York City rally, 1960. (AP)

Eleanor focused on the television coverage, lecturing her guests at one point that they shouldn't overreact to winning traditionally Democratic districts. She cautioned them to wait for the result from rural enclaves in the South and Midwest. The swing cities and towns that could go either way were the crucial tallies that she wanted to know. They would determine the outcome in a close election, ER reminded friends in her living room.[46] JFK finally went to bed at four a.m., still uncertain of the outcome.

Eleanor's personal appeals to Black, Protestant, Jewish, women, urban, and rural voters, as well as supporters of the UN and Stevenson devotees, could well have made the difference in JFK's razor-thin popular vote victory (by only .17 percent) and his determinative 303–219 margin over Nixon in the Electoral College. Of the eight states in which ER campaigned, Kennedy won five: New York, West Virginia, Maryland, Illinois, and Missouri. He also won more than half of the eleven former Confederate states—North Carolina, South Carolina, Georgia, Louisiana, Arkansas, Texas, and a portion of Alabama's electoral votes.

Prior to the 1964 Civil Rights Act and the 1965 Voting Rights Act, FDR's coalition continued to include a major portion of the South. Eleanor had feared that JFK would lose Dixie, but her strong defense of religious freedom and church-state separation may have contributed to his strong showing in the Protestant Bible Belt, especially among Southern Baptists, who then espoused a centuries-old belief in the high wall between religion and government. Discrimination against them in the American colonies like Virginia, where Anglicanism had been the established faith, prompted their firm advocacy of religious freedom.

Abba Schwartz, a Washington lawyer specializing in refugee policy, developed close friendships with Jack and Bobby Kennedy and Eleanor Roosevelt. Serving as an advisor for the trio, he arranged many of her 1960 campaign appearances and often accompanied her on the trips. Schwartz reported after the victory that he had received numerous thank-you letters indicating that the former First Lady had garnered votes for the new president-elect in the locales where she headlined rallies. ER was gratified to learn from Schwartz that a number of her speeches for Kennedy, particularly on religious freedom, had been rebroadcast in Pennsylvania, which JFK won, and other states.[47]

Mrs. Roosevelt was so pleased with the election's outcome that she even praised her nemesis, Vice President Nixon, for accepting defeat, and noted that his gracious concession demonstrated for less democratic nations a model for free and fair (if narrowly decided) elections. In some countries, she observed, a close election might produce a revolution supported by the loser who refused to accept the outcome. She concluded with a Cold War *cri de coeur:* The United States was the free world's leader, and it had to face the communist threat with courage. Americans must trust the new president to improve their lives at home and save the world from the Marxist menace. "We trust in God, we know how to dream and how to work, and I pray we will rise to sustain and follow a great man with great ideals," Eleanor declared.[48]

How far the former Kennedy adversary had come, and ER continued her support as the new president-elect began to construct his administration. She approved of his first controversial decision—nominating his brother Robert as attorney general. Despite his youth (he was thirty-five) and relative inexperience, Bobby had been his father's adamant choice to head the Justice Department and, from that prominent position in the administration, advise and protect Jack. JFK knew the choice would prompt charges of nepotism, but he yielded to the Kennedy patriarch. Protestations followed the announcement, with one *New York Times* writer commenting that Senator Kennedy had "struck the first jarring note today in five weeks of masterly political orchestration." Renowned Yale Law School professor Alexander Bickel fumed, "On the record, Robert F. Kennedy is not fit for the office."[49]

Eleanor countered: "I think the storm of protest which has been aroused by the appointment of Robert Kennedy to the attorney generalship is beginning to seem foolish." She granted his youth and inexperience, but ER thought he possessed "integrity" and understood his brother's programs "better . . . than anyone else that the president-elect has been able to find." She refuted the nepotism charge and added a reference to her own cause, civil rights, one that Bobby Kennedy had supported when investigating corrupt labor union practices as chief counsel for the Senate Rackets Committee in the late 1950s. "With an attorney general who will use his powers to the limit, a good deal can be accomplished along the lines that I am sure the future president wants," the former First Lady observed. She called for time and "a little more calm to find out whether President-elect Kennedy's objectives are better obtained through the way he has chosen, or whether he should have observed the unwritten tradition that having members of your family in positions of government where they carry real responsibility is dangerous."[50] Three decades since she had chastised her husband for hiring their son James as his assistant, Eleanor displayed more patience toward the Kennedys. And she didn't raise the fact that Bobby had once worked for Sen. Joe McCarthy.

What role Adlai Stevenson would play in Kennedy's New Frontier continued to roil Eleanor's friends whom she had convinced to support JFK. After the election, mail flooded in complaining that Stevenson "was being dumped" by the Kennedy camp. Stevenson devotee Mary Lasker "wasn't very pleased," Mrs. Roosevelt reported to Abba Schwartz, "because I was rather sharp with her" when Lasker "complained that Adlai wouldn't be secretary of state." She was correct; the president-elect chose Dean Rusk for the position, and Stevenson had to settle for the lesser post of

John F. Kennedy and Eleanor Roosevelt meeting in New York City prior to the inauguration, 1961. (AP)

ambassador to the United Nations. As the wife of a former president, Eleanor tried to explain to the Stevenson supporters that a chief executive had to choose the team with whom he felt most comfortable, and she refused to add to his burdens by second-guessing his choices.[51]

In early January 1961, Eleanor and Jack conducted a photo-op at New York's Carlyle Hotel, but as she exited and hailed her own taxi, she insisted that they didn't discuss politics.[52] Yet even before JFK's swearing-in, she began writing to him about her various policy concerns. On January 17, 1961, she forwarded to Kennedy a report handed to her by a veteran in the Kingsbridge, New York, Veterans Administration Hospital, when she went there with a group that made weekly visits to the facility. During World War II, she found the VA inefficient, "so I would hope," she told JFK, "that you would be able to find someone who could do something about extra efficiency and the necessary information [for veterans to receive their benefits]." Always quick to offer advice, she alerted him that this matter "has a political impact, which I think you will want to consider, and the recommendations [in the report] seem to me vital for fair treatment of the veteran and his dependents."[53]

Signaling the new administration's desire to please the former First Lady, Kennedy's special assistant Fred Dutton wrote to the president's secretary, Evelyn Lincoln: "The president may personally want to know about the attached letter since it is from Mrs. Roosevelt." Her correspondence and report had already been sent by the White House to Gen. James S. Gleason Jr., the new administrator of Veterans Affairs, and Dutton noted that the general's reply would be submitted to the president, who would forward it to Mrs. Roosevelt.[54] From rivals to allies, could the new president and former First Lady now form an effective team that would allow them to accomplish their mutual goals—she from a more idealistic perspective outside government, he facing the realities of the Free World's leader?

7

ELEANOR ROOSEVELT AND JOHN F. KENNEDY ON THE NEW FRONTIER

ELEANOR'S DISAPPOINTMENT OVER STEVENSON'S FAILURE to procure the secretary of state slot didn't preclude her from attending Kennedy's inauguration. In fact, all her children (except for Republican John) journeyed to snowy Washington, making the event a genuine convergence of the Roosevelt and Kennedy dynasties. Instead of sitting on the platform with other former First Ladies Edith Wilson and Bess Truman, as Kennedy urged, Eleanor chose to sit in the diplomatic section, swathed in a mink coat and Navy blanket that she had procured at National Airport from officers the previous day to ward off twenty-degree temperatures and a biting wind chill. "These will be useful when we sit in the cold for the ceremony tomorrow," ER predicted. Facing the inaugural stage, she and her friends the Gurewitsches could see the entire official retinue gathered for JFK's swearing-in, including former Ambassador Joe Kennedy and new UN Ambassador Adlai Stevenson.[1]

After the ceremony, from the warmer climes of Arizona, her favorite winter retreat, Mrs. Roosevelt praised the president's inspiring inaugural address in a handwritten message to him: "Dear Mr. President, I think 'gratitude' best describes the sense of liberation and lift to the spirit which you gave. I have reread your words several times and am filled with thankfulness. May we all respond to your leadership and make your task easier."[2]

ER's response to his first direct call for leadership was to accept the president's appointment of her as a delegate to the UN for its upcoming 1961 short session. "There is really no committee work that I can do," she wrote, "but Adlai Stevenson seemed to think it might be useful to the atmosphere generally, particularly with the new African delegates [representing recently independent nations], if I was on the General Assembly for the plenary meetings." She was most grateful to Ambassador Stevenson and the president "for your feeling that I might be of use."[3] Once the UN session commenced, Eleanor penned another thank-you to the president for naming her a delegate, stating modestly that she hadn't "been very useful, but I think I accomplished what Adlai wanted in just appearing at the UN."[4]

ER wasted no time in praising the new president on his first congressional address, delivered just ten days after the inauguration. Perhaps she was touched that President Kennedy ended his speech with a quote from FDR's last State of the Union Address and recognized what would have been his seventy-ninth birthday on that date.[5] "I was deeply impressed by your fine . . . message," she wrote. "I was particularly glad that you were able to include your proposal for a national 'Peace Corps.'" "The possibilities for useful service overseas which can be developed for people in this country and most particularly our young people," interested her, so much so that she was planning an episode of her *Prospects of Mankind* television show on the subject.[6] Could she have ten minutes of the president's time to interview him at the White House?

Kennedy agreed. Returning her courtesy at Val-Kill, he welcomed her to the door of his new home, hers for twelve years from 1933 to 1945. Deferring to Mrs. Roosevelt's age and gender, he stepped aside for her to cross the White House threshold first. "Oh no, Mr. President," she gently corrected the chief executive. "Don't you know that no one precedes the president of the United States?" He followed her requested protocol, "but I could see it made him uncomfortable," the former First Lady told Edna Gurewitsch.[7]

Mrs. Roosevelt's visit and interview marked Kennedy's March 1, 1961, executive order creating the Peace Corps and introducing legislation on the Hill to make it a permanent institution.[8] ER had supported such a program since 1957 and was thrilled when JFK named her to the organization's National Advisory Council.[9]

Kennedy borrowed the Peace Corps concept from Senator Humphrey and found that it resonated with college students during the fall campaign. JFK saw it both as a method to tap into American altruism and youthful idealism, while serving a Cold War goal of turning postcolonial nations toward the Free World. Since the Soviets sent scientists around the globe to share their expertise and communist ideology, why shouldn't the United States gain a foothold in underdeveloped nations by sending eager American volunteers there to provide knowledge as well as to boost democratic ideals?[10]

In her filmed conversation with the president, ER linked his inaugural call to service and this new initiative for sending young American volunteers to developing nations to provide medical, educational, and agricultural assistance. Her face glowed with enthusiasm, as if she wished she were a half-century younger so she could join the new Peace Corps and devote herself to the causes of her life in a far-flung emerging country.[11]

President Kennedy hoped that five hundred to a thousand young Americans would launch the program, followed eventually by their elders. As an internationalist, who, like JFK, had studied abroad in England as a teenager, Eleanor commented to the president: "And you think of [the Peace Corps] also as being . . . valuable to us as Americans in our gain in knowledge of the world, don't you?" "That is right," Kennedy responded. "They will all come back with the most valuable experience, and as I say, one of the most encouraging facets of the entire concept of the Peace Corps has been the response. I think that we have really thousands and hundreds of thousands of people in this country who want a chance to be of service to the country, and to causes with which we are associated. This gives them one area."[12]

Eleanor encouraged him to work with the UN to coordinate development efforts and to expand the program to provide volunteer assistance in "depressed areas" of our own country. Thinking of her

John F. Kennedy and Eleanor Roosevelt at the White House for a filmed episode of her TV show *Prospects of Mankind,* where they discuss the new Peace Corps, 1961. (Courtesy of FDRL)

labor constituency, she suggested that skilled craftsmen in plumbing, electrical work, and other technical fields could be of service. She advocated teaching Peace Corps volunteers languages they would need to live and work among foreign populaces, and Kennedy, ever pragmatic, replied that a balance would have to be struck between learning "esoteric dialects" and sending volunteers abroad as quickly as feasible.[13]

The new president clearly enjoyed being on the same policy page as his former rival in the Democratic Party and concluded that it had been a "pleasure . . . to welcome Mrs. Roosevelt back to the White House." Their cheerful laughter indicated a mutual delight.[14] What a difference a year, a presidential election, and the Val-Kill summit had made. In early January 1960, JFK and ER had a tense encounter after his first appearance on her show. He had rearranged his schedule around the announcement of his presidential candidacy to do an interview in Boston with her. In return, she gave the senator a dismissive brush-off when the press asked her to comment on his run for the White House. An irritated Kennedy told his friend Henry Morgenthau III, producer of the show, "I do think she could have been a little warmer."[15]

As the 1961 Peace Corps interview ended, Eleanor prepared to depart. "What's your hurry?" the president queried. "Stay awhile."[16] The

John F. Kennedy and Eleanor Roosevelt stroll along White House colonnade, 1961. (AP)

good will engendered by Val-Kill's rapprochement and subsequent campaign partnership clearly carried over to the new presidency. Edna Gurewitsch heard a "lilt" in Eleanor's voice as she reported on her return to the White House, indicating "that the visit had pleased her."[17] It must have felt especially gratifying after eight years of the Republican Eisenhower administration.

Eleanor's formal thank-you letter for the president's generosity in filming the introduction to her Peace Corps broadcast included kudos for "the perfectly lovely redecorating that you are doing in the White House," rendering it "so light and bright and airy, and I hope you will find it a pleasant place to live." Understanding more than most "all the responsibilities and aggravations" that burden a president, she reminded him that "it does make a difference if one's surroundings are pleasant and cheerful." She was especially appreciative of the president's kindness and "extra time" he devoted "to let me have a glimpse of the children" (three-year-old Caroline and two-month-old John Kennedy Jr.).[18]

Not shy about requesting more time with the president, however, Eleanor asked that, if he had a "few minutes" and "it did not inconvenience [him]," could she chat with him the very next week? She would be in Washington to tape the remainder of her program on the Peace Corps with Senator Humphrey and the president's brother-in-law and new director of the initiative, R. Sargent Shriver Jr. Immediately after taping, she was also hosting a dinner party, to which President and Mrs. Kennedy were invited, but they sent regrets.[19]

Demonstrating his responsiveness to her policy requests, JFK sent a March 14 letter to ER explaining that he had followed up on her request to assist military veterans. "I hope you will never hesitate to call matters like this to my personal attention." He would appreciate her "personal assistance" in helping his presidency "cut through whenever possible to the problems of individuals in need of genuine help."[20] Now he was pitching straight into her strike zone of linking power to the people.

Despite her self-imposed rule against importuning presidents on behalf of jobseekers, Eleanor did so for her and Kennedy's mutual friend Abba Schwartz. "Forgive me for bothering you," she wrote the president, "for I know how many pressures come on a president and have tried never to telephone or write you on matters of this kind." But she felt so strongly that Schwartz was "particularly well fitted for this post" (of assistant secretary of state for security and consular affairs) that she hoped "very much that [the president] would give his name careful consideration." She concluded, "With great admiration for everything you have done and are doing," a sign of her now solid alliance with Kennedy.[21] Schwartz took the State Department position in 1962.

Eleanor commended the president for the appointment of Robert Morgenthau, son of her husband's treasury secretary and Hyde Park neighbor, to one of the most consequential legal positions in the country—US Attorney for the Southern District of New York. After attending Morgenthau's swearing-in, she reminded the president what an effective job the lawyer had done in the fall campaign by increasing "the Negro and Puerto Rican vote" in the Bronx.[22]

At the same moment that Eleanor celebrated Kennedy's appointment of Morgenthau, her worst fear about JFK's presidency materialized. She had complained about his inexperience in Cold War foreign policy, especially his anticommunism and unilateralism expressed toward Cuba during the campaign. Just three months into his presidency, Kennedy executed the Eisenhower administration's ill-fated plan to invade Cuba with CIA-trained freedom fighters from that Soviet-allied island nation, ninety miles off Florida, and remove Castro. For a host of reasons (some a result of JFK's faulty decisions, others not), the incursion utterly failed, resulting in the capture by Castro's forces of more than 1,113 invaders.[23]

Although the president's approval rating soared to 83 percent after he took responsibility for the fiasco, he faced the dilemma of how to handle the freedom fighters now incarcerated in Castro's jails. President Kennedy called on Mrs. Roosevelt's diplomatic experience and international prestige when he appointed her honorary chair of the private Tractors for Freedom Committee, joined by co-chairs Milton Eisenhower (the former president's brother and president of Johns Hopkins University) and Walter Reuther (president of the United Auto Workers). Castro initially demanded "farm machinery" in exchange for the prisoner release. The committee attempted to raise funds to supply Cuban farmers with agricultural tractors.[24]

ER reported in her June 23, 1961, column that donations had poured in from the United States and South America to fund a portion of the machinery. But she reminded readers that the committee had no power to negotiate, and she hoped Castro would stop attempting to modify the prisoner swap terms: "I've a great many telegrams from the wives, mothers and children of these prisoners begging the committee not to desert the prisoners and offering to help in any way possible to raise any sum of money demanded by Castro. These appeals are sad, but this would be a question for government and beyond the committee's mandate."[25] She was caught between her natural inclination toward humanitarianism and the realities of Cold War politics. Republican leaders and former

Vice President Richard Nixon criticized the Kennedy administration for bartering with Castro to release the prisoners.[26]

Asked about the "Cuban tractor deal" at his June 28 press conference, President Kennedy replied that he understood that Castro had upped the ante from farm tractors to "far larger" equipment that "could be used for other purposes besides agriculture. The committee has therefore felt that Mr. Castro is not interested in permitting these prisoners to be released in return for agricultural tractors and, unless he changes his view, the situation will remain as is."[27]

JFK found himself in a Cold War domestic political quandary. William E. Miller, chair of the Republican National Committee, criticized Kennedy for cancelling Eisenhower's original plans for the Cuban invasion that included providing US air cover for the freedom fighters. Now JFK was having to negotiate for the release of those fighters with the communist dictator he was trying to oust. The president's elaboration at the press conference revealed the painful dilemma:

> I wish the prisoners could be free. I wish that it had been possible to secure their release, because they are . . . men in whom we have great interest and who are devoted to the cause of freedom. But I think the committee did everything that reasonable men and citizens could do. They were motivated by humanitarian interests. I think that they demonstrated by exploring with Castro in detail exactly the nature of Castro's interest. If our first response had been negative, it might have been possible for Mr. Castro to say that we had refused to send agricultural tractors in return for these men. This committee went to every conceivable length in order to demonstrate their good faith. Mr. Castro did not accept it.[28]

Kennedy thanked Mrs. Roosevelt for chairing the disbanded committee, and she, in turn, expressed her gratitude for his appreciation: "I was happy to serve on the committee, and I am only sorry that our efforts were unsuccessful."[29] Her skepticism over his international relations decisions only deepened as the president increased the number of

American military advisors in South Vietnam to shore up that country's resistance to the communist North Vietnamese and the Viet Cong insurgency. Moreover, JFK failed to fulfill his campaign promises to advance civil rights through executive action, nor did he advance the cause of Black Americans in his legislative agenda, having the same fear that FDR had expressed to Eleanor about losing the support of Southern members of Congress and their constituents.[30] In Kennedy's case, one-third of his Democratic majority in the Senate consisted of powerful, senior senators from the old Confederacy, and he faced the loss of their votes for his New Frontier agenda if he pressed for a strong civil rights bill.

As Kennedy was about to depart on May 30, 1961, for his historic summits in Europe with Khrushchev and French President Charles de Gaulle, he stopped in New York City to deliver a brief speech at the Eleanor Roosevelt Cancer Foundation dinner honoring Gen. Omar Bradley. After encomia for the retired five-star general and former chair of the Joint Chiefs of Staff, Kennedy turned to Mrs. Roosevelt to express his gratitude for her philanthropy and support: "She has lent her name and her efforts and her talents and her generosity to so many causes, and all of us here, individually and collectively, have been the beneficiary of them in one way or another."[31]

ER offered more unsolicited advice about JFK's public speaking style and format. Via a detailed letter, she instructed the president on how to reach the people: "I hope you will forgive me if I seem presumptuous, but I am concerned because I feel that there is not as yet established a real feeling among the people that you are consulting them and that they must react and carry on a dialogue with you on such subjects as you choose to bring before them."[32] Her description of his initial press conferences was accurate. Reflecting the fraught international scene during the Cold War that always threatened to devolve into hot conflicts around the world, Kennedy's somber mien could come across as rather stilted and aloof. As he grew more comfortable with the press and the format, he mastered it with his knowledge, wit, and charisma.

Eleanor discussed the president's demeanor with journalists in New York and reported to Kennedy that he and his policies were not resonating with "the people." She had relied on this approach for determining public perceptions for decades and had transmitted the results to her husband. ER also knew that FDR's fireside radio chats perfected his ability to sway a mass audience and maintain an intimate relation with it. Kennedy would eventually create the television age's equivalent through his live primetime press conferences. On a long car trip, Eleanor had listened to Kennedy's July 19, 1961, conference in the wake of Soviet threats to West Berlin, and she remained unimpressed: "It did not take the place of fireside chats." The journalists' questions, encompassing numerous topics, "were much too sophisticated for the average person to understand." She suggested that the president speak directly to the people on one subject at a time and ask for popular reactions that the administration would analyze and consider. Specifically, she wanted him to call on the people to ask their members of Congress to pass the education bill.[33]

Sounding like Kennedy's mother, who frequently urged her children to follow her self-improvement routines, Eleanor prompted the president, "I wish you could get someone like my old teacher (probably her daughter) to help you deepen and strengthen your voice on radio and TV. It would give you more warmth and personality in your voice. It can be learned, and I think it would make a tremendous difference."[34]

Mrs. Roosevelt apologized for "wishing an awful lot of work on [the president]," but she stressed the need for his leadership in uncertain times. Relying on her usual modesty, she told Kennedy that his advisers "probably understand the whole situation far better than I do," but she reminded him that she attracted "the reaction . . . of the ordinary man in the street," which the president might find hard to obtain.[35]

After his July 25, 1961, address to the nation on Soviet threats against West Berlin, a speech that Eleanor described as "moving and exciting," she observed in yet another letter to Kennedy that "there is too much strain on your throat which should be completely free." She suggested once again that the president "try to take some lessons in breathing and projection because in the long run it will be useful in saving time and effort."[36] Patiently replying to Eleanor's maternalism, the commander in chief noted that his vocal strain was an old problem that he had tried to address and improve during the campaign "with voice instructions, but I have relaxed my efforts since then. It is difficult to change nature, but I will attempt to nudge it."[37]

Focusing on peace, ER took issue with the president's emphasis on American and NATO military forces to defend West Berlin from Soviet aggression. She was also concerned about his bolstering civil defense by designating public bomb shelters and encouraging families to create their own safe spaces, stocked with essentials. Eleanor wrote in her column, "I wonder if we constantly increase the efficacy of destruction whether there will be any space left that is not affected by the falling bombs that will be rained upon us." And she posed the existential question of the nuclear age: If the world is decimated by atomic bombs, "would life be worth preserving under these circumstances?" Assuring the president that she had "great admiration for [his] willingness to shoulder the responsibilities" of leading the Free World, and that she understood better than anyone "what a lonely business these decisions are," she hoped that he would have the American people's "full understanding, their confidence, their cooperation." She concluded her column, which she enclosed with her letter to the president containing public speaking tips, "We are either going to make a unified effort to live together or the future is indeed black."[38]

President Kennedy thanked Mrs. Roosevelt for her "thoughtful and helpful" letters and wrote that he understood her "feelings about fallout shelters. The prospect of nuclear exchange is so terrible that I conceive that it would be possible [preferable?] to be among the dead rather than the quick. The difficulty is that this has been the weapon on which we have relied for our security and without it as an ultimate action we are unprepared. We are going to attempt to improve this however."[39]

What a unique position the former First Lady occupied. She had the ear of the president, who knew he needed to maintain her political support because of her influence in the Democratic Party, her vast number of admirers throughout the world, and the multitudes who read her column. Yet while reaching a large and varied coalition within the Democratic Party, she faced none of the constraints of a traditional officeholder.

In foreign affairs, Mrs. Roosevelt advocated what came to be called "soft power." Coined in the late 1980s by Harvard's Kennedy School of

Government political scientist Joseph Nye, the term referred to "the deployment of the 'attractive' power of cultural values and diplomacy, as opposed to economic and military coercion, to achieve political ends."[40] Eleanor also epitomized the exercise of such power in her own political sphere, applying her personal values of civility, respect, and graciousness to achieve the ends she desired. She stood firm in defending her principles and could play hardball when necessary, but as Ambassador Mary Ann Glendon observed, ER believed "that personal connections could help to reduce professional tensions. . . . It was not her style to take people to the woodshed" (although she certainly had done so to JFK); "instead, she invited them to tea."[41]

Evidence of Mrs. Roosevelt's relationship with the public is an August 23, 1961, handwritten letter and newspaper clipping sent to ER, via *McCall's* magazine. The writer, Mrs. Earl Norris of Everest, Washington, brought to Eleanor's attention the case of Preston Cobb Jr., a fifteen-year-old Black male sentenced to the electric chair for murdering a white farmer, Frank Dumas, age seventy, on whose land the teen and his family lived in Hillsboro, Georgia. Cobb was the sixth of nine children being raised by their widowed mother. In an unsworn statement, he admitted to the crime, saying that Dumas frightened him in an argument over some fish. (Self-incrimination occurred frequently before the 1966 US Supreme Court case establishing Miranda rights, including the right to remain silent and the guarantee of a lawyer, especially because police often used third degree interrogation methods.) Cobb's trial lasted one day, and the all-white male jury took only forty-five minutes to determine its guilty verdict. The state was to implement the sentence in a mere forty days. Mrs. Norris described herself as a "white woman, raised in the South," who thought it was "criminal to electrocute a boy of fifteen just because he is a Negro." She asked if something might be done "to keep this boy from being murdered" and concluded that if a white boy had committed a similar crime he would have to serve "only a few years in a reform school."[42]

The last point must have particularly resonated with Mrs. Roosevelt, who was a staunch patron of Wiltwyck, a reform school for delinquent boys (initially housing only Black students but eventually serving an integrated student body) from impoverished sections of New York City. She not only supported the school, which lay across the Hudson River from Hyde Park, with fundraising and board membership, she invited a hundred or so of the students to her Val-Kill home for a picnic every summer. They would feast on her informal fare of hot dogs, potato salad, ice cream, and cupcakes, romp around the grounds and pond near her cottage, and listen to her read stories aloud as they gathered about her.[43]

Eleanor sent a cover letter to the president, enclosing Mrs. Norris's missive and newspaper clipping: "I thought the enclosed should be brought to your attention. It seems to me unthinkable that a boy of fifteen, whether black or white, should be condemned to death. I have written a column and asked all citizens to appeal for mercy in this case."[44] The former First Lady couldn't ask the president to pardon Cobb or commute the harsh sentence because that constitutional authority applies only to federal cases. But she certainly was familiar with the clemency concept; her husband had issued more than 3,600 pardons or commutations of federal sentences during his twelve years as president.[45]

ER's "My Day" outlined the facts in Cobb's case, noting that "a southern woman" had shared them with her and that the teen's execution was already scheduled. Eleanor was stunned to learn that Georgia's death penalty could apply to children as young as fourteen, which she was sure would stir opposition "worldwide": "This is unenlightened penal legislation. I think that there also ought to be a reaction in the whole of the U.S. against allowing any youngster to be electrocuted at the age of fifteen, regardless of whether his skin is white or black." Mrs. Roosevelt then employed her patented call for action to the proper authority, asking everyone to telegraph Georgia's governor with an appeal for clemency and "reeducation" of the convicted teen.[46]

On this racially charged matter, Kennedy doesn't seem to have responded to Mrs. Roosevelt directly, as he ordinarily did. Instead, his personal secretary, Evelyn Lincoln, sent a brief note to her, saying that the president "appreciated" the Norris letter and clipping. "He is giving the matter his careful consideration," was the noncommittal conclusion.[47]

NAACP lawyers appealed the case to the Fifth US Circuit Court of Appeals, which found obvious racial discrimination in jury selection and granted relief from the death sentence in 1964.[48] As Mrs. Roosevelt hoped, protest messages swamped the state's governor, S. Ernest Vandiver. Women's groups, international student advocates, and a delegation from the Netherlands all expressed their outrage over the violations of Cobb's due process rights, blatant racism, perfunctory trial, resulting death penalty for a juvenile, and his incarceration in a penitentiary for "hardened criminals." The national and international pressure partially succeeded. Vandiver recommended changing Georgia's death penalty statute to exclude convicts under age seventeen, and the General Assembly passed the law in 1963. Although Cobb escaped the electric chair, he served eighteen years in jail.[49]

When she believed a federal case constituted an injustice, Eleanor didn't hesitate to ask the president for commutation. She had fought courageously against the 1950's Red Scare witch-hunts and Congressman Richard Nixon's and Sen. Joseph McCarthy's appalling tactics. But the Smith Act, passed by Congress and signed into law by FDR in 1940 as Europe spiraled into war, contained antisubversion measures. Attempts to undermine morale of the armed forces could trigger fines up to $10,000 and ten years' imprisonment. The same penalties applied to advocating or attempting violent overthrow of the government. Even joining an organization with that mission was prohibited.[50]

As a University of North Carolina undergraduate in 1939, Junius Scales joined the Communist Party in sympathy with its policies supporting labor, Black people, and the impoverished. His membership didn't preclude Army enlistment during World War II, but military intelligence kept him far from the front lines when he was stationed overseas in Italy at war's end. After the war, he worked with the party to organize labor and civil rights activism in several Southern states, taking his efforts underground as the Red Scare erupted. In 1954, FBI agents arrested him in Memphis and charged him with violating the Smith Act's membership clause. Just two years later, as his case wound through the judicial process, Scales resigned his Communist Party membership when the Soviet Union acknowledged Josef Stalin's murderous tenure. Still, the United States refused to drop the Scales case because he wouldn't implicate other members of the party.[51]

In June 1961, the US Supreme Court narrowly ruled 5 to 4 to uphold Scales's conviction under the Smith Act's membership ban. The majority found no constitutional violation for prosecution of an individual's active participation in the illegal activities of an organization.[52] Notably, Scales was the only person ever convicted for *belonging* to the Community Party rather than committing subversive activities.[53]

Scales had already begun serving his six-year sentence at the federal penitentiary in Lewisburg, Pennsylvania, when Mrs. Roosevelt received a petition to sign on his behalf. Rather than do so, she signaled President Kennedy: "I prefer to write you directly about this case rather than sign the petition." As was her style, why not go right to the top, to the official who could act unilaterally? She noted that, although Scales's conviction came under the Smith Act's membership clause, by the time he began his sentence, he "had been out of the Communist Party for over four years. He left the party of his own accord." With classic Eleanor Roosevelt civil libertarianism, she asserted that "in a democracy the fate of the individual is important. Therefore, it seems to me to be a great pity to allow a man to suffer for no purpose whatsoever." What followed was her pitch to presidential conscience: "I am sure, if you look into this case, that you will agree this man is deserving of compassion, so I urge you to do what you can to get a commutation of sentence for Junius Scales." Then she signed off with cheery, "warm" wishes to JFK, Mrs. Kennedy, and their children for "every happiness at Christmas and the New Year."[54]

Other prominent leaders urged the president to free Scales, including theologian Reinhold Niebuhr. The *New York Times*'s editors also promoted his release. It took a year for the president to grant the request. On Christmas Eve 1962, JFK commuted Scales's sentence; he walked out of Lewisburg after having served fifteen months as a political prisoner.[55]

The president and former First Lady connected not only through their correspondence about policy, civil liberties, racial injustices, and his public speaking. In fall 1961, Mrs. Roosevelt performed a ceremonial duty for the president, who had asked her to serve as his personal representative at the opening of Memorial University in St. John's, Newfoundland, where she received an honorary Doctor of Laws degree.

She happily reported in her column "how popular our country stands with the people of Newfoundland."[56]

ER thanked President Kennedy for bestowing on her the honor of representing him and for arranging a government plane to transport her in comfort, but she reported that "it is a long time since I have 'endured' red carpets and inspecting honor guards, and I was a little appalled by it! I am quite sure I enjoy life better outside the official functions than I do inside, so I am quite glad I do not have to return very often!"[57]

Just prior to Christmas 1961, Eleanor received a photograph inscribed by the president, and, in thanking him for taking the time to do so, she congratulated him and Mrs. Kennedy on "the success" of their recent trip to South America. "You both did a fine piece of work under difficult circumstances," she wrote, "and you deserve everyone's gratitude."[58]

The Kennedys had visited Venezuela and Colombia to promote the president's new Alliance for Progress aid program in Latin America, intended to position the United States as a benevolent force for development rather than a supporter of right-wing authoritarians against communist advances. President and Mrs. Kennedy received warm welcomes in both countries' capitals and the hinterlands, where they visited Alliance for Progress housing and land reform projects. The new First Lady made a stellar impression with her brief remarks in Spanish spoken without a script to cheering crowds.[59] Although Vice President Richard Nixon's 1958 grand tour of South America included a well-received stop in Colombia, protesters attacked his limousine in Caracas, Venezuela, and he barely escaped serious injury. US support of and offer of asylum for the recently ousted Venezuelan dictator had prompted the attack against Eisenhower's vice president.[60]

Undoubtedly, this recent diplomatic incident prompted Eleanor's reference to "difficult circumstances" that the Kennedys successfully navigated on their goodwill tour. The day before meeting the released prisoners from the failed Bay of Pigs invasion, the president replied with "many thanks for your generous comments concerning our recent trip to South America. You were extremely kind," he wrote. "I am very grateful to you."[61] After ER's efforts on behalf of the prisoners had stalled, Attorney General Robert Kennedy assumed the process of trying to release the freedom fighters and sent former OSS general counsel James B. Donovan to Havana for negotiations. Ultimately, the United States brokered a deal for an exchange by sending $60 million worth of pharmaceuticals, medical equipment, and baby food to Cuba. The released freedom brigade returned to a heroes' welcome at the Orange Bowl in Miami over the Christmas holidays 1962. President and Mrs. Kennedy greeted them, with the First Lady delivering brief remarks in Spanish. When the brigade commander presented its flag to JFK, the president, clearly moved by the gesture, declared that it would one day return with the brigade to a "free Havana."[62] US Information Agency films on the success of the Kennedys' trip necessarily ignored that JFK's policies toward Latin America reflected a mix of high ideals in foreign aid and pragmatic Cold War fears about communist revolution there.[63]

As Kennedy neared the end of his first year in office, he named Mrs. Roosevelt chair of the President's Commission on the Status of Women, which he established via executive order, per the insistence of labor lobbyist Esther Peterson.[64] In accepting the president's next call to service, Eleanor sent her sincere concern for Ambassador Kennedy, who had just suffered a life-threatening stroke. The Kennedy patriarch, whom Eleanor despised, survived but was rendered virtually mute and nearly immobile by the cerebral hemorrhage. On another thank-you letter to the president, for his and Mrs. Kennedy's Christmas telegram, Eleanor penned a postscript: "I hope your father is improving, but I know these are critical days for all of you."[65] She must have flashed back to those frightening weeks at Campobello in 1921 when she nursed FDR through the first paralytic stages of his polio and ultimately lost him to a fatal stroke twenty-four years later. If she could maintain her own health, despite a mysterious blood disorder, 1962 might prove an exciting and productive year for the former First Lady with her new assignment from President Kennedy.

8

FIGHTING FOR WOMEN'S RIGHTS

ALL MRS. ROOSEVELT'S WORK TO better the human condition would be meaningless if the world ended in a nuclear holocaust. At 1962's dawning, Eleanor continued to urge President Kennedy to find a way toward peaceful coexistence with the Soviets. While apologizing "for the number of items I keep sending your way," she forwarded to the commander in chief a report on "using computers to help establish safety from war."[1]

In addition to her concern about nuclear annihilation, ER worried about the testing of atomic weapons. The president explained in a March 1962 speech to the nation the need for testing to advance research and development in the arms race to protect US security. Given the Soviet Union's resumption of such tests, the Kennedy administration believed it had no alternative but to resume experimentation underground and in the atmosphere. He hoped that genuine security could someday be achieved by test-ban treaties and verifiable nuclear disarmament.[2]

JFK shared with Mrs. Roosevelt his detailed rationale for high-altitude testing in response to her letter about the policy.[3] She was grateful for the explanation and the meeting that Kennedy's National Security Advisor McGeorge Bundy had with the American Association for the United

Nations delegation. Although she usually opened her letters with a salutation of "Dear Mr. President," on this topic of principled disagreement with the chief executive, she began with "My Dear Mr. President"—the first and only time she appeared to do so, and it was reminiscent of her patronizing "My Dear Boy" 1959 telegram to him.[4]

Given Mrs. Roosevelt's passionate advocacy of international cooperation and human rights, it was only appropriate that the president would second her nomination for the 1962 Nobel Peace Prize. She had been proposed for the prestigious award in 1948, and her friend, Adlai Stevenson, now US ambassador to the United Nations, repeated the nomination thirteen years later. He renewed his effort the next year, in 1962, with the president's support. Kennedy's letter to the Nobel Committee lauded her as "a living symbol of world understanding and peace." Her "untiring efforts" for those causes, he contended, made her "a vital part of the historical fabric of this century." Recognizing her unparalleled contributions "in itself would contribute to understanding and peace in this troubled world."[5]

Although truly honored simply to be nominated, it humbled Eleanor, a lifelong practitioner of self-effacement: "I am overcome by such an idea, and I must frankly tell you that I cannot see the faintest reason why I should be considered. . . . I shall not be surprised in the least if nothing comes of it, but my gratitude to you for having thought of this gesture will be just as great."[6] She correctly predicted that nothing would come of it, but she would have approved of the eventual winner—nuclear disarmament advocate Linus Pauling, who had also won the 1954 Nobel Prize in chemistry.

JFK agreed to appear on another episode of Eleanor's *Prospects of Mankind* television series, this time to discuss their joint efforts on behalf of the President's Commission on the Status of Women (PCSW). The 1960 Democratic Party platform had opened with a reference to the 1796 presidential election theme, "The Rights of Man," and proclaimed that this Jeffersonian concept remained at the party's heart more than a century and a half later. In 1960, still a few years before the modern women's movement, no one seemed to question that the term "man" might not include women. One of the briefest sections of the 1960 platform, however, encompassed gender among the classifications leading to employment discrimination: "The right to a job requires action to break down artificial and arbitrary barriers to employment based on age, race, sex, religion, or national origin. Unemployment strikes hardest at workers over forty, minority groups, young people, and women. We will not achieve full employment until prejudice against these workers is wiped out."[7]

Eleanor cared more about her personal principles, however, than political statements without action.[8] For nearly six decades, ER had fought for women in the workplace. Starting in 1903 with her volunteer work at the Rivington Street Settlement House in Manhattan, she heard about the abominable conditions forced on women and young girls in factories and cottage industries: laboring up to fourteen hours a day, six days a week, at mind-numbing and back-breaking work for no more than a $6 weekly wage. She learned from reformers in the settlement house movement the importance of collective action in political advocacy to change public policy. Eleanor joined the Consumers League, established to fight labor abuses and advocate equal pay for men and women, ten-hour workdays, and a minimum weekly wage of $6. Instead of boycotting businesses that refused to follow these practices, the Consumers League took a positive approach of touting those employers who did so.[9]

ER's activism for female workers didn't automatically translate into support for their role in electoral politics. Her upbringing had skewed her ideology toward her Uncle Ted's brand of "Republicanism and respectability," and the latter made her skeptical of militant suffragists in the early twentieth century.[10] Yet TR promoted women's suffrage in his 1912 progressive third-party run for the presidency, and FDR did, too, as a member of the New York Senate from 1911 to 1913. His stance shocked Eleanor, who claimed she "had never given the question serious thought, for I took it for granted that men were superior creatures and knew more about politics than women did, and while I realized that if my husband was a suffragist I probably must be, too, I cannot claim to have been a feminist in those early days."[11]

As the proposed Nineteenth Amendment, which enfranchised women at the federal level, moved through a torturous ratification process, Eleanor remained "noncommittal" and advised her mother-in-law to do likewise. Thus, they joined neither the suffrage movement nor the National Association of Anti-Suffragists, which tried to recruit ER. Some women who opposed the amendment equated women's suffrage with socialism, a dangerous linkage in the 1919–20 period of the first Red Scare. Eleanor simply "considered any stand at that time quite outside my field of work."[12]

At age seventy-two, Mrs. Roosevelt still embraced some remaining gender-based generalities. In 1956, she told an interviewer: "Most men have, I think, a greater sense of history than women. I think men see things in a historical setting. And Franklin, I always felt, was thinking of what this would mean in history and the future, and [chuckling] I'd be darned if I cared what it would mean in history and the future any more than I care today, do you see?"[13] It's hard to believe that a woman who made so much history didn't truly care about it, but her point as a septuagenarian was that she always cared about the present and was impatient to see reforms effected.

Toward the end of her life, Mrs. Roosevelt explained about her early married life, "I had a lot of little children, and I was not very active, but finally I was persuaded that women's suffrage was something that one needed to attain many of the things that I already believed in but that had not thought of at all because I was brought up—it sounds odd to say—but my mother's family was entirely outside of politics."[14]

Although New York State granted women the vote through a 1917 referendum, Eleanor did not avail herself of that privilege in the next year's midterm election. Perhaps she had failed to register in Hyde Park, the Roosevelts' legal domicile. She now had five children, ages one to twelve, which surely preoccupied her in their New York City home. The Nineteenth Amendment's ratification in April 1920 gave her the federal franchise just in time to campaign with and vote for her husband's vice-presidential candidacy.[15] "Soon after [his loss to the Harding-Coolidge ticket], I undertook work which proved to me the value of a vote," ER wrote years later.[16]

She joined the League of Women Voters (LWV), founded in 1920. As the Roaring Twenties ensued, the LWV rekindled her earlier interests in improved working conditions for women, child welfare, and world peace.[17] And she would make an important leap into public policy on these issues a full decade before she undertook to improve the lives of Black Americans. She had not yet met Mary McLeod Bethune, who would enlighten her on race. Easing women's burdens assumed a priority on ER's agenda.

Joining the LWV's New York board expanded ER's political horizons in the Empire State. Her new volunteer position entailed identifying and tracking congressional legislation of interest to the League. Collaborating with new friends who were women's rights activists and working with trained lawyers opened Eleanor's world to new possibilities.[18] She would never again retreat from activism, as she had done from settlement-house volunteerism, at the urging of her grandmother and cousins.[19] "I became a much more ardent citizen and feminist than anyone about me in the intermediate years would have dreamed possible. I had learned that if you wanted to institute any kind of reform you could get far more attention if you had a vote than if you lacked one."[20]

ER's conscientious work led to her selection as the League's vice president of legislative affairs. Instead of simply tracking bills, she began lobbying Congress and the New York legislature for reforms to improve women's lives and their roles in politics. Most important for her future work, she learned how to organize and activate women voters via the LWV's nonpartisan training. "I've always found that the best workers in a political party frequently are graduates of the League of Women Voters," she later wrote. "The group provides an opportunity to learn to organize and do research work. Members learn how to find out what they really want to know on a wide variety of subjects. They study both sides of questions very impartially, and, while they never back individuals in politics, they do work for certain measures that they believe in, and that is what makes them valuable when they come into a political party."[21]

ER also appreciated that LWV members learned "how you deal with people who, either because they are in office or because they want to be in office, must be reached and persuaded to take the right side on a question. As a constituent and a League member you have studied the subject and have reached a conclusion that you may want to impress on a candidate."[22] No matter how strongly she held a position, Eleanor always believed she could argue it more effectively if she thoroughly understood counterarguments to it. She enjoyed playing devil's advocate against her own opinions. Eleanor's support for women's rights initially took a moderate tack. Radical feminists still disquieted her, and she didn't want to earn her husband's disdainful label of "she-male," which he and his right-hand man Louis Howe applied to women they considered too strident or masculine. (Included among them were ER's friends, life partners Marion Dickerman and Nancy Cook of the New York Democratic Committee's women's division, and Esther Lape and Elizabeth Read of the LWV.) "I prefer doing my politics with you," ER wrote to Franklin from the 1921 national LWV convention in Cleveland, although she reported to him that she had "heard some really good women speakers."[23]

Eleanor's stated preference for work on her husband's behalf materialized later that year when FDR's polio and paralysis forced her back into a domestic caretaking role. Once he had recovered enough to plan the next phase of his political career, she accepted a surrogate role to keep his name before the public, which allowed her to mitigate her natural introversion and hone a more effective speaking style, with Louis Howe's coaching.[24]

Howe, Eleanor's mother-in-law, Sara Delano Roosevelt, and eventually JFK fell into a similar category of characters in her life story, from the turn of the twentieth century to the 1920s to the 1960s. Initially, they all made her life more difficult or, at least, irritated her in some way. Her mother-in-law meddled in her marriage and spoiled her children, Howe disrupted her household, and Kennedy frustrated her politics. Much to her credit, she developed enough flexibility and found ways to deal with the formidable trio, ultimately making peace with "Mama" (Eleanor's moniker for Sara, accented on the second syllable), collaborating with Louis to make Franklin president, and establishing common ground with Kennedy to serve their mutual electoral and policy goals.

ER described the Dowager Roosevelt as a "remarkable woman," "a very strong character," who was "very sure that she knew what was right and wrong." Eleanor simply relented to Mama's wishes early in her marriage to Franklin and then physically removed herself from Sara's orbit at Hyde Park by escaping to Val-Kill after its construction in 1925.

The mistress of Springwood couldn't comprehend why her daughter-in-law wanted to live in a "hovel," but Eleanor had "emancipated" herself, as she described the arrangement. "I think she was very fond of me, and I was very fond of her," ER claimed some fifteen years after her mother-in-law's 1941 death.[25] Yet Eleanor had told a friend immediately after Sara's passing that she felt no "grief or sense of loss," despite a close association with her mother-in-law for more than three decades.[26]

Louis she admired for his unalloyed devotion to Franklin, which had started so early in FDR's career that Howe never held him in awe and could tell the unvarnished truths that all politicians need to hear but seldom do from their advisors.[27] Howe vacationed with the Roosevelts and happened to be at Campobello when polio struck Franklin in August 1921. Louis and Eleanor bonded during that frightening siege while caring for their helpless patient. Howe encouraged (ER would say "pushed") her to join the women's division of the New York Democratic State Committee to serve as a link between the party and her ailing husband. As vice chair of the committee and chair of the finance committee, she acquired additional political skills in fundraising, programming for women and young voters, and editing a monthly magazine for the division. Each time she struck out on her own, no matter if the initial reason included serving her husband's interests, she carved out more professional space between them, and she learned how to play the political game as a woman, for women, in a man's world. She noted that if the women's division raised funds, it could "make its own plans and carry them through" without relying on male party members who often denigrated their female colleagues' activities. She would serve on the committee for six years and make new friends with the talented women she encountered.[28]

Even when these women were fighting for their own place in the party and for women's equality, they would be known by name as appendages to their marriage partners. Until her death in 1962, Eleanor's letterhead read "Mrs. Franklin D. Roosevelt," even though FDR had been deceased for seventeen years. Despite these etiquette traditions, not to mention legal norms, that bound women to their husbands, FDR's polio indirectly gave Eleanor an apprenticeship in practical politics that would culminate nearly four decades later in her status as a preeminent power broker vis-à-vis JFK's place in the Democratic Party. The etymology of the term "power broker" dates only to 1961. At the very moment the label came into American usage, the first woman to wield such power in the Democratic Party reached the zenith of her influence.[29]

The 1920s proved a crucial decade for Eleanor's education as a politico in women's rights advocacy. She worked closely with cohorts in the LWV, the state Democratic Committee, the Women's Trade Union League (WTUL), and the New York Women's City Club. ER, Dickerman, Cook, and two other leaders from these groups, Elinor Morgenthou and Caroline O'Day, spent six years on a Trooping for Democracy crusade, traveling by car throughout the Empire State. Their progressive political and public-policy agenda was as long as it was potentially impactful for women and families. It included promoting public housing, sanitation systems, public transportation, parks, playgrounds, school lunches, nursing facilities, unemployment benefits, workers' compensation, workplace safety, forty-eight-hour work weeks, protective legislation for women workers, mandatory schooling, female jury service, and women's representation on all Democratic Party committees. As ER commented in 1922, "Women are by nature progressives," and, therefore, had "decided to go forward with the Democrats to better things rather than remain with the Republicans."[30]

She participated in New York gubernatorial campaigns every two years and presidential elections every four. She even went as deeply into the grassroots as possible when FDR asked her to bolster the Democratic Party in GOP Dutchess County, where Hyde Park is located, and surrounding districts in upstate New York. In 1922, she hosted a picnic at the Roosevelt estate for the wives of forty mayors in the region. At that year's Democratic state convention, which chose Al Smith as its gubernatorial candidate, she contributed to a show of force with other female delegates. Smith won the governorship by a landslide.[31]

Two years later, with the presidential election approaching, Democrats sought to unseat incumbent Calvin Coolidge, who had assumed the presidency upon Warren Harding's sudden death in 1923. ER worried about the apathy among newly enfranchised female voters. "The most difficult problem before women leaders today is 'How are we to interest the women of the state in voting and get them to change from their uninterested and apathetic attitude to an attitude of intelligent and active interest in their Government?'" she wrote for the Democratic Party. A tad condescendingly, she continued,

> I sometimes think that women have used their vote a little as a small child uses his first garden. He plants his seeds with great care, but instead of watering them and giving them constant care and attention, he forgets all about them, or else digs them up to see what they are doing. We have treated our vote the same way. We dig it up now and then, but we give it very little care in between times. Of course, no one woman has the right to say what the mass of women want to accomplish with their vote, but I can at least say what I hope the Democratic women wish to achieve.[32]

ER and her colleagues fought vociferously and successfully at the 1924 state party convention to select women delegates to the presidential convention that summer. Evidence of her rising profile in the national party came in the Democratic National Committee's appointment of her as chair of the women's platform committee. Assembling a panel of distinguished women activists from across the country, Eleanor led their endorsement of the League of Nations, which progressive women believed could preserve peace after the devastation wrought by World War I; a cabinet-level education department; equal pay for women; a living wage; abolition of child labor; forty-eight-hour work weeks; healthcare; occupational safety measures; and employment bureaus. But at the convention, the all-male resolutions committee utterly rejected the women's agenda, with the added humiliation that they were literally locked out of the meeting to consider it. Mrs. Roosevelt concluded that women "were of very little importance" at the national convention.[33]

That fall, Eleanor crisscrossed the state for Smith's gubernatorial reelection, giving speeches for one of the few men who supported at least part of the gender-equity agenda. She wasn't past negative campaigning (with a dash of humor), as she drove a car topped with a steaming teapot to draw attention to the GOP political scandal involving corrupt oil leases on Wyoming's Teapot Dome. Smith's Republican challenger was none other than Eleanor's cousin, Theodore Roosevelt Jr. TR's son lost to Smith,[34] but Coolidge maintained Republican control of the White House.

ER's work with the Democratic State Committee's women's division, the WTUL, and the Women's City Club consumed more of her time, and she resigned as the LWV's vice president in 1924. Continuing her active membership, Eleanor supported the organization's causes and contributed regularly to its newsletter. She also remained active in pursuing state legislation to reduce work hours for women and children.[35] The WTUL, founded in 1903, brought upper-class activists together with working women to train the latter to be labor leaders at a time when unions banned female members.[36]

Eleanor's goal of protecting working women from the unhealthful, dangerous conditions and long hours in factories put her at odds with proponents of the Equal Rights Amendment in the 1920s. After ratification of the Nineteenth Amendment, Alice Paul, founder of the National Women's Party, began advocating another constitutional reform that she hoped would abolish all laws that discriminated against women. Her proposed amendment read, "Men and women shall have Equal Rights throughout the United States and every place subject to its jurisdiction."[37]

A Kansas congressman, the nephew of suffragist Susan B. Anthony, introduced the proposal in 1923. Eleanor's concern, along with others who had supported protective legislation for women, centered on fear that the ERA would void any laws that treated men and women differently, even those that were intended to protect women in the workplace, by regulating their hours and even the types of jobs they could perform. The amendment's supporters, however, argued that any law that that singled out the "fairer sex" for different treatment from men stigmatized females as weaker and inferior.[38] These two positions on the ERA also reflected class distinctions that arose in the women's movement between the two world wars. Mrs. Roosevelt's bloc focused on gender differences in advocating protective legislation for poor women and their children in dangerous working conditions. In contrast, activists for equality among the sexes tended to support professional women's interests.[39]

The ERA would be introduced in every subsequent Congress through 1972 but remains unratified.[40] Mrs. Roosevelt explained her ongoing opposition to the ERA when the House Judiciary Committee reported it to the full House in 1945, one month after her husband's death.

> Some of the women who write me seem to think that if this amendment is passed there will be no further possibility of discrimination against women. They feel that the time has come to declare that women shall be treated in all things on an equal basis with men. I hardly think it is necessary to declare this, since as a theory it is fairly well accepted today by both men and women. But in practice it is not accepted, and I doubt very much whether it ever will be.[41]

She continued:

> Other women of my acquaintance are writing me in great anxiety, for they are afraid that the dangers of the amendment are not being properly considered. The majority of these women are employed in the industrial field. Their fear is that labor standards safeguarded in the past by legislation will be wrecked, and that the amendment will curtail and impair for all time the powers of both state and federal government to enact any legislation that may be necessary and desirable to protect the health and safety of women in industry.[42]

With a moderate patina, she concluded, "I do not know which group is right, but I feel that if we work to remove from our statute books those laws which discriminate against women today, we might accomplish more and do it in a shorter time than will be possible through the passage of this amendment."[43]

Between the 1924 and 1928 presidential elections, ER literally found her political voice by launching what would become a long career as a radio personality, using the novel medium in the 1920s to educate women about housing, family planning, child labor, worker's compensation, and the protection of women in the workplace. Once again, she moved forward in polishing her organizational and communication skills.[44]

Another appointment would globalize ER's vision of women rights—her nomination to the board of the Leslie Commission, notably by two Black Republicans. The commission was named for Mrs. Frank Leslie, who willed her publishing fortune in 1914 to suffragist leader Carrie Chapman Catt to work toward achieving the vote for American women. Once it reached that goal, the organization focused on women's suffrage around the world.[45] With offices on New York's Madison Avenue, the commission had a global reach by the time Eleanor joined its board in 1926. The organization's new mission gave her a taste of her future human rights advancement at the UN and served as a model for Kennedy's commission to study women's status in the United States. Having expended most of Mrs. Leslie's estate, her namesake commission dissolved in 1929 and used the remaining funds to aid "suffrage emergencies."[46]

Yet as her political acumen in promoting public policies that would benefit women expanded, Mrs. Roosevelt bemoaned her view that, even if women participated in politics beyond simply voting, they still had very few results to show for their efforts. In a *Red Book* article,[47] she explained:

> Women have been voting for ten years. But have they achieved actual political equality with men? No. They go through the gesture of going to the polls; their votes are solicited by politicians; and they possess the external aspect of equal rights. But it is mostly a gesture without real power. With some outstanding exceptions, women who have gone into politics are refused serious consideration by the men leaders. Generally, they are treated most courteously, to be sure, but what they want, what they have to say, is regarded as of little weight. In fact, they have no actual influence or say at all in the consequential councils of their parties.[48]

ER's experience throughout the 1920s had certainly moved her closer to the precincts of male power, but it also made her an eyewitness to how little influence women truly possessed. Their roles in national elections were to organize female voters and raise money. But male party leaders excluded women from the candidate selection process and certainly couldn't imagine them as viable nominees, Eleanor observed.[49]

Her stark conclusion? "Politically, as a sex, women are generally 'frozen out' from any intrinsic share of influence in their parties."[50] She never surrendered to these facts, however. Her personal ties to Gov. Al Smith enabled her to act as a bridge between him and her husband. He asked her to encourage Franklin to run for governor, but she responded that he made his own decisions. She did, however, facilitate the phone call between FDR, who was at Warm Springs, and Smith, who succeeded in convincing Franklin that he should run for governor in 1928.[51]

Eleanor had developed into a powerful political force in her own right by this time and deserved credit for supporting her husband's full return to the electoral arena, knowing that it would inspire him as no other endeavor could. Recognizing her position in the party, the Democratic National Committee called on her in 1928 to direct the Bureau of Women's Activities, as well as a women's advisory committee at presidential candidate Al Smith's national headquarters in New York.[52] Now her previous organizational experience served her well as she established subcommittees to reach various constituencies among female voters: independent and new voters, women in business and other professions, college graduates, laborers, and social workers.[53]

Smith's Roman Catholicism and anti-Prohibition position doomed him to a landslide defeat by Herbert Hoover. The incumbent New York governor even lost his own state, but FDR squeezed out a narrow victory to succeed him as governor, and Eleanor would soon move to Albany to assume her new duties as the Empire State's First Lady.[54] She hoped that her husband's new, prominent role wouldn't relegate her to secondary status, but she knew she had to pare down her partisan activities and resigned from the Democratic State Committee before the election.[55]

Not wishing to relinquish her teaching and administrative duties at the Todhunter School, from which she derived considerable gratification, during the semesters Mrs. Roosevelt made the round trip by train from Albany to New York City each Sunday afternoon and stayed to Wednesday. She inspired students at the all-girls school to engage in life-long learning because eventually "there will be nothing closed to women because of sex."[56]

Conflict of interest concerns forced her out of many pressure-group offices, but she maintained her activities on behalf of women's issues. Her NBC radio show *Women in Politics* gave her a platform for commentary, as did editing, without attribution, the *Women's Democratic News*, from which she had officially resigned. She didn't hesitate to take sides in labor despites, as when the International Ladies Garment Workers struck in 1930.[57]

Working conditions for sweatshop clothing makers, primarily women, had captured her attention at least as far back as the tragic 1911 Triangle Shirtwaist Factory fire in New York City, which killed 146 employees at a company that banned union membership. Immigrant women and girls and more than twenty of their male colleagues—who jumped to their deaths, were burned alive, or died of smoke inhalation—perished because of unsafe conditions in which they labored fifty-two hours a week, Monday through Saturday, for meager wages.[58] Such a tragedy had prompted ER in the 1920s to teach evening literature classes to immigrant girls who couldn't read English. She brought cocoa and cake for refreshments and listened to the challenges her young students faced. She looked back on those encounters as "some of the most valuable" she experienced.[59]

With FDR ensconced in the New York governorship as of 1929, Eleanor embraced the luxury of approaching her causes knowing that her husband held a political office that could effectuate her policy agenda. One way to do so included suggesting progressive women leaders for state positions. ER and her friend Molly Dewson, former suffragist and president of the New York Consumers' League, recommended to FDR (separately, because Eleanor knew that method would be most effective) Frances Perkins as industrial commissioner.[60] Franklin accepted the recommendation of this tireless advocate for abolishing child labor, shortening women's work weeks, and bringing manufacturing sites up to code.[61]

ER and Dewson succeeded in promoting New York State's passage of the forty-eight-hour work week in 1930.[62] That limit sounds burdensome to twenty-first century workers, used to the forty-hour week (promoted by labor unions and promulgated by the federal government in 1940), but it was a step forward for those seeking protective laws in the pre-Depression era. After the 1929 stock market crash, FDR named Perkins to chair an employment committee and develop a state compensation program for the thousands of jobless workers.[63]

Eleanor's discernment blossomed when Governor Roosevelt sent his wife into the field to inspect state programs: from prisons to hospitals to forestry projects. She could physically access places he couldn't and take the time he didn't have to uncover deficiencies needing remedies. FDR had an insightful, capacious, and retentive mind, enhanced by his role as assistant secretary of the Navy on inspections throughout the world, and he encouraged his wife to equal his talent for careful observation, fact gathering, and reportage. She accepted the challenge and developed another skill set that she would soon take to Washington.[64] She recalled: "I learned to look into the cooking pots on the stove and to find out if the contents corresponded to the menus. I learned to notice whether the beds were too close together and whether they were folded up and put in closets or behind doors during the day, which would indicate that they filled the corridors at night; I learned to watch the patients' attitude toward the staff; and before the end of our years in Albany, I had become a fairly expert reporter on state institutions."[65] FDR came to rely on his wife above all others to bring him the necessary information and interpretation from field visits to fashion remedial policies. Yet neither partner ever claimed the centrality of her role in his work as governor.[66] In the future, however, Eleanor would avoid becoming a hidden figure.

After an easy victory for a second gubernatorial term in 1930, for which Eleanor organized the women's division of the New York State Democratic Committee, FDR now looked ahead to a presidential run. She later wrote that the "prospect did not interest me particularly.... From a personal standpoint, I did not want my husband to be president.... It was pure selfishness on my part, and I never mentioned my feelings on the subject to him." Married almost three decades, she knew she couldn't dissuade him from his calling of public service, and she also knew that he possessed what the nation needed as the Depression deepened into an unemployment rate approaching 25 percent.[67]

Mrs. Roosevelt had forged her own independent career, especially in teaching young girls, advocating women's rights, and becoming the most influential female power broker in New York State's Democratic Party as well as at the national level. What would a countrywide campaign and potential role as First Lady mean for her professional responsibilities in education, journalism, broadcasting, and politics?

In the year before the 1932 campaign, Eleanor led the women's division of the Friends for Roosevelt, her husband's exploratory committee, using the experience she had gained in working for the state party. She applied her polished writing skills to drafting and editing the committee's publications about FDR, as she would for the national Democratic Party's women's division. She also campaigned for Lt. Gov. Herbert Lehman in his bid to become the Empire State's next governor.[68]

ER eschewed direct work in her husband's campaign.[69] Her activities behind the scenes, however, reflected the status she had achieved in organizing women in New York and nationally. She and Dewson collaborated on a plan for the state and the national party. Each of the forty-eight states would have a vice chairwoman to lead women voters, and county chairwomen were to report to them. Eleanor reviewed the state plans to turn out women voters.[70]

In addition, her public role included frequent trips with her husband on the campaign trail. Breaking the tradition of candidates not appearing at the party's presidential convention, Franklin and Eleanor boarded an American Airways Stinson Tri-Motor plane that a ground crew had to hand-crank to start the propellers spinning. The wind-impeded trip from Albany to the Chicago convention took seven hours, and the delegates had to stay an extra day to catch a glimpse of their new candidate.[71]

ER stood just behind her husband on the stage, while son James steadied his dad as Sen. Thomas J. Walsh of Montana, chairman of the convention, officially bestowed the nomination. Mrs. Roosevelt thus became the first woman to see in person her husband nominated for president at his party's national convention. Listening to FDR's acceptance speech, in which he promised "a new deal for Americans" mired in the Great Depression, Eleanor smiled and waved to familiar faces in the crowd.[72]

Once the general election campaign began, ER joined the Democratic candidate on the trail for numerous rallies, literally supporting her husband when he gripped her arm on the back of train platforms as they whistle-stopped across the country. Paralyzed from the waist down, FDR knew that balancing on his leg braces always made standing upright precarious and tiring. Eleanor could easily lean over a train's platform to shake hands while he leaned on the railing. Combining this flesh-pressing with her work to turn out the women's vote, she played a larger role in a presidential campaign than any candidate's spouse prior to 1932.[73]

FDR defeated Hoover in a landslide. Eleanor would again have to upend life for her husband's career. "Happy Days Are Here Again" had been the buoyant campaign song played throughout Franklin's appearances at the convention and on the arduous road to the White House. Would the days that followed be happy for the new First Lady? Before discovering the answer to that question, she simply squeezed in as much public work for her causes as she could manage.

Several weeks before the inauguration, Mrs. Roosevelt made one of her weekly appearances on the *Pond's Dance Hour* radio program. She chose "Woman's Career vs. Woman's Home" as her topic in a brief closing to the show's musical segments.[74] Eleanor hoped that her subject of why women should be afforded jobs didn't provoke controversy. "It seems to me as perfectly obvious that if a woman falls in love and marries, of course, her first interest and her first duty is to her home, but her duty to her home does not of necessity preclude her having another occupation." She always saw men and women as equal in their desire to put their talents to work in gainful employment. "A woman, just as a man, may have a great gift for some particular thing," she argued. "That does not mean that she must give up the joy of marrying and having a home and children. It simply means, when we set them in opposition to each other, that we haven't as yet grown accustomed to the fact that women's lives must be adjusted and arranged for in just the same way men's lives are. Women may have to sacrifice certain things at times—so do men."

ER observed that homemaking had previously occupied all of women's time. By 1932, women could devote their extra time to leisure activities or to work outside the home. "If so—the only people to be concerned about it are the members of the family."

Although the four Roosevelt boys all shipped off to Groton prep school at age twelve, Eleanor seemed to speak from personal experience as the mother of five when she admitted, "To be sure, sometimes children resent the fact that their mother has a job and is not at their beck and call at any hour of the day or night." If children's needs were met, though, "they have no right to expect that she will give up that which she loves because they would like to have her home at five o'clock instead of six o'clock."

Anticipating the theme of Betty Friedan's *Feminine Mystique*,[75] still three decades away from publication, ER asserted, "The very best thing that comes to a woman with a job is the fact that she has to use her brain to work it in with her home, that she keeps her brain from stagnating, that she has something new to talk to her husband about, and that he never will get the feeling that she is just like the old chair which he has always sat in—comfortable, but thoroughly familiar and never changing." She believed that an active woman contributed to "a happier relationship at home." Because her husband's infidelity and illness had nearly ended their marriage, Eleanor salvaged it by developing an independent, yet coordinate, professional role alongside FDR.

Mrs. Roosevelt hoped all working women could become creative and productive, both for their own benefit and that of their communities. Still reflecting a more traditional view during the Great Depression, however, she conceded that women whose partners earned enough might have to leave their jobs for men or single women who needed them, but she rebelled against this arrangement as a "permanent concession."

As she was about to embark on her First Ladyship in 1933, Eleanor made a plea to American husbands (she called them "Mr. Man") to allow their wives to flourish in order for them to be fulfilled and happy. In her radio messages, ER liked to provide lessons from her own family's experiences. Just as she neared accepting the most visible job any women could undertake in the United States, she recalled that as her children left home, she had the freedom to undertake work in the public sphere.

Eleanor thought she might have to alter her radio link to the American people once she became First Lady. She began to alert her audiences to the "regret" she would experience at not hearing from her listeners who had expanded her knowledge, perspectives, and friendships. She couldn't have anticipated how much wider her understanding of people at home and abroad would grow in her extensive travels as First Lady. How ironic that she had been advocating productive work for women, but now she thought that her husband's new position might stymie her connection to those from whom she drew sustenance.

Mrs. Roosevelt performed what she thought would constitute her radio swan song on the eve of FDR's first inauguration, and she thanked even "those who have been critical and objected to anything which I have said, because they have taught me some valuable lessons. Criticism is good for us all if it does not have the effect of discouraging us."[76] An avalanche of critiques from journalists, political opponents, and voters would flow into the White House throughout her First Ladyship. When reflecting in 1958 on the attacks she provoked, specifically from right-wing columnists like Westbrook Pegler, Mrs. Roosevelt remarked that she only disliked criticism from loved ones. But if what they said was truthful, she said, "I think about it very carefully."[77]

Undoubtedly remembering the nitpicking that she endured as a young girl and woman from her mother, grandmother, aunts, and mother-in-law, ER opined that "criticism of the young is often of doubtful value. They haven't yet reached the point where they can recognize their own mistakes or deficiencies and use criticism to good advantage. But for those of us who have lived a little longer, it should serve to clarify our ideas, make us surer of our own judgment and on the whole be helpful to us."[78]

The night before her husband's inauguration, Eleanor assured her radio listeners: "I shall always hope in one way or another to keep in touch with you, the American people, for I feel you are very close to me. Your interests are my interests and I hope that in many ways we see eye to eye as to many of the questions that come up in our daily lives. The one great danger for a man in public life or for the woman who is that man's wife, is that they may be set apart from the stream of life affecting the rest of the country."[79]

Mrs. Roosevelt's vision of the nation's capital, where she and FDR had spent seven years during the Wilson administration, captured the essence of how average Americans saw it—distant, removed from their lives, atypical from most of the country, and mired in corrupt politics. "It is easy in Washington to think that Washington is the country," she observed, "and forget that it is a very small place and only becomes important as the people who live there truly represent the other parts of the country."[80]

Hoping she could maintain some contacts with her "radio acquaintances," Eleanor defined what she valued most, "the human contacts which we make as we journey through life." She observed, "People are different, and different things seem important to them, but to me the most important thing in the world is other people's lives. My friends and my family and my contacts with other human beings mean far more to me than anything else in life. . . . In one way or another we are going to keep in close touch during these coming years."[81] She would more than make good on that promise.

The impracticality of commuting from the nation's capital to Todhunter in Manhattan forced Eleanor to abandon her beloved teaching position. She used the extra time to pen her first book, *It's Up to the Women,* a brief collection of her articles and speeches, including those she had recently delivered on radio. As historian Jill Lepore expressed about a modern edition, "To say that Roosevelt's act of writing this book was shocking hardly covers it. In 1933 women rarely spoke in public, held very few public offices, and had barely begun voting."[82] Part pep talk for women facing the Depression's traumas, part political manifesto,

Eleanor's book encouraged women to remember their courageous foremothers who survived the nation's settlement, founding, and "war between the states." She gave practical advice, using her store of real-world anecdotes, on how homemakers could economize to balance family budgets, maintain sound minds and bodies through healthful living (for example, screening windows to avoid disease-carrying mosquitos), provide nutritious meals (complete with suggested menus), and raise well-behaved children.[83]

The book also focused on ER's goals for women in the workplace and in public life. Although Mrs. Roosevelt listed traditional jobs for females (librarians, teachers, secretaries, nurses, social workers, stewardesses) and a few nontraditional roles (newspaper reporters, photographers), she assured readers that "we can be lawyers, doctors, scientists . . . ; and in the arts women have excelled as sculptors, and we have good women poets, writers, painters, playwrights." Her advocacy of quality education for Americans also gave her the opportunity to promote peace. Another world war might end civilization. She was convinced that only "better education" would "prevent recurrence of war," with its "waste and futility. . . . The *will to peace* will have to start with women, and they will have to want peace sufficiently to be crusaders on the subject."[84]

Mrs. Roosevelt stressed the need for women to understand the impact that government policy has on them and their families' welfare. She urged them to become involved in political parties to influence their platforms but cautioned that it would be more difficult for them to break into the inner circles of male influence at the state, county, and local levels than in national politics. Although she understood that "the percentage of women holding office is small," Eleanor's "dreams of the future" called for women learning "to work together even before they can work with men." Her request for unity resulted from the ongoing disagreement among women's rights advocates on protective legislation for female workers. ER continued to hold the view that they needed such protection. She went a step further to assert that, although she had nearly come to agree that men and women should be treated equally in employment, she "realize[d] that when all is said and done, women are different from men. They are equals in many ways, but they cannot refuse to acknowledge their differences. . . . Their physical functions in life are different. . . ." She hoped that "in the next few years" the United States would witness "not only a social order built by the ability and brains of our men, but a social order which also represents the understanding heart of the woman."[85]

Despite her emphasis on physical gender differences, ER continued to oppose pay inequities. "Equal pay for equal work" expressed her guiding principle. Eleanor observed that women expected to marry and be financially sustained by their husbands and therefore didn't think in terms of a lifetime in the workplace. Yet in the Great Depression's early years, 1929–33, the marriage rate fell 22 percent because couples couldn't afford matrimony.[86] Thus, more single women needed jobs just as unemployment skyrocketed. Even if they could find gainful employment, in accepting lower pay they also lowered wage scales for men. Eleanor's answer? Women needed to form their own labor unions or join men's so that they could organize to fight for fair and equal wages, safe working conditions, and shorter work weeks.[87]

Letter writers often queried Eleanor on whether the United States would ever have a female president. She found the question amusing, "for it is really unimportant what sex a president may be." Until a "worthy" female appeared on the political stage to assume the office, she presumed that both "worthy and unworthy" men would occupy the Oval Office.[88]

She thought it "nonsense" that women couldn't bear the presidency's "physical strain." What about farm women? Or those who toil in factories? Or those who work night shifts as custodians and then race home to ready their children for school? Unstated was the fact that she saw her own husband debilitated by polio's ravages but capable of shouldering the office's burdens. "While women may not have as much muscular strength as men, they have as much endurance and ability to bear strain as the male of the species," she concluded.[89]

Eleanor hoped that women would acquire more experience in public affairs and the rough and tumble of politics before seeking the presidency. She cited Russia's Catherine the Great and Britain's Queen

Elizabeth I as "independent rulers": "In fact, birth seems to have created more confidence in some countries of the past than does ability today! . . . So let us hope that when a woman does assume any important office, it will be because the services she can render are apparent to all."[90]

Louis Howe once asked during her husband's first term whether she wanted to be president. If so, he would begin planning for her 1940 campaign, presuming, incorrectly, that Franklin would serve only two terms. The brilliant political strategist was convinced that women understood the New Deal's humanitarian core better than men and that a woman could be elected to the nation's highest office. He had trained Eleanor in grassroots politics and press relations, and Howe knew she was up to the Oval Office's profound challenges. She declined to add another elective political career to the family agenda. Moreover, she didn't think that most Americans would trust a women's leadership. Until a qualified woman could garner votes from both male and female voters, she would carry on with her own work outside the elective arena.[91]

ER's understanding of women in politics, the electorate's view of gender, and her most effective approach to policy advocacy were accurate. It is hard to imagine that she could have won the nomination in a male-dominated Democratic Party. In addition, a 1937 Gallup poll found that 64 percent of respondents would not vote for a qualified woman for president. Only two females served in the Senate and six in the House in 1939.[92] Finally, she had attracted strong opposition to her activism, as do all First Ladies (who are unaccountable to voters).

Mrs. Roosevelt admitted that she was "no philosopher," but she believed that her extensive travels and vast experience in meeting with people at home and abroad gave her a "philosophy of living." In later years, she observed, "I'm quite a good listener. . . . It comes very naturally to me to listen to people and let them talk."[93] As her grandmother had told her, "You are a girl, and I expect you to be more sensible and more thoughtful than your brothers." Eleanor believed in that gender distinction, too, but unlike her grandmother's generation, she thought women could become self-actualized and crucial participants in society, especially when it faced a desperate financial crisis like the Great Depression.[94]

Eleanor Roosevelt's efforts to empower women's participation as voters and political leaders only strengthened after her husband assumed the presidency. She convinced the DNC chairman to create the women's division as a permanent office, and she consistently campaigned for the Roosevelt administration to hire women for executive-level appointments. ER and Dewson compiled a roster of a hundred prominent Democratic women. Progress in appointing females remained slow, but two years into the Roosevelt presidency, more than fifty held elevated positions at the national level, with hundreds more appointed in state and local government agencies.[95]

With Dewson's encouragement, FDR named Frances Perkins the first woman cabinet member when he nominated her to head the Department of Labor. Nevertheless, initial New Deal programs utterly excluded women,[96] instead focusing on male unemployment because of the prevailing view that men were primary breadwinners. Never mind that single, divorced, or widowed women had to earn a living. Many were homeless, like their male counterparts. ER found a reliable colleague in Harry Hopkins, director of the Federal Emergency Relief Administration and the Civil Works Administration (CWA).[97] She convinced him to create a women's division in both agencies. The First Lady convened social workers and reformers (like those in the Women's Trade Union League) at the White House and spoke to them about creating jobs for unemployed women. When his schedule and inclination allowed, the president would welcome the visitors to the Executive Mansion. After her husband's first year in office, the CWA had employed a hundred thousand women.[98] As Cook explained, "If her views represented heresy and radicalism to some, for ER and the women's progressive network they represented the substance and soul of America, the long-postponed American Dream."[99]

Eleanor constantly remained alert to setbacks for American women. The National Recovery Administration, created to produce industrial codes under the National Industrial Recovery Act, achieved many of the workplace standards Eleanor and her colleagues had fought so hard for in the 1920s, but they also codified gender-based wage differences. The Civilian Conservation Corps (CCC) recruited only young men for public works in the nation's parks, forests, highways, utilities, and environmental projects. ER encouraged her husband's administration to create so-called She She She camps in parallel to the CCC enclaves for men. She convened a White House meeting on the initiative, and finally Congress passed the necessary legislation. Although some 8,500 women ultimately participated, their programs were a pale recreation of the men's version. CCC males earned a wage of $7 a week ($170 in 2026 dollars); women received a weekly "allowance" of fifty cents. Budget cuts shuttered the women's camps by 1937, but the men's CCC projects continued until 1942, when World War II's military draft and revived industries rendered the Depression-era work program redundant.[100]

Eleanor fought hard to make the original Social Security Act apply to as many Americans as possible, but as enacted in 1935, the law rendered ineligible many minority men and women because it excluded agricultural and domestic workers. Likewise, she pressed for the Works Progress Administration to reach Black females for both work projects and supervisory roles.[101]

Those activities solely in her domain gave Mrs. Roosevelt opportunities to create completely new precedents. She became the first First Lady to hold weekly press conferences and insisted that only female reporters attend. She hoped to preserve their jobs and perhaps encourage media outlets to hire additional women journalists. Her goals included informing women voters, urging them to speak their minds, and encouraging them to engage with policy issues. Although she tried to avoid partisanship, she continued to advocate for the abolition of sweatshops and child labor, she urged buyers to boycott businesses with unsafe workplaces, and she supported higher salaries for teachers. She also brought women who had received prominent jobs in the Roosevelt administration to meet with female journalists. Now that Eleanor had taken her place on a national stage, her connection, especially with women, grew accordingly. During her first year in the White House, ER received 300,000 letters. As historian Mary Beard explains, Americans were used to thinking of presidents as "Great White Fathers"; now Mrs. Roosevelt embraced the role of "Great White Mother."[102]

While traveling in the Pacific during World War II, ER spoke to the young soldiers, sailors, airmen, and marines, especially those who had been wounded, as a concerned and compassionate mother would. And she promised to contact their families when she returned stateside. One of the military aides who accompanied her wrote: "She left behind her many a tough battle-torn GI blowing his nose and swearing at the 'cold' he had recently picked up."[103]

That maternal persona, combined with proximity to power, made Mrs. Roosevelt the perfect choice to produce a daily newspaper column for United Feature Syndicate. Starting at the end of 1935, she began recording her observations of both the mundane and fascinating world she inhabited for her "My Day" column, described by one admirer as "the diary of the accomplished White House character who manages to sublimate the typical American woman in the person of the First Lady of the Land."[104]

As her husband approached his 1936 reelection campaign, Eleanor's column appeared in nearly sixty newspapers around the country, whose combined circulation approached four million. "The Missus," as Franklin referred to his wife, especially when she pressured him on policy, arranged for Molly Dewson to meet with the president on how to organize the DNC's women's division to its best effect for the campaign. They inspired each state to create women's committees to produce campaign literature on FDR's accomplishments during his first term and to outline his administration's plans for a second. Eleanor and Molly shaped the appealing content and design for these pamphlets and encouraged the Roosevelt campaign to use them effectively for Franklin's reelection, which he achieved in a landslide over Republican Alf Landon.[105]

Like her husband, ER used radio for disseminating her messages, although she couldn't command free airtime for the asking, as FDR could for his fireside chats or other official addresses to the American people. She had to rely on commercial programs to grant her a broadcasting platform. Just prior to becoming First Lady, she told her audience:

> I find there is something fascinating and mysterious in talking over the radio to a whole nation at once. As I have talked to you I have tried to realize that way up in the high mountain farms of Tennessee, on lonely ranches, on the Texas plains, in thousands

> and thousands of homes, there are women listening to what I say, listening and weighing my words against their own experience. It seems impossible—incredible that this is true, and yet I know it is true because from many of these same isolated homes will come in a few days, letters, sometimes telling me I have helped them, sometimes disagreeing with my view of life.[106]

Once in the White House, she would invite the Associated Country Women of the World to a garden party there, and President Roosevelt commended their work to produce food and conserve farmland around the globe.[107]

"I was doing things that had not been done before," the former First Lady recalled in 1958. She lauded her long-suffering husband for giving her free rein to pursue her issues and career, including three-week lecture tours each spring and fall. Those trips allowed her to see if government programs were effective and then report her eyewitness accounts to the president.[108]

In 1934, Simmons Mattress Company sponsored a program for Mrs. Roosevelt, and she donated the company's payment to charity that would help fund her Arthurdale project in West Virginia.[109] As she fought for women to take up roles in business and politics, the First Lady contemplated how these new positions would influence the way women thought of themselves and how their male colleagues would treat them. Once again, she flashed back to her grandmother's admonition: Never forget that "you are a lady," she had told young Eleanor. At the time, the little girl never anticipated that she would embrace any undertaking in the male-dominated worlds of business or politics. She feared that, even in 1934, women had to avoid aggression or perseverance in business lest "people say that her attitude is not quite ladylike." She offered her own admonition to females in the workplace: "If women are going to compete with men, they must either use their minds and insist on being equal in every way and lose that something of glamor which surrounds women who are set apart behind certain restraints and reserves, or they must compete as women, using as part of their competitive armor, that mysterious something" that she defined as "charm."[110]

ER counselled women to save "their charm and their womanly personalities" for home and "disabuse the minds of their competitors of the old idea that women are only 'ladies in business.'" She believed that this approach "is even truer where it concerns women who are going into public life either as elective or appointive officials. . . . They must stand or fall on their own ability, on their own character as persons, and a good motto is 'be yourself,' and your associates and the public in general will render the verdict as to whether that self meets with approval. Insincerity and sham, whether in men or in women, always fails in the end in public life."[111] What if a woman's true self was charming? Mrs. Roosevelt didn't solve that riddle for women in public life.

Eleanor's previous sponsor, Pond's, brought her back for new shows. On May 12, 1937, she appeared with her friend of two decades, Polish-born socialist Rose Schneiderman, longtime president of the Women's Trade Union League and secretary of the New York State Department of Labor, for a lengthy discussion on women in the workplace, some eleven million at that time.[112] They foreshadowed the issues in gender, socioeconomic class, and labor politics that would arise in JFK's women's commission a quarter century later.

Both ER and Schneiderman supported protective legislation for women laborers, particularly limiting burdensome work weeks. Eleanor had been supporting such laws for two decades, but some professional women worried that limiting hours for female factory workers would adversely impact white-collar jobs held by females. Here gender and socioeconomic class collided, as Schneiderman responded that "professional women" could "jolly well take care of themselves" because of their training and education. Unskilled women, however, needed help in organizing for higher wages, reduced hours, and improved working conditions. "There are very few men who go home at the end of the day to do the housework," Schneiderman observed.

To address these ongoing problems from the First Lady's perch, Mrs. Roosevelt received an unexpected opportunity to extend her tenure in the White House when, at the 1940 Democratic Convention, FDR received his party's nomination for an unprecedented third term. The

Republican faithful at their quadrennial convocation sported campaign buttons with sayings like "Out at Third" and "We Don't Want Eleanor Either." The First Lady substituted for the president, who had wars in Europe and Asia occupying his time, and she thus became the first presidential spouse to address a national party convention. Frances Perkins, in Chicago for the event, called on Mrs. Roosevelt to unify the party, riven over how to address the coming world war and troubled by FDR's choice of progressive vice-presidential candidate Henry Wallace. Eleanor ameliorated the tensions and called "on all good men and *women* [to] give every bit of service and strength to their country that they have to give. This is the time when it is the United States that we fight for, the domestic policies that we have established as a party that we must believe in, that we must carry forward, and in the world we have a position of great responsibility."[113]

The bombing of Pearl Harbor in December 1941 forced the United States' entry into World War II and mooted many of the Depression's employment issues. Mothers, wives, and unmarried women flocked to wartime industries for jobs, while the able-bodied men in their lives headed into military service. Rosie the Riveter was needed on the assembly line to produce war materiel, and most employers didn't care if she needed wages as a breadwinner or not.

Now Eleanor turned her advocacy to supporting government and private-sector services for these women. Who would care for their children? How could they provide meals for their families? And, as usual, she demanded equal pay for equal work. She also directed her energies and public megaphone toward women in military service. She didn't want female soldiers to be an auxiliary appendage to the Army. They should be part of the regular service—a goal accomplished in 1943 with creation of the Women's Army Corps (WAC). The First Lady campaigned for more female doctors in the service and questioned why Army nurses weren't allowed to marry.[114] On her visits overseas—to England in 1942 and the South Pacific theater of war in 1943—she made sure to speak to women service members about their experiences in the Army and Navy.

The Democratic Party had no desire to change candidates or presidents mid-war, so it nominated FDR an unimaginable fourth time in 1944. The First Lady's role included vouching for her husband's health, though photos and newsreels showed a gaunt and tired chief executive. He was suffering from congestive heart failure, a fact his doctors hid from the public. The war limited campaigning, but Mrs. Roosevelt accompanied her husband to Ebbets Field in Brooklyn on a cold, rainy fall day to watch him give brief remarks to the assembled New Yorkers. The Republican ticket, headed by New York governor Thomas Dewey, tried to make ER an issue by declaring that Mrs. Dewey would exercise only the First Lady's traditional duties. Nevertheless, President Roosevelt achieved an Electoral College landslide by continuing to unify the New Deal coalition.[115]

On April 12, 1945, FDR was barely three months into his fourth term and was taking a traditional Easter break in Warm Springs before his scheduled speech at a UN organizational meeting in San Francisco, scheduled for the following week. Mrs. Roosevelt, who'd thought her husband sounded more robust and cheerful on the phone a few days earlier, was surprised to receive a call from his cousin saying the president had fainted. His doctor, however, urged the First Lady to carry out her schedule that afternoon before flying to Georgia later. Off she went to a women's benefit at Washington's Sulgrave Club. When FDR's press secretary reached her there and asked her to return to the White House, she knew in her heart that the worst had happened. The thirty-second president of the United States, her husband of some four decades, had passed into history. "I am more sorry for the people of this country and of the world than I am for ourselves," she told the messengers of the news she already knew.[116] Her grief only deepened when she learned from Franklin's cousins that Lucy Mercer had been with the president when he was stricken and that Eleanor's daughter Anna had arranged these rendezvous during his final years.

By the end of 1945, the former First Lady tied for fourth place in a nonpartisan poll to name a presidential candidate for the next presidential election. Generals Douglas MacArthur and Dwight Eisenhower were the top two choices, industrialist Henry Kaiser was third, and ER followed in a three-way tie with Henry Ford and Bernard Baruch—quite a feat for someone who shunned elective politics. But the mantle of her deceased husband had passed to ER, and she would use this symbolic passage effectively.

Her most enduring policy advocacy—for her own gender in the workplace—had still not embraced the ERA. Instead, she continued to support protections for employed females, but her vision of women's rights was expanding. By 1948, Mrs. Roosevelt was busy leading the UN delegation to draft and adopt the Declaration of Human Rights, including gender equity.[117]

9

ER AND JFK'S LAST ALLIANCE

AS A RESULT OF HER international exposure, Mrs. Roosevelt brought more progressive gender policies to the New Frontier. By the time President Kennedy called on her service in this realm, ER's position on gender equity, especially the Equal Rights Amendment, was shifting. Her evolution over the twentieth century's first half tracked the belief of many women's rights proponents in that era who focused on biological differences between men and women and advocated protections for females against exploitation in the workplace. It was considered the height of progressivism in 1910 when labor lawyer and future US Supreme Court Justice Louis Brandeis authored the *Muller v. Oregon* brief, supporting protective policies for female employees based on social science data.[1] Yet by the 1960s, on the cusp of the modern women's movement, ERA proponents emphasized equal treatment of both genders, as had the amendment's originators.

Mrs. Roosevelt continued to provide leadership for female political party activists and labor organizers. In May 1962, Kennedy spent several days in Manhattan promoting his government health insurance proposal for the elderly (what would become Medicare in 1965), and ER

John F. Kennedy, Eleanor Roosevelt, and New York Governor Nelson Rockefeller (far left) in New York City for the dedication of International Ladies Garment Workers Union housing project, 1962. (Courtesy of FDRL)

sat on the stage next to the podium as JFK dedicated a housing project financed by the International Ladies Garment Workers' Union. She was pleased that the housing complex would be open to all races but fretted over JFK's failure to use his executive powers to expand civil rights for Black Americans.[2]

From early in his presidency, JFK began to receive the same kinds of messages from ER that she had imparted to his Democratic predecessors, including her husband, asking him to hire more women. Kennedy hadn't endorsed the ERA in his 1960 campaign, but women labor leaders like Esther Peterson, who maintained some influence in the Democratic Party, convinced him that he should support their causes, such as equal opportunity and minimum wages for all workers.[3] As director of the Labor Department's Women's Bureau and later promoted to assistant secretary of labor to head the Bureau of Labor Standards, Peterson was the highest-ranking female in the Kennedy presidency and took the lead on creating a commission to pursue employment equity for women. She first consulted not Mrs. Roosevelt but Secretary of Labor Arthur Goldberg when the Kennedy administration began getting pressure to support the ERA, which Peterson saw as a "fluffy" generality.[4]

She persuaded Goldberg that "we've got to get at this women's question another way, we've got to find a new way." He encouraged Peterson to think creatively, and she suggested a commission. The labor secretary approved her written elaboration of the concept and backed Peterson's contact with Kennedy aide Mike Feldman. She then lunched with Ralph Dungan, special assistant to the president. Esther convinced them by arguing, "You've got to have this [commission]. You've got to be ready for the [future]." After years on the Hill, she knew "that argument always works with political people." Feldman briefed the president, who gave the green light, telling Peterson in a short meeting, "I think it looks good. I think it looks all right, Esther."[5]

Because of his premature death, Kennedy never had an opportunity, through a memoir or oral history, to provide his rationale for embracing Peterson's proposal with such alacrity. The 1960 Democratic Party platform on which JFK ran supported "the right to a job," requiring "action to break down artificial and arbitrary barriers to employment based on age, race, sex, religion, or national origin." He saw these barriers as preventing women from "achieving full equality in our American life."[6] Eleanor and Esther were pioneer women on Kennedy's New Frontier and convinced him to take this stand a year and a half before he would do so for African Americans in his proposed civil rights legislation. In advocating women's rights, he did not face the political (or, indeed, violent) reactions that surrounded efforts at racial progress, especially in the South. After all he did to win her over to his candidacy the previous year, keeping Mrs. Roosevelt on his side was an added bonus. The president also saw an opportunity for the commission to recount "the story of women's progress in a free, democratic society" while asking for "advances still to be made."[7] He understood that some communist countries provided more rights to women and minorities, so the United States should close that gap when possible. Increasing America's advances in armaments, outer space, athletics, and through the Peace Corps weren't the only ways to attract the developing world to our side.

As a pragmatic labor lobbyist and women's advocate, Peterson held the line against getting "into psychological kinds of things. And I think one of my victories was that we'd stay in substantive areas that we could really look at in a positive way. . . . And away from the *Feminine Mystique*, which I just didn't want the commission to be part of, nor, I'm sure, would the president. I just didn't think he should be involved in that. And it wasn't what we needed either."[8] The American housewife's psyche, which Betty Friedan would capture in her book published two years later and which Peterson would cite in her 1970 oral history, was of no interest to her in promoting the practical aspects of women in the labor market.

Next came the decision about chairing the commission. Peterson insisted on Mrs. Roosevelt, as did Goldberg, who agreed that "she was the only person in the United States who had the stature." But they wondered if the Kennedys had mended all fences with the Roosevelts. Dungan and Feldman discussed the matter at length with Peterson, and then Dungan gave her the White House imprimatur to invite the former First Lady's service as chair. "But I was the one who was to call her, not the president," Peterson recalled.[9]

After listening to Esther's description of the task ahead, Eleanor accepted with enthusiasm, but added a poignant fact: "This may be the last thing that I really do." Eleanor had noticed her energy waning from what had been an endless supply throughout her life. But she was now seventy-seven, and she couldn't shake the fevers and other flu-like symptoms for which her doctor was treating her, thinking she had a blood disorder.

The two women collaborated on developing a list of potential members, drawing from business, labor, and academe. "I wanted people who were in a position to act," Peterson recorded. Some wanted an all-female commission, but Esther demanded that both genders be represented. For vice chair, she chose Princeton labor economist Richard Lester, who had worked with her on minimum-wage legislation. "He had been one of our [labor's] expert witnesses from time to time and always had a very good point of view towards women as people—not women as women, but as a force in labor and employment areas. And I felt that we had to have someone with academic credentials. And then, let me be frank, I wanted to have the votes. I thought it was very necessary to be sure that we had enough people there who would vote along the lines that I thought the commission should go. I guess I'm very practical, I wasn't in politics for nothing," Peterson explained.[10]

Lester met for at least two hours over lunch with Peterson and ER at the latter's Manhattan home in fall 1961 to discuss potential members of the commission. "Mrs. Roosevelt, of course, was acquainted with a great many of these people, much more so than I was. And she had some very acute things to say," remembered the economist. She was "tremendously" involved in the selection process.[11] For example, ER recruited her Black friend and activist civil rights lawyer Pauli Murray to serve on the commission's Committee on Political and Civil Rights and assist with report drafting.[12]

Esther's long experience lobbying for labor causes, particularly with JFK in Congress, taught her that careful arguments for women's employment rights had more influence on him than the ERA. She believed that these specific positions from her work in the campaign helped push the new president toward accepting her idea of a women's commission to study and promote economic rights.[13]

Peterson's stands complemented Mrs. Roosevelt's long-held beliefs on gender. Eleanor's leading role in women's advocacy, both in the party and society, meant that Kennedy would need her support in what he hoped would be the first of two presidential terms and his 1964 reelection run. On December 14, 1961, just prior to President and Mrs. Kennedy's departure for Colombia and Venezuela, JFK issued an executive order creating the President's Commission on the Status of Women, which recognized the "prejudices and outmoded customs [that] act as barriers to the full realization of women's basic rights." Those rights, the order declared, "should be respected and fostered as part of our Nation's commitment to human dignity, freedom, and democracy." The order linked women's rights to the national interest in "promot[ing] the economy, security, and national defense through the most efficient and effective utilization of the skills of all persons." It observed that in national emergencies "women have served with distinction in widely varied capacities but thereafter have been subject to treatment as a marginal group whose skills have been inadequately utilized."[14]

The president charged the commission with "developing recommendations for overcoming discriminations in government and private employment on the basis of sex and for developing recommendations for services which will enable women to continue their role as wives and mothers while making a maximum contribution to the world around them." To achieve this goal, the executive order outlined six areas for the commission to "make recommendations as needed for constructive action":

1) Employment under federal contracts;
2) Impact on women's income of federal social insurance and tax laws;
3) Protective federal and state labor laws on hours, wages, and night work and "whether they should be adapted to changing technological, economic, and social conditions";
4) Different legal recognition of men and women in political, civil, property, and family rights;
5) Education, counseling, training, home services, and childcare "for women as wives, mothers, and workers"; and
6) Assurance of "nondiscrimination on the basis of sex" and "constructive employment opportunities for women" in federal employment policies and practices via legislation, executive orders, or administrative action.[15]

The bipartisan commission consisted of twenty members appointed by the president, joined by the secretary of labor; attorney general; secretary of health, education, and welfare; secretary of commerce; secretary of agriculture; and chair of the Civil Service Commission. A total of fifteen women and thirteen men would serve, including two senators and two congressmen, from each party.[16] Peterson had suggested

John F. Kennedy, Eleanor Roosevelt (left of Kennedy), and Esther Peterson in the Oval Office for the first meeting of the President's Commission on the Status of Women, 1962. (Abbie Rowe, White House Photos/JFKL)

Republican George Aiken, and the president, who liked the Vermont senator, agreed. Esther knew that Aiken had been a reliable vote for minimum wage and equal pay. In addition, he was a reasonable legislator and easy to work with, which Peterson prized.[17]

The executive order designated October 1, 1963, as the commission's termination date, giving the group fewer than two years to complete its research, recommendations, and final report for the president.[18] "Many of the old legal disabilities have been swept away," Kennedy noted in his statement accompanying announcement of his executive order. "Some still remain. But more than their removal is required. Attention must be given to opening up greater opportunities in employment for women as well as removing remaining discriminations against them."[19]

Just two months later, the president welcomed the new commissioners to the Oval Office and invited them to meet in the West Wing.

"I remember the day we first took [ER] there," reported Peterson. "She went in and had a good talk alone with Kennedy for a while. She told me afterwards that they talked only politics, they didn't talk women. [Laughter]." The relationship between JFK and ER was now "much, much better." The "tension" between the two that Peterson had witnessed at the Senate hearing several years earlier was "pretty well gone."[20]

Mrs. Roosevelt and President Kennedy had forged a common goal to pursue gender equity, especially in education and employment. What a dramatic turn of events that her "dear boy," known as a womanizer, and the grande dame of the Democratic Party, plagued by infidelity in her own marriage, would now join forces to advance the cause of women's rights. She couldn't have known that JFK continued his marital infidelities throughout his presidency, but at least Eleanor saw a charming family occupying the White House. He was no longer the son of a political opponent but the husband of a beautiful First Lady and father of two beguiling children. Even if she had known of his incorrigible womanizing, it is unlikely that it would have ended her new-found political alliance on gender equality.

As early as 1939, Mrs. Roosevelt had admitted to the younger members of the Washington Women's City Club, "I'm so tired of programs of study I don't know what to do."[21] Who could blame her if, by 1962, the woman who Adlai Stevenson said would rather light a candle than curse the darkness felt her life glow subsiding and urged the PCSW at their first meeting to take "action" and make "concrete suggestions and recommendations."[22]

The president that day was already looking ahead to his 1964 reelection campaign. Reports appeared in the morning papers that Michigan Governor George Romney, a Mormon, might enter the GOP presidential nomination race. "I remember the president was not interested—I'm a Mormon from Utah—in talking commission," Esther recalled. "All he wanted to know was everything about Romney. I remember it so well because Arthur and I were trying to get him to look at the agenda."[23]

In spring 1962, Mrs. Roosevelt again invited the president to an interview on her educational television program, this time to discuss for a public audience the new PCSW and all the issues the commission would address. Sitting together at the White House, the former First Lady and president chatted about the need for "equal pay and equal conditions" for women, who, Kennedy observed, constituted one-third of the American workforce. Eleanor pressed the president on why women failed to be represented in "higher positions." He reverted to the traditional response that it resulted from "the interruption in their careers that takes place in the lives of most women because of their keeping a family—raising children. . . . But I still think we ought to do better. . . . I know, Mrs. Roosevelt, I am always getting letters from you about getting women in these policy-making jobs, and we are very conscious of that responsibility."[24]

Impatient to see reforms effected, Eleanor now pushed even harder for change. With no easing of her enervating symptoms, she couldn't wait for the commission's report. Might something be done more quickly to assist women with families who wanted or needed to work outside the home? she asked Kennedy. He responded that the role of women in society "is the most sensitive and important matter," and, while he was already proposing legislation to support gender equity in pay for businesses engaged in interstate commerce (which Congress has the constitutional authority to regulate), JFK preferred to wait for suggestions from the commission on more controversial matters.[25]

Following her conversation with the president, Mrs. Roosevelt's program continued with questions for Secretary Goldberg, including about which areas the commission could offer something "really new for American women." Goldberg responded, in part, "Mrs. Roosevelt, you were one of the pioneers in getting special laws for women, to protect them. Do we still need them, or do we now emerge in a period where we ought to abolish discrimination in laws in favor of women? I want to study that."[26] Peterson's conception of the commission ensured that only one of its members supported the ERA mandate to eliminate *all* disparate treatment based on gender, which would include protective legislation for women. The other commissioners "had proven loyalties to the labor movement, to the Progressive Era women's organizations, or to the Kennedy administration," meaning that they tended to share Mrs. Roosevelt's priorities.[27]

On her interview program, Eleanor turned to her guest Agda Rossel, Sweden's permanent representative to the United Nations, who was previously president of the UN Commission on the Status of Women. She described her country's successful childcare and meal preparation programs for working mothers so that they would know that their preschool children were well cared for in state-run nurseries and would always have a nutritious dinner with parents each evening. Mrs. Roosevelt also pointed out that Swedish schools served a hot lunch to all students. Perhaps she flashed back to her days as New York's First Lady, thirty years earlier, when she peeked under the pot lids at state facilities' kitchens on her inspection tours for FDR.

Revealing how far some Americans still had to go in contemplating women's equality, another guest on the show, Smith College president Thomas Mendenhall, whom the announcer introduced as having "spoken frequently about women's problems," queried Secretary Goldberg: "There are some occupations, let's admit it, more suited for women than others. Are you going to argue that they're all equally suited, Mr. Secretary?" Goldberg responded, "Well, I would argue about the desirability of having in an open society every opportunity for every person, man or woman, to opt to a profession." Mendenhall suddenly changed his tune, interjecting, "Agreed. Agreed." Yet Goldberg returned to the generalization that "we would be foolish to deny that for women raising a family is a tremendously important thing. And I would certainly urge every woman to evaluate that enormous joy in determining an occupation."

Rossel clarified that women should make such determinations and be given the tools to do so. She questioned why men and women had to pursue professional training in their younger years: "Why do [women] have to start so early, and why can't they start later on in their life? Why can't they come back and complete their training later on?" Goldberg agreed, noting that "you do not have to feel that because you are not able at one point in your career to pursue in a continuous pattern that this excludes you at a later point in your life picking up and pursuing and continuing study."

ER, who had borne six children in a decade, observed that it takes tremendous self-discipline, which is not taught, for a woman to leave professional training for childrearing and then return when her children are older. She encouraged the secretary of labor to address wages for part-time employment, which might be more conducive for working mothers' schedules if the pay and status were higher. Eleanor also advocated "a partnership in marriage" rather than female deference to husbands, "so that each of them has a right for self-development."

Mendenhall reverted to Depression-era rationales, asking Goldberg why women should be encouraged to work when men's unemployment rates were unacceptably high. The labor secretary responded that most women in the workforce are there by necessity; they are heads of households, single, or their husbands are unemployed. In addition, the jobs they performed tended to be those "only available to women." Goldberg concluded "that prejudice ought not to be a barrier against any persona—a man or a woman—realizing his full potential."

The nation needed to rethink its education system, Mrs. Roosevelt summarized: "I like the idea that one could train faster, perhaps, at an older age—not too old—but a little bit more mature. I'm enormously encouraged by the fact that it really seems to be the feeling that children are not really harmed by the fact that their mothers work." Thus ended the third season of Eleanor's *Prospects of Mankind*. She bid what she thought was a temporary farewell to "all of our faithful audience. . . . I hope we will have you all together joining us next year." But she would not live to produce a fourth season.

In June, shortly after the historic TV program aired, the PCSW met at Hyde Park, and ER thanked JFK for his letter of good wishes. She found the meeting successful in working toward equalization in employment. The commission established seven committees to perform research on the status of women, consult with numerous experts, and make recommendations in the areas designated by the president's executive order. The members were pleased to learn from Deputy Attorney General Nicholas Katzenbach that the president had directed that appointments and promotion in the federal civil service be made without regard to gender.

At the Hyde Park gathering, held in the FDR Presidential Library, Mrs. Roosevelt declared, "Because I anticipate success in achieving full employment and for use of America's magnificent potential, I feel confident that in the years ahead many of the remaining outmoded barriers to women's aspirations will disappear. Within a rapidly growing economy, with appropriate manpower planning all Americans will have a better chance to develop their individual capacities, to earn a good livelihood, and to strengthen family life."[28]

Eleanor Roosevelt and Esther Peterson at Hyde Park for a meeting of the PCSW, 1962. (Courtesy of FDRL)

ER was no mere figurehead. She chaired every meeting during the first year and kept discussions on track when they tended to drift beyond the commission's mandate. Peterson, whom the president named its executive vice chairman, would meet Eleanor in her New York apartment and in Washington to review "papers and plans. We'd give her the agenda early."[29]

Richard Lester observed that "none of us will forget the experience at Hyde Park when we had our meeting there for two days, when [Mrs. Roosevelt] met with us and had us over to her [Val-Kill] cottage. We saw how effective and how able and gracious she was."[30] Unfortunately, ER's failing health soon stymied her full participation. As Peterson explained, "She worked hard until she started going downhill physically—after the Hyde Park meeting, she began getting a little weaker—then she got a cold . . . and things gradually got worse. But we never replaced the chair. So while she was well, she was really involved; she was really interested in the commission."[31]

Several issues particularly engaged the former First Lady, and they reflected her long-standing efforts for women and minorities. ER emphasized the link between women's employment and domestic responsibilities. Peterson recalled that Eleanor "was concerned that we hold onto family life. She kept saying that the work we were doing would strengthen family life. I remember her using those words a great deal, that if we solved some of the unemployment and low pay problems women would be happier and they'd strengthen family life. I suppose, if there was any one thing that concerned her most it was the employment of the disadvantaged, of the minority groups."[32]

Commissioner Dorothy Height, the well-known head of the National Council of Negro Women, took the lead on Black women's issues. "But Mrs. Roosevelt was the one who did a lot on that," said Peterson. "We had a discussion on whether or not we should have a task force or committee on the disadvantaged woman, the minority woman. And Mrs. Roosevelt . . . said that that should be a concern of every committee. And as it is it runs through all the reports. There isn't a report that doesn't deal with the disadvantaged woman, in civil rights and political, home and community. . . . This was part of her philosophy and we adopted it."[33]

Just nine weeks after the Hyde Park gathering, Mrs. Roosevelt sent the commission's preliminary report, based on its first six months of work, to President Kennedy. "It was just to let him know the direction we were going. And it gave us a good vehicle to go to other Cabinet officers and say, 'Look, this is the way it's beginning to look. If you're going to say anything, you better start saying it now,'" was the commission's strategy, according to Peterson. One sticking point with the White House behind the scenes focused on family planning. "We wanted to get it in in some way or other and it was a delicate maneuver," Peterson observed. "And we finally cleared with the Catholic groups and the others the wording that's finally in the report. The casual reader wouldn't know it, but we who worked on it know what it really says. . . . I think the report was the first government document that had any, any indication at all that the direction we go will be toward family planning. And that was part of that period [of the preliminary report]."[34]

Mrs. Roosevelt, a proponent of family planning for her entire public career, placed her emphasis elsewhere in writing the first Catholic president that "the commission has asked me to tell you that we are undertaking the responsibility you have placed upon us, aware of its significance and confident that more rapid progress can indeed be made toward full partnership of women in our American democracy."[35] The Defense Department was considering increasing opportunities for higher-level officers in the women's components of the armed forces, and a September meeting would address gender pay equity in companies that held federal contracts. The commission was gathering information on state laws that treated men and women differently. It also announced its support for the general principle of pay equity between genders.[36]

The report concluded: "We cannot consider our economy sound if women who have a contribution to make are not fully able to do so. The commission's success in contributing to the full partnership of women will depend in no small measure on expanding opportunities for all our people. A rapidly rising national output is the strongest weapon against substandard jobs, poverty-stricken homes, and barren lives."[37]

President Kennedy thanked the commission for their achievements thus far in expanding opportunities for women in the federal workforce and armed forces. His August 25, 1962, letter to Mrs. Roosevelt noted that "it will be forty-two years tomorrow since women gained the right to participate fully in the governing of our country through the right to vote. It is appropriate on this date, therefore, that we take note of the progress made and the distance to be traveled to achieve full equality for all of our citizens."[38] Indicating the public relations benefit of this report and exchange of letters, Press Secretary Pierre Salinger's office released the documents to the public.

That summer of 1962, Eleanor and the Gurewitsches made a sentimental journey to Campobello. They received permission to cross over a new bridge connecting the Roosevelts' beloved island to Maine. Named for FDR, the span had not yet officially opened. Mrs. Roosevelt had planned to cut the ribbon at the dedication, with President Kennedy in attendance, and she invited him to lunch with her on the island. But this August 1962 lunch between Democratic titans wouldn't occur. JFK wrote to say his plans had changed, making it impossible for him to come to the Canadian province. He then heard from Sen. Edmund Muskie of Maine, who hoped to welcome him to the bridge ceremony, that Mrs. Roosevelt was unwell and that this event might be the last to honor her husband during her lifetime.[39] The president immediately wrote to her:

"I've read that you have not been feeling up to par recently and want to take this opportunity to send along my best wishes for a speedy recovery."[40] But her health continued to decline, making her presence at the bridge dedication impossible. Eleanor and Franklin's son, Congressman James Roosevelt, did the honors.[41]

Unbeknownst to Mrs. Roosevelt at the time, September 25 would mark publication of her last "My Day" column. Prior to Warren Court decisions that declared third-degree police interrogations a violation of the Fifth Amendment's right against self-incrimination, Eleanor addressed racism in law enforcement's questioning of suspects. She also decried segregation in housing and schools, including in the North.[42]

That her health was failing became clear from a form letter sent to JFK asking him to serve as honorary chairman of fundraising for the Wiltwyck School. Even more concerning was the letter's signature, effected by an assistant "due to Mrs. R's illness."[43] In what would be her last signed letter to the president, dated October 2, Eleanor thanked President and Mrs. Kennedy for thinking of her and sending flowers. Her crabbed signature belied her optimistic tone, writing that the cause of her "fever" had been determined, and she would be back to her schedule soon.[44]

Perhaps recognizing that the former First Lady needed a personal touch, the president hand-wrote a note for her seventy-eighth birthday on October 11—"78 years of a vital, useful, and remarkable life. I hope you are better and that we shall meet again soon."[45] Hospitalized and too ill to respond, Eleanor turned to daughter Anna, who penned a note to the president expressing her mother's gratitude that he would "take the time and effort" to send birthday wishes. Unfortunately, Eleanor's condition wasn't improving as the family had hoped, and Franklin Jr. would update the president on her condition. Anna sent "prayers and best wishes during these difficult times,"—a reference to the letter coming amidst the Cuban Missile Crisis's agonizing "13 days" in October 1962.[46] A few days later the commission, realizing that Mrs. Roosevelt couldn't join them for the next phase of their work, wrote to say she was "very much in our thoughts."[47]

On October 18, 1962, doctors finally accommodated Mrs. Roosevelt's fervent wish to leave the hospital and return to the Manhattan townhouse she shared with the Gurewitsches. After two years of treating her for low blood counts, fevers, chills, and fatigue (misdiagnosed as aplastic anemia, said to be a form of leukemia), Dr. Gurewitsch ultimately concluded that she suffered from a rare type of tuberculosis that had invaded her bone marrow. Steroid treatments prescribed for the blood disorder may have reactivated TB she had perhaps contracted in 1919 when she visited World War I battlefields in Europe with her husband. All those years earlier, physicians identified her respiratory illness as pleurisy, and she had never been treated for a tubercular condition.[48] Or she might have developed the infection in her last years when steroids prescribed for her misdiagnosis of anemia may have made her more susceptible to a particularly virulent form of the TB bacterium.[49]

As she declined, thousands of well-wishes poured in from around the world, sent by heads of state and their constituents. Prayers from virtually every faith tradition on the planet arrived at ER's last home, where she lay in her upstairs bedroom too weak to sit for more than a few minutes. "David, I want to die," she told Gurewitsch.[50] Knowing that she could no longer live the "strenuous life," as her Uncle Ted had labeled the Roosevelt approach to seizing each day with energy and activism, Eleanor begged doctors, nurses, and family members to let her slip away from the pain and discomfort. She began refusing to ingest prescribed medications. Years before she had described herself as a fatalist, but one who believed that there must be some form of "going on" after death. She admitted, though, that she was unclear about the nature of an afterlife.[51] On November 7, 1962, her generous heart, so attuned to all who suffered around the globe, beat its last.

EPILOGUE

Farewell to the World's First Lady and Camelot's King

"TRULY, ELEANOR ROOSEVELT WAS THE imperishable conscience of the world," President Kennedy declared at her passing. Was he required to remember the late First Lady in such glowing terms? Or had former enemies become eternal allies? He ordered US flags to fly at half-staff in Mrs. Roosevelt's honor until her burial.[1] He and Mrs. Kennedy received a telegram inviting them to the funeral service at St. James Episcopal Church in Hyde Park and the interment in Springwood's Rose Garden.[2] They would attend, along with Vice President Johnson, former Presidents Truman and Eisenhower, UN Ambassador Stevenson, Chief Justice Earl Warren, and UN Secretary General U Thant. But first, they and Eleanor's friends gathered at Val-Kill for visitation with the Roosevelt family.[3] First Lady Jacqueline Kennedy, who had praised her predecessor in a letter to ER earlier that year as "so rare and so good for all women of my age to have to emulate—a great lady," penned a kind note to Anna Roosevelt Halstead, thanking her for the intimate memorial arrangements that "made us all feel as if we were private people." Nothing impressed Mrs. Kennedy more than protecting the privacy of

John F. Kennedy, Jacqueline Kennedy, Harry Truman, Dwight Eisenhower, and Eleanor Roosevelt's children Anna, Franklin Jr., John, and Elliot at her funeral in Hyde Park, 1962. (Abbie Rowe, White House Photos/JFKL)

presidential families[4]—especially hers, with two young children being raised in the White House fishbowl.

JFK had come full circle since that fateful August day two years earlier when he met with Mrs. Roosevelt for their showdown lunch at her cottage and then delivered his Social Security commemorative address on Hyde Park's lawn. Now he watched her simple oak coffin, covered in pine boughs from the woods surrounding Val-Kill, as ER requested, arrive at its final resting place next to the graves of FDR and his famous Scottish terrier, Fala.[5] Eleanor had cared for her husband's beloved canine friend after Franklin's death. Like Greyfriars Bobby, Fala always seemed on guard for his master's return, lying by the Val-Kill door in expectation and standing at the ready when he heard a motorcade approaching, until he died in 1952.[6]

The look of sadness on President Kennedy's face at the Roosevelt gravesite reflected that a genuine alliance, not simple political opportunism, bonded ER and JFK in the last two years of her life. Just a week after Eleanor's death, the president announced that, at the request of her family, he had appointed a committee, headed by Ambassador Stevenson, "to explore and make suggestions regarding the manner in which the major interests to which Mrs. Roosevelt dedicated her life could be continued," especially "the securing and protection of human rights and on improvement of living conditions among the underprivileged." JFK asked the committee to meet in Washington before November's end to organize and streamline the efforts that many of her friends wished to undertake in her honor. We will never know what the former First Lady would have thought about the fact that only one woman, her friend Mary Lasker, appeared among the fifteen-person committee, and one, "Mrs. Joseph Lash," among the handful asked to serve as consultants.[7] Kennedy also accepted a suggestion from Senator Muskie to recommend that Canada and the United States jointly create an international park around Eleanor and Franklin's Campobello home.

In the redesigned White House Rose Garden, just springing to renewed life in April 1963, President Kennedy announced his signing of a bill granting a federal charter to the Eleanor Roosevelt Memorial Foundation, which was dedicated to her causes: "Relief of the poor and underprivileged, promotion of public health, promotion of economic welfare, and furtherance of international good will." The president's written remarks concluded that "Mrs. Roosevelt, I believe, would be pleased to know that her friends and associates have chosen this way to continue her work, especially because it enables all citizens to take part in deeds rather than just words."[8] Kennedy received a certificate naming him a "Founding Member" of the Eleanor Roosevelt Memorial Foundation, signed by Ambassador Stevenson, who attended the White House ceremony establishing the foundation. Its mission was "to keep alive the courageous ideals and efforts of Eleanor Roosevelt."[9]

Now that "Mrs. R" had exited the political stage, JFK had no personal obligation to honor her posthumously, but she and her late husband Franklin remained patron saints of the Democratic Party's liberal wing. The Americans for Democratic Action (ADA), of which Eleanor was a founding member and honorary chair, celebrated the New Deal's ideals each January with Franklin D. Roosevelt Day dinners on his birthday at chapters across the country.[10] Democratic presidents sent greetings and a brief statement to the celebrations. In January 1963, JFK devoted his remarks to Mrs. Roosevelt. Her loss "cannot be measured," he began, but "grief is the last thing that she, most of all, would wish to preoccupy us. Her orientation was never with bygones. It was always with things to come. The beliefs she lived by—the dedication to people which was her genius, and the understanding of them which was her charm—are ever-living. . . . Her commitment to humanity and her hopes for the world went way beyond her mortal self." Mrs. Roosevelt "would want these dinners to continue to be annual reminders of the spirit and principle of her husband, Franklin D. Roosevelt," Kennedy declared. Attendees, he observed, were "champions and exponents of the great liberal tradition of Franklin and Eleanor Roosevelt." "The need for expression of liberal—often unpopular—ideas is one that will survive us all," JFK concluded.[11]

Official tributes were not the only ways that the Kennedys and Roosevelts remained bonded. Eleanor's son, Congressman James Roosevelt, who had been such a close associate of Ambassador Kennedy, wrote a poignant letter to Joe's wife Rose, thanking her for condolences after his mother's death: "Your very wonderful letter meant so very much to me. You and Joe through the years have always made me feel a part of your family, and I have, and always will, the same deep respect and affection for you and your family." James wrote frankly about ER: "Mother had a full and rare life. She truly loved people for themselves, not what they seemed to be. One of the last things she said to me, about two weeks before she died, was, 'I think the president would have an easier time if Nixon is not governor of California.' And so it is. Her mistakes were those of judgment but rarely involved ill will, and her loyalties ran deep." Perhaps this was his explanation of her late arrival aboard the 1960 Kennedy bandwagon. Her dislike of Nixon and his 1950s Red-baiting, especially of her friend Helen Gahagan Douglas, also ran deep. Sadly, she probably wasn't aware that Nixon lost the Golden State gubernatorial race the day before she died and declared his retirement from politics (prematurely, as it happened).

Congressman Roosevelt's description of his siblings' and perhaps his father's relationship with ER reveals stark honesty: "She loved her family and stood by us even when we brought her grief and tribulation." Her five children had nineteen marriages among them and fought frequently over money and the family's tangible assets, including the Hyde Park and Val-Kill properties. "We, her children, have so much to be proud of and the responsibility not to mar but to uphold her image." As the Kennedy family's supreme image-maker, Rose could certainly understand the congressman's wish.

He concluded with heartfelt warmth toward Rose and Joe: "You and Joe have given us much through yourselves and your family that perhaps you will know what I mean when I say that my duty to my mother's memory will best be served if I join in your prayers for her and continue to deserve your affection as well as do my part to help your son and my president. I will try to see you both very soon. Many thanks and my love always, Jimmy."[12]

During his presidency, JFK wanted to reward Franklin Jr. for his crucial help in winning the 1960 West Virginia primary over Hubert Humphrey. Given Franklin's distinguished World War II Navy service,

John F. Kennedy, Jacqueline Kennedy, and Franklin Roosevelt Jr. on a Navy ship watching America's Cup races, 1962. (Robert Knudson, White House Photos/JFKL)

Kennedy thought it appropriate to appoint him secretary of the Navy, but Defense Secretary Robert McNamara nixed the nomination, opposing most courtesy appointments at the Pentagon and perhaps knowing of Franklin's less than stellar congressional career. Moreover, McNamara was a Republican until 1978, which would have made him disinclined toward FDR fandom. Franklin Jr. settled for undersecretary of commerce.

Mrs. Roosevelt didn't live to see the first substantive outcome from the President's Commission on the Status of Women. Her testimony and Peterson's legislative acumen, however, had already inspired the president and Congress to move forward even before the PCSW completed its final report. "I concluded very definitely that we had to have a federal [equal pay] law. That, too, I think, I can take some credit for," Esther stated in her oral history. "I got Arthur [Goldberg] to really agree to put it on our legislative list, and I talked with the legislative people over there [at the White House]. I had to convince them that it was a good political issue, that they had to do something for women and that this would be one of the best things they could do." Although the president's legislative staff, led by Lawrence O'Brien, posed no obstacles to the equal pay for women proposal, they didn't make it a priority.[13]

Undersecretary of Labor Willard Wirtz, who replaced Goldberg as head of the department when JFK appointed the latter to the Supreme Court in 1962, "was not as warm toward this idea as was Arthur," according to Esther. Wirtz "didn't think we could ever get it. . . . He didn't think it was possible. I don't think he objected to it in principle as much. But I didn't ever have enthusiastic support during those times. All you hear is, 'Oh, another women's sort of thing.'" Having drafted the pay equity bill at the same time as she and her colleagues were establishing the commission, Peterson wanted the record to show that the legislation moved forward separately: "We got Mrs. Roosevelt to testify for it, but it was well on its way before the commission acted."[14]

In February 1962, the PCSW endorsed the equal pay bill, which passed both houses of Congress, but a conference committee to reconcile differences in the legislation failed to meet before adjournment, and the reform died. After reintroduction in the new Congress, the 1963 version made it all the way to President Kennedy, whom Peterson kept on board

John F. Kennedy and Esther Peterson (standing behind Kennedy in white suit) in the Oval Office for the signing of the Equal Pay Act, 1963; Kennedy hands Dorothy Height, of the National Council of Negro Women, a ceremonial pen. (Abbie Rowe, White House/JFKL)

with supportive statements he could issue about the bill. He signed the Equal Pay Act in June.[15] The landmark legislation prohibited "discrimination on account of sex in the payment of wages by employers." Kennedy labelled the law "a first step" that "affirms our determination that when women enter the labor force they will find equality in their pay envelopes." As an amendment to the 1938 Fair Labor Standards Act, the 1963 law required that employers pay workers equally, regardless of gender, for labor requiring "equal skill, effort, and responsibility."[16] This was the goal of "equal pay for equal work" that Eleanor had advocated for decades.

Meanwhile, Esther, with an editorial committee, prepared the commission's unanimous final report, titled *American Women*.[17] She knew they had the White House's support when, after sending a draft to the president's staff, his advisors asked that JFK's photo be included in the report's frontispiece.[18] The commission also featured a picture of the smiling Eleanor Roosevelt as a tribute to their deceased leader. At the White House ceremony and reception for the commission, held on what would have been ER's seventy-ninth birthday, October 11, 1963, President Kennedy departed from prepared remarks to speak extemporaneously about the importance of the PCSW's work. After expressing his "very great appreciation to Miss Peterson and to Professor Lester" along with members of Congress on the commission, especially Senator Maurine Neuberger and Congresswoman Edith Green, both Oregon Democrats who fought for women's rights on Capitol Hill, he declared, "I think this is a very vital matter with which we're dealing." He thought a civilization could be judged on "its opportunities for women."[19]

Kennedy repeated the themes he had discussed with ER the previous year on her television program: How can "we" help women make maximum use of their "emotional and intellectual powers" and talents, along the lines of excellence, which he paraphrased from the Greeks as the definition of happiness? What happens to women who graduate from college with skills and training, the "unusual women," he oddly labeled them? Eleanor had interjected in their previous conversation that such an education was "wasted" when women became homemakers. JFK believed women applied their knowledge in raising families and local volunteer work, but he called on Congress and the executive branch to bring "attention" to improving American society for women. He offered posthumous gratitude for Mrs. Roosevelt: "This represents a legacy of hers in a very real sense." The president concluded with "very warm thanks . . . on behalf of our country and women everywhere."[20]

That same day, JFK celebrated a new commemorative stamp honoring the late First Lady. After the ceremony, the president spotted a friend of Eleanor's, the Rev. William Turner Levy, clasped him on the shoulder, and remarked, "What a great life. What a great woman. I envy you."[21] Clearly, the ensuing years and her passing had mellowed Kennedy's feelings toward the political matriarch.

As he received the final report, he made a veiled reference to other societies that we admire less but that focused more on women's issues. As one historian notes, "Anxiety over the perceived Soviet threat led

John F. Kennedy and Esther Peterson in East Room of the White House for the presentation of the PCSW report, 1963. (Abbie Rowe, White House Photos/JFKL)

many to believe that America needed to harness all its scientific talents, including those of women. These circumstances helped to bring the public's attention to the 'underutilization of women's abilities.'"[22] The Soviet Union's 1957 launch of Sputnik, the first manmade satellite, had only heightened these fears. Whether JFK was establishing the Peace Corps, racing to the moon, creating (with Mrs. Kennedy) the White House as a symbol of American democracy, or struggling over Black Americans' civil rights, for which he would introduce meaningful legislation the day after the PCSW reception, JFK always bore in mind the bipolar contest between the Free World and the Communist Bloc.

The PCSW report, published as a hundred-page booklet, was available from the government at its release for $1.15 ($12 in 2025 dollars). It contained twelve illustrative tables and twenty-one charts with census data showing how far women had to come to achieve parity. Two years later, Scribner's released the slim book to a larger audience. It created an action plan for gender equity policies in hiring, wages, and childcare. Peterson had four children and understood the difficulties of working mothers, especially when she had to care for her ailing husband. In 1968, her efforts resulted in a day care facility at the Department of Labor, named in Peterson's honor, the first such benefit offered to employees in a federal agency.[23]

Neither the 1963 equal pay law nor the PCSW's report eliminated pay discrepancies, nor did the Civil Rights Act of 1964, which banned gender discrimination in employment. President Barack Obama's first signing ceremony for a congressional bill, in January 2009, enacted the Lilly Ledbetter Equal Pay Act; it expanded the time that women had to bring a Civil Rights Act complaint of gender-based wage disparity.[24] Congress's amendment of the act, led by Hillary Clinton, then a senator from New York, had followed a 2007 Supreme Court decision against Mrs. Ledbetter's substantiated claim that the Goodyear Tire and Rubber Co. had paid her less than her male counterparts over the course of her career. When she discovered the pay inequity, by virtue of receiving considerably less in pension benefits, the short statutory timeframe to report such a pay discrepancy had long expired.[25] Some progress had been made between 1960, when women earned 59 cents to the dollar for men, and 2013, when that figure rose to 79 cents, but, the nearly 20 percent gap remains (at 84 cents for females to each dollar earned by males). COVID-19 layoffs and the pandemic shutdowns that prompted women to leave the workforce to provide childcare placed a further drag on wage parity.[26]

Moreover, other burdens shouldered by women, identified by the PCSW in 1963, have yet to be addressed comprehensively in the United States. Reliable and affordable childcare, paid maternity and paternity leave, extended family responsibilities, and discrimination against women of color all remain obstacles in American society for achieving gender equity. One area of vast improvement for women since the report's release is in higher education. Women's rate of college attendance has increased by more than a third since John Kennedy ran for the presidency in 1960.[27] Females now outnumber males among college students, 60 percent to 40 percent, with men's enrollment dropping even more during the COVID-19 pandemic.[28]

The PCSW disbanded after issuing its final report, but all fifty states subsequently created commissions on the status of women. "To assure effective and continuing leadership in advancing the status of women," Kennedy issued an executive order on November 1, 1963, just three weeks before his assassination, creating the Interdepartmental Committee on the Status of Women and the Citizens' Advisory Council on the Status of Women.[29] They began to hold national meetings of the state commissions.

Also on the positive side of the ledger, many of the women who served on President Kennedy's commission or acted as consultants to it, including Pauli Murray and Betty Friedan, assumed future positions of leadership in the modern women's rights movement. Friedan's February 1963 publication of her landmark feminist manifesto, *The Feminine Mystique,* earned her a place on the commission's consulting group. Friedan devoured the commission's report, annotating it in detail. Three years later, she became founding president of the National Organization for Women (NOW), realizing by 1966 that governmental organizations alone would never implement the far-reaching remedies needed to solve problems cited in *American Women.*[30]

Yet as one labor and feminism historian has explained, part of the PCSW's legacy is organizational. It drew on faith in past government commissions and spawned new public institutions, as well as NGOs, devoted to expanding women's rights. More important, President Kennedy's commission created an "intellectual agenda" through its report, which reflected an understanding of wage inequality and homemaking in the contexts of women's experiences during the Great Depression, World War II, and the postwar 1950s.[31]

American Women reflected the heart and soul of the New Deal and the New Frontier—that *government* could address and ameliorate societal and economic injustices. Lyndon Johnson's Great Society programs would expand this theory to the maximum extent Americans would accept before Ronald Reagan's 1981 inaugural message that "government is not the solution to our problem; government *is* the problem"[32] captured the electorate's psyche.

If the commission had supported the Equal Rights Amendment, would a different outcome have awaited that still-unratified constitutional revision? Would it have achieved comprehensive women's equality? The PCSW's report stated that the ERA "need not *now* be sought." It recommended instead that courts should apply the Fifth and Fourteenth Amendments to their fullest extent to achieve gender equity.[33] ER's friend Pauli Murray supported this litigative approach. Ruth Bader Ginsburg, as founding director of the American Civil Liberties Women's Rights Project, took up the cause in the 1970s and achieved demonstrable success on a case-by-case basis for gender equity.[34] But winning lawsuits for individual litigants falls short of across-the-board women's rights reform. By 1971, ERA-skeptic Esther Peterson and other PCSW commissioners began to support the amendment.[35]

The PCSW embodied the essences of both Eleanor Roosevelt and John Kennedy as well as their political relationship. The commission's conception embraced both pragmatic and idealistic goals. JFK first needed to woo ER as a Democratic power broker in 1960 and then maintain her support for his planned reelection campaign. What better way to do so than naming her to head the commission? Although he didn't face a significant gender gap in his narrow win over Nixon, the majority of women voters had supported GOP presidential tickets from 1952 through 1960, and women had cast the majority of Republican votes in those contests.[36] It couldn't hurt to place his administration and party on the correct side of women's history to maintain or expand female support in 1964.[37] Plus, as an added ideological Cold War bonus, Kennedy could tout to the world that the United States had the courage to admit its weaknesses in women's rights, produce a roadmap for addressing them in a free and democratic society, and utilize women's talents to the fullest extent. No one could expect all the goals outlined in *American Women* to be achieved by November 1964, but two policies (the Equal Pay Act and nongendered civil service hiring rules) had already been promulgated before the final report appeared.

In turn, Eleanor could pursue her nearly life-long passion for achieving the ideal of women's equality while healing a schism in the Democratic Party that prevented Richard Nixon from becoming president—or worse, the more conservative Republican Barry Goldwater in 1964. She didn't have to *like* John Kennedy or revise her jaded view of his father to play a role in another presidential administration after eight years in the wilderness of the Eisenhower era. An additional practical bonus for her included countering the move toward the ERA so that protective legislation for women remained intact. What did either Eleanor or Jack have to lose in their PCSW gambit? The passage of time might eventually prove some of their views wrong, but fate would prevent them from witnessing such a verdict or giving them the opportunity to evolve more progressively.

Neither the president nor the former First Lady would experience the PCSW report's demonstrable impact or enduring progeny. JFK succumbed to an assassin's bullet in Dallas on November 22, 1963. Yet the truce reached between Eleanor Roosevelt and John Kennedy in August 1960 at her lunch table in the modest Val-Kill cottage on her husband's Hyde Park estate not only helped elect the 35th president of the United States but allowed the passing of the torch from one dynasty to another—"like the Plantagenets to the Yorks," as Arthur Schlesinger Jr. wryly noted after attending Mrs. Roosevelt's funeral.[38] The lessons of how political cooperation can vanquish personal, ideological, and generational conflict should remain as eternal as the flame that First Lady Jacqueline Kennedy lit at her husband's Arlington gravesite. The grande dame and her "dear boy" not only found common ground for pursuing their common interests but established a model, needed today more than ever, for burying old personal and political grudges to serve the common good.

NOTES

ABBREVIATIONS

AER — Eleanor Roosevelt, *The Autobiography of Eleanor Roosvelt* (New York: Da Capo, 1992)

ERPDE — Eleanor Roosevelt Papers, Digital Edition, George Washington University, Columbian College of Arts and Sciences, https://erpapers.columbian.gwu.edu/

ERPP — Eleanor Roosevelt Papers Project, George Washington University, Columbian College of Arts and Sciences, https://erpapers.columbian.gwu.edu/

FDRL — Franklin D. Roosevelt Library

HTF — Amanda Smith, ed. *Hostage to Fortune: The Letters of Joseph P. Kennedy* (New York: Penguin Books, 2001).

JFKL — John F. Kennedy Library, https://www.jfkl.org

MD — "My Day," newspaper column by Eleanor Roosevelt, https://www2.gwu.edu/~erpapers/myday/browsebyyear.html

OH — Oral History

INTRODUCTION

1. "Sally Roosevelt Dies After Fall," (Syracuse, NY) *Globe-Standard*, August 13, 1960, 1. Except for this introduction that sets the stage for the drama of Eleanor Roosevelt and John Kennedy, the narrative generally reflects a chronology, starting with their two political dynasties. Only chapter 8 provides a flashback to Mrs. Roosvelt's long career in advocating women's rights, which leads into the story of her work with President Kennedy in directing the PCSW.

2. ER, MD, August 16, 1960, ERPDE.
3. James Tobin's magnificent exploration of FDR's struggle with polio and its aftermath notes the truism that "the determinants of anyone's life are legion," but he accurately writes that "the crippling of his [Roosevelt's] lower body, and his complicated response to that crippling, altered the course of his career, shaped his view of life, and changed his relationships with others, from his intimates to the entire American public." See Tobin, *The Man He Became: How FDR Defied Polio to Win the Presidency* (New York: Simon & Schuster, 2013).
4. ER, interview with Arnold Michaelis, December 1956, C-SPAN Radio.
5. ER, interview with Arnold Michaelis, December 1956, C-SPAN Radio.
6. ER, interview with Arnold Michaelis, December 1956, C-SPAN Radio.
7. ER, telegram to JFK, January 29, 1959, ERPDE.
8. Joseph P. Lash, *Eleanor and Franklin* (New York: Norton, 1971), 245.
9. David Michaelis, *Eleanor* (New York: Simon & Schuster, 2020), 91.
10. Allida M. Black, *Casting Her Own Shadow: Eleanor Roosevelt and the Shaping of Postwar Liberalism* (New York: Columbia University Press, 1996), 173.
11. Various versions of what FDR said to Eleanor about Ambassador Kennedy, all with the same gist, exist in the following sources: Michael R. Beschloss, *Kennedy and Roosevelt: The Uneasy Alliance* (New York: Harper & Row, 1980), 229; Edna Gurewitsch, *Kindred Souls: The Devoted Friendship of Eleanor Roosevelt and Dr. David Gurewitsch* (New York: Open Road Integrated Media, 2014); David Nasaw, *The Patriarch: The Remarkable Life and Turbulent Times of Joseph P. Kennedy* (New York: Penguin Press, 2012), 316–17; Joseph P. Lash, *Eleanor: The Years Alone* (New York: Norton, 1972), 292–93; Smith, *HTF*, 511.
12. See Mark White, *Icon, Libertine, Leader: The Life and Presidency of John F. Kennedy* (London: Bloomsbury Academic, 2024), 29–30, 49–52.
13. Gurewitsch, *Kindred Souls*, 220.
14. Jan Jarboe Russell, *Eleanor in the Village: Eleanor Roosevelt's Search for Freedom and Identity in New York's Greenwich Village* (New York: Scribner, 2021).
15. "ER National Historic Site, New York," "The Val-Kill Years," NPS, US Department of Interior (Washington, DC: GPO, 2006); "Val-Kill: Eleanor Roosevelt National Historic Site," NPS, (2021), https://www.nps.gov/places/val-kill.htm.

1. DYNASTIES CONVERGE

1. Barbara A. Perry, *Rose Kennedy: The Life and Times of a Political Matriarch* (New York: Norton, 2013).

2. Richard Neustadt, *Presidential Power* (New York: John Wiley & Sons, 1960), 32.
3. David B. Roosevelt with Manuela Dunn-Mascetti, *Grandmère: A Personal History* (New York: Warner Books, 2002), 34–41, 238–39.
4. "Eleanor Roosvelt: Her Life in Pictures," *McCall's* magazine editorial film, 1958, YouTube.
5. ER, *AER*, 9–13.
6. ER, MD, May 24, 1949, ERPDE.
7. ER, *AER*, 20–25.
8. "Digest of Education Statistics," Table 310: Degrees conferred by degree-granting institutions, by level of degree and sex of student: Selected years, 1869–70 through 2021–22, National Center for Education Statistics, https://nces.ed.gov/.
9. Blanche Wiesen Cook, *Eleanor Roosevelt, Vol. 1, 1884–1933* (New York: Penguin Books, 1992), 156.
10. Cook, *Eleanor Roosevelt*, 1:125–33; Millicent L. Hathaway, "Trends in Heights and Weights," *Yearbook of Agriculture 1959*, https://naldc.nal.usda.gov/download/IND43861419/PDF.
11. Cook, *Eleanor Roosevelt*, 1:141, 155, 162, 169.
12. James MacGregor Burns, *Roosevelt: The Lion and the Fox* (New York: Harvest Book, 1956), 24–25; Geoffrey C. Ward, *A First-Class Temperament: The Emergence of Franklin Roosevelt* (New York: Harper and Row, 1989), 312–13.
13. ER, *AER*, 60–61; Elliot Roosevelt and James Brough, *An Untold Story: The Roosevelts of Hyde Park* (New York: G. P. Putnam's Sons, 1973), 226.
14. Joseph E. Persico, *Franklin and Lucy: President Roosevelt, Mrs. Rutherford, and the Other Remarkable Women in His Life* (New York: Random House, 2008), 122–28; David Michaelis, *Eleanor* (New York: Simon & Schuster, 2020), 163–68.
15. Burns, *Roosevelt*, 86–91.
16. Joseph P. Lash, *Eleanor and Franklin* (New York: Norton, 1971), 318; Michaelis, *Eleanor*, 130.
17. Mary Ann Glendon, "God and Mrs. Roosevelt," *First Things* (May 2010), https://www.firstthings.com/article/2010/05/god-and-mrs-roosevelt.
18. Lash, *Eleanor and Franklin*, chapter 31.
19. Perry, *Rose Kennedy*, 11–17.
20. Neal Thompson, *The First Kennedys: The Humble Roots of an American Dynasty* (Boston: Mariner Books, 2022).
21. Thomas H. O'Connor, *The Boston Irish: A Political History* (Old Saybrook, CT: Konecky and Konecky, 1995); Perry, *Rose Kennedy*.

22. "The Roosevelts and the Kennedys," FDRL, November 22, 2013.
23. Robert Dallek, *An Unfinished Life: John F. Kennedy, 1917–1963* (Boston: Little, Brown, 2003), 33–35, 73–81; Fredrik Logevall, *JFK: Coming of Age in the American Century, 1917–1956* (New York: Random House, 2020), 83, 85, 106–9; Perry, *Rose Kennedy,* 71.
24. Kay (Katherine Murphy) Halle, recorded interview by William M. McHugh, February 7, 1967, 1, JFKL OH.
25. Dallek, *Unfinished Life,* 79–81.
26. Mark Updegrove, *Incomparable Grace: JFK in the Presidency* (New York: Dutton, 2022), 207.
27. Dallek, *Unfinished Life,* 95–105, 195–97.
28. Perry, *Rose Kennedy.*
29. Perry, *Rose Kennedy,* 65–67, 76–78.
30. FDR to JPK, September 13, 1928, in Smith, *HTF,* 77 and n29.
31. David Nasaw, *The Patriarch: The Remarkable Life and Turbulent Times of Joseph P. Kennedy* (New York: Penguin Press, 2012), 135.
32. Smith, *HTF,* 66; "The Roosevelts and the Kennedys," FDRL; Nasaw, *Patriarch,* 170–77.
33. Nasaw, *Patriarch,* 179–82; "Roosevelts and the Kennedys," FDRL; Smith, *HTF,* 66.
34. Nasaw, *Patriarch,* 179–80; Thomas Maier, "The Secret Boozy Details of a Kennedy, a Churchill, and a Roosevelt," *Time,* October 21, 2014.
35. FDR to JPK, telegram, in Smith, *HTF,*100.
36. Smith indicates that her grandfather contributed $25,000 to FDR's campaign. Nasaw puts the figure at $15,000. *Patriarch,* 182–83. FDR, Commonwealth Club Address, September 23, 1932, American Rhetoric Online Speech Bank, https://www.americanrhetoric.com/.
37. Smith, *HTF,* 66; Nasaw, *Patriarch,* 172–73; Logevall, *JFK,* 100–101.
38. Halle, recorded interview by William M. McHugh, February 7, 1967, p. 1, JFKL OH.
39. "1932: FDR's First Presidential Campaign," Roosevelt House, Hunter College, CUNY; JPK to Elliott Roosevelt, November 10, 1932, in Smith, *HTF,* 102.
40. JPK to FDR, telegram, March 14, 1933; and JPK to FDR, May 19, 1933, in Smith, *HTF,*116–17.
41. Nasaw, *Patriarch,* 186.
42. Smith, *HTF,* 108.
43. Maier, "Secret Boozy Details."
44. Halle, recorded interview by William M. McHugh, February 7, 1967, p. 1, JFKL OH.

45. Smith, *HTF,* 67; Thomas Maier, *The Kennedys: America's Emerald Kings* (New York: Basic Books, 2003), 113.
46. JPK, memorandum, in Smith, *HTF,* 127–28.
47. JPK, memorandum, in Smith, *HTF,* 127–28; Perry, *Rose Kennedy,* 86.
48. JPK, memoranda, 129, 111; JPK to JPK Jr., May 4, 1934, 134, all in Smith, *HTF;* Nasaw, *Patriarch,* 105–11.
49. Nasaw, *Patriarch,* 209–10.
50. JPK, memorandum, in Smith, *HTF,* 136–39.
51. Michaelis, *Eleanor,* 234–35.
52. Perry, *Rose Kennedy,* 87; Smith, *HTF,* 154; and Arthur Krock, memorandum, in Smith, *HTF,* 154–57.
53. JPK, memorandum, in Smith, *HTF,* 149–51.
54. Rose Kennedy: Jean's First Communion, April 28, 1935, in Smith, *HTF,* 153. In truth, Kennedy had wanted to stay in Washington to attend the annual White House Correspondents' Dinner, where presidents were the guests of honor. Joe also needed to discuss with FDR his request to have him oversee $4.88 billion authorized for public works in the Emergency Relief Appropriation Act. Kennedy chose not to accept the new responsibility because he didn't wish to work with prickly Secretary of the Interior Harold Ickes, whom FDR had named Public Works Administration director and who had opposed naming Kennedy to the SEC. But Joe agreed to serve in a more informal capacity of advising the president on public works that were intended to employ thousands of Americans and stimulate the ailing economy: see Smith, *HTF,* 153n99; Nasaw, *Patriarch,* 207–8.
55. FDR to Robert Kennedy, July 12, 1935, in Smith, *HTF,* 159.
56. Jordan Steffan, "FDR's Stamp Collection: A Childhood Hobby He Took to the Oval Office," *Smithsonian Magazine,* August 4, 2009.
57. Robert Kennedy to FDR, July 19, 1935, in Smith, *HTF,* 15.
58. Perry, *Rose Kennedy,* 19.
59. Nasaw, *Patriarch,* 236.
60. JPK to FDR, September 6, 1935, in Smith, *HTF,* 159–60.
61. Smith, *HTF,* 113.
62. JPK to FDR, October 2, 1935, in Smith, *HTF,* 161–62.
63. Smith, *HTF,* 114; Nasaw, *Patriarch,* 211–12.
64. JPK to FDR, January 20, 1936; JPK to Missy LeHand, June 15, 1936, both in Smith, *HTF,* 185.
65. JPK to Robert Worth Bingham, October 6, 1936, in Smith, *HTF,* 188.
66. JPK to Father Charles Coughlin, August 18, 1936, in Smith, *HTF,* 187.
67. Nasaw, *Patriarch,* 250–51; "1936 President Roosevelt Visits Hyde Park and Warm Springs Campaigning for Reelection," YouTube.

68. Perry, *Rose Kennedy*, 93–94.
69. JPK to James Roosevelt, January 8th, 1937, in Smith, *HTF*, 190.
70. Rosemary, Kathleen, Eunice, Patricia, Robert, Jean, and Edward Kennedy, "President Roosevelt's Second Inauguration," in Smith, *HTF*, 190–91.
71. ER, *This I Remember* (New York: Harper and Brothers, 1949), 165.
72. Smith, *HTF*, 195n187.
73. Nasaw, *Patriarch*, 269–70.
74. Barbara A. Perry, *The Priestly Tribe: The Supreme Court's Image in the American Mind* (Westport, CT: Praeger, 1999), chapter 1.
75. Nasaw, *Patriarch*, 272.
76. Michael R. Beschloss, *Kennedy and Roosevelt: The Uneasy Alliance* (New York: Harper and Row, 1980), 128.
77. Nasaw, *Patriarch*, 272.
78. Smith, *HTF*, 223; Nasaw, *Patriarch*, 272–73.
79. Nasaw, *Patriarch*, 273–75.
80. JPK to Joseph Tumulty, December 21, 1937, in Smith, *HTF*, 219.
81. JPK to FDR, telegram, January 13, 1938, in Smith, *HTF*, 235–36.
82. Nasaw, *Patriarch*, 283.
83. Will Swift, *The Kennedys Amidst the Gathering Storm: A Thousand Days in London, 1938–1940* (New York: Smithsonian Books, 2008), 12.
84. JPK, Diary, February 18, 22, 1938, in Smith, *HTF*, 236–37; JPK to James Roosevelt, March 3, 1938, in Smith, *HTF*, 237–39.
85. Perry, *Rose Kennedy*, 99–100.
86. Blanche Weisen Cook, *Eleanor Roosevelt, Vol. 2, 1933–1938: The Defining Years* (New York: Penguin, 1999), 31–32; "Roosevelt's Son Married in Wilmington (1937)," British Pathé, YouTube; "Nuptial: Ann Clark Weds John Roosevelt (1938)," British Pathé, YouTube; Curtis Roosevelt, *Too Close to the Sun: Growing Up in the Shadow of My Grandparents, Franklin and Eleanor* (New York: Public Affairs, 2008), 155–56; Ruth K. McClure, ed., *Eleanor Roosevelt, An Eager Spirit: Selected Letters of Dorothy Dow, 1933–1945* (New York: Norton, 1984), 66–72; for Temple's handwritten thank-you note to Mrs. Roosevelt, see "Shirley Temple Black," FDRL. ER wrote about the Val-Kill picnic for Shirley in her column: see MD, July 11, 1938, ERPDE.
87. Cordell Hull to JPK, Diplomatic Dispatch, March 14, 1938, in Smith, *HTF*, 243.
88. JPK, Diary, March 18, 1938, in Smith, *HTF*, 245.
89. Smith, *HTF*, 227–28.
90. Department of State, Office of the Historian, "Isolationism in the 1930s," https://history.state.gov/milestones/1937-1945/american-isolationism.
91. Cook, *Eleanor Roosevelt*, 2:543.

92. Cook, *Eleanor Roosevelt,* 2:472–74, 501.
93. Cook, *Eleanor Roosevelt,* 2:501–2; Emma Garman, "'I Am the Kind of Woman I Would Run From': The Life of Lady Astor," *Daily Beast,* July 12, 2017; Perry, *Rose Kennedy,* 115, 125.
94. Cook, *Eleanor Roosevelt,* 2:503.
95. Perry, *Rose Kennedy,* 114–15.
96. Cook, *Eleanor Roosevelt,* 2:504.
97. ER, *This I Remember,* 161.
98. ER, *AER,* 212.
99. Perry, *Rose Kennedy,* 109.
100. Cook, *Eleanor Roosevelt,* 2:504–5.
101. Cook, *Eleanor Roosevelt,* 2:555.
102. ER, "Keepers of Democracy," 15, *Virginia Quarterly Review* (Jan. 1939): 1–5, ERPP.
103. Cook, *Eleanor Roosevelt,* 2:516.
104. Smith, *HTF,* 228.
105. Logevall, *JFK,* 254–55.
106. Dallek, *Unfinished Life,* 62–66.
107. "Roosevelts and the Kennedys," November 22, 2013, FDRL.
108. Cook, *Eleanor Roosevelt,* 2:529.
109. Cook, *Eleanor Roosevelt,* 2:544.
110. "Kristallnacht," United States Holocaust Memorial Museum, https://www.ushmm.org/.
111. "James Roosevelt (1907–1991)," ERPP; Cook, *Eleanor Roosevelt,* 2:538–39.
112. Smith, *HTF,* 229; Perry, *Rose Kennedy,* 134–35, 142.
113. Perry, *Rose Kennedy,* 145.
114. JPK to FDR, September 30, 1939, in Smith, *HTF,* 385–86.
115. Smith, *HTF,* 229.
116. JPK to Rose Kennedy, August 2, 1940, in Smith, *HTF,* 455.
117. Blanche Weisen Cook, *Eleanor Roosevelt, Vol. 3, 1939–1962: The War Years and After* (New York: Penguin, 2016), 347; Michael Barone, "FDR Among the Catholics," *Crisis* magazine, January 1, 1999.
118. Rose Kennedy to JPK, [October 7, 1940], in Smith, *HTF,* 474–75.
119. FDR to JPK, October 17, 1940, in Smith, *HTF,* 475.
120. FDR to JPK, October 17, 1940, 475; FDR to JPK, October 25, 1940, 479, both in Smith, *HFT.*
121. Perry, *Rose Kennedy,* 156–57; JPK, Diary, in Smith, *HTF,* 480–81.
122. Cook, *Eleanor Roosevelt,* 3:348, 625 note.
123. Hank Searls, *The Lost Prince: Young Joe, the Forgotten Kennedy* (New York: World Publishing, 1969), 164–65.

124. Perry, *Rose Kennedy,* 158–59.
125. Perry, *Rose Kennedy,* 157–58.
126. JPK Jr. to JPK, [November 2?, 1940], in Smith, *HTF,* 490.
127. JPK to FDR, resignation draft, in Smith, *HTF,* 492.
128. JPK, press release, December 1, 1940, in Smith, *HTF,* 497.
129. "The Kennedys: Is Democracy Finished?," *American Experience,* PBS.
130. "Kennedys: Is Democracy Finished?," *American Experience,* PBS.
131. Cook, *Eleanor Roosevelt,* 3:359.
132. Nasaw, *Patriarch,* 511–21; JPK, Diary notes, January 21, 1941, in Smith, *HTF,* 524–29.
133. JPK, Diary notes, January 21, 1941, in Smith, *HTF,* 525.
134. Nasaw, *Patriarch,* 514–15; JPK, "My Views on Foreign Policy: We Ought to Stay Out of the War," January 18, 1941, TeachingAmericanHistory.org, Ashbrook Center, Ashland University.
135. Nasaw, *Patriarch,* 518–19.
136. JPK to John Boettiger, February 10, 1941, in Smith, *HTF,* 529.
137. Cook, *Eleanor Roosevelt,* 3:376–77, 390.
138. ER, interview with Arnold Michaelis, December 1956, C-SPAN Radio.
139. Lash, *Eleanor and Franklin,* 263; David Michaelis, *Eleanor,* 122.
140. Perry, *Rose Kennedy,* 167.
141. JPK to FDR, March 4, 1942, 541–42; JPK to FDR, March 12, 1942, 543–44; JPK, Diary, April 10, 1942, 544–46, all in Smith, *HTF;* Perry, *Rose Kennedy,* 167.
142. JPK, Diary, in Smith, *HTF,* 557.
143. Perry, *Rose Kennedy,* 175–78.
144. Perry, *Rose Kennedy,* 172–75, 180–81. See also William Doyle, *PT 109: An American Epic of War, Survival, and the Destiny of John F. Kennedy* (New York: William Morrow, 2015); and Edward J. Renehan Jr., *The Kennedys at War, 1937–1945* (New York: Doubleday, 2002).
145. FDR to JPK, August 17, 1944, in "The Roosevelts and the Kennedys," November 22, 2013, FDRL.
146. FDR to JPK, in Smith, *HTF,* 600.
147. JPK to Arthur Houghton, May 26, 1945, in Smith, *HTF,* 600.
148. JPK to Cissy Patterson, November 26, 1945, in Smith, *HTF,* 622.
149. JPK, Diary notes on the 1944 political campaign, in Smith, *HTF,* 605–12.
150. ER, *This I Remember,* 342–43.
151. JPK, Diary notes on the 1944 political campaign, in Smith, *HTF,* 609.
152. JPK, Diary notes on the 1944 political campaign, in Smith, *HTF,* 611–12.
153. Merle Miller, *Plain Speaking: An Oral Biography of Harry S. Truman* (New York: Berkeley Medallion Books, 1974). Historian Robert H. Ferrell is quoted in a 1995 article by Francis H. Heller that Miller fabricated

numerous quotes that he attributed to Truman: "Plain Faking," *American Heritage* 3 (1995): 46. Nasaw, *Patriarch,* 576.

154. JPK to Kathleen Kennedy Hartington, May 1, 1945, in Smith, *HTF,* 615–16.
155. "1944: FDR's Fourth Presidential Campaign," Roosevelt House, CUNY; "Gallup Poll—Approval Rating—Franklin D. Roosevelt," WikiMedia Commons, accessed June 30, 2020.
156. JPK to Kathleen Kennedy Hartington, in Smith, *HTF,* 617.

2. DIVERGENT PATHS TO POWER

1. Joseph P. Lash, *Eleanor: The Years Alone* (New York: Norton, 1972), 133.
2. Thomas S. Langston, *With Reverence and Contempt: How Americans Think About Their Presidents* (Baltimore: Johns Hopkins University Press, 1995), 115.
3. Russell L. Riley, "American Regicide: Post-War Presidents and the Bitter Politics of Returning to Normalcy," in *The Presidency: Facing Constitutional Crossroads,* eds. Michael Nelson and Barbara A. Perry (Charlottesville: University of Virginia Press, 2021).
4. David McCullough, *Truman* (New York: Simon and Schuster, 1992), 353.
5. Doris Kearns Goodwin, *No Ordinary Time: Franklin and Eleanor Roosevelt: The Homefront in World War II* (New York: Simon and Schuster, 1994), 604.
6. McCullough, *Truman,* 292–320.
7. Blanche Wiesen Cook, *Eleanor Roosevelt, Vol. 3, 1939–1962: The War Years and After* (New York: Penguin, 2016) 542–43; ER, *AER,* 286.
8. Mike Wallace interview with ER, 1957, C-SPAN 3, available at YouTube.
9. Lash, *Eleanor,* 134.
10. David B. Roosevelt, with Manuela Dunn-Mascetti, *Grandmère: A Personal History* (New York: Warner Books, 2002), 199.
11. Cook, *Eleanor Roosevelt,* 3:548.
12. Harry Truman to ER, December 21, 1945, ERPP.
13. Roosevelt and Dunn-Mascetti, *Grandmère,* 200.
14. Cook, *ER,* 3:548.
15. Letter from Harry S. Truman to ER Regarding the US Relationship with the Russians, March 16, 1948, Teaching American History.org.
16. Frank Newport, David W. Moore, and Lydia Saad, "Most Admired Men and Women: 1948–1998," December 13, 1999, Gallup Poll.
17. ER, "Why I Do Not Choose to Run," *Look,* July 9, 1946, quoted in Allida Black, *Courage in a Dangerous World: The Political Writings of Eleanor Roosevelt* (New York: Columbia University Press, 1999), 236–39.

18. Maureen Dowd, "Citizen Journalist," in *A Vision for America: JFK in Words and Pictures,* eds. Stephen Kennedy Smith and Douglas Brinkley (New York: Harper, 2017), 45–47.
19. Barbara A. Perry, "The Kennedy Dynasty," in *Modern American Political Dynasties,* eds. Kathleen A. Gronnerud and Scott J. Spitzer (Santa Barbara, CA: Praeger, 2019), 87.
20. "James Roosevelt (1907–1991)," ERPP.
21. "Elliott Roosevelt (1910–1990)," ERPP.
22. Lash, *Eleanor,* 134–36, 139, 140–41, 142–45; "Democrats Urged to Run Eisenhower; Americans for Democratic Action of State Call for Douglas as Running Mate," *New York Times,* April 4, 1948.
23. Lash, *Eleanor,* 137.
24. "Executive Order 9808, Establishing the President's Committee on Civil Rights, Harry S. Truman," Federal Register, https://www.archives.gov/federal-register/executive-orders/1946; *To Secure These Rights: The Report of the President's Committee on Civil Rights,* 1947, Harry S. Truman Library and Museum; "Special Message to the Congress on Civil Rights," Public Papers of the Presidents, Harry S. Truman, 1945–53, February 2, 1948, Harry S. Truman Library and Museum.
25. "John F. Kennedy's Pre-Presidential Voting Record and Stands on Issues," JFKL, 5; Barbara A. Perry, *Edward M. Kennedy: An Oral History* (New York: Oxford University Press, 2018), 85–90.
26. "1948 DNC: Truman's Democrats Tackle Civil Rights," *Life*/NBC, YouTube.
27. "1948 Democratic Platform," American Presidency Project, UC Santa Barbara, https://www.presidency.ucsb.edu/.
28. Oral history with James P. Coleman, September 5, 1990, interview A-0338, Southern OH Program Collection (#4007), Southern Historical Collection, Wilson Library, University of North Carolina at Chapel Hill.
29. Steve Inskeep and Ron Elving, "In 1948, Democrats Weathered Civil Rights Divide," NPR, August 27, 2008.
30. "Executive Order 9980, Regulations Governing Fair Employment Practices Within the Federal Establishment, Harry S. Truman" and "Executive Order 9981, Establishing the President's Committee on Equality of Treatment and Opportunity in the Armed Services, Harry S. Truman," Federal Register, https://www.archives.gov/federal-register/executive-orders/1948.html.
31. ER, "Liberals in This Year of Decision," *Christian Register,* June 1948, quoted in Black, *Courage in a Dangerous World,* 147–48.
32. ER to Harry Truman, October 4, 1948, ERPP.

33. "1948 Democratic Platform," American Presidency Project, UC Santa Barbara, https://www.presidency.ucsb.edu/.
34. See chapter 8 for an explanation of ER's views on women's rights and how they evolved over her life.
35. "Chronology of the Equal Rights Amendment, 1923–1996," NOW.org.
36. ER to Harry Truman, October 4, 1948, ERPP.
37. Lash, *Eleanor,* 147–48.
38. Stacy A. Cordery, *Alice: Alice Roosevelt Longworth, from White House Princess to Washington Power Broker* (New York: Viking, 2007), viii.
39. Lash, *Eleanor,* 147.
40. Jeffrey M. Jones, "Presidential Job Approval Related to Reelection Historically," May 29, 2020, Gallup Poll; Simon Topping, "Never Argue with the Gallup Poll: Thomas Dewey, Civil Rights, and the Election of 1948," *Journal of American Studies* 38 (2004): 179–98; "Truman Beats Dewey," Decades TV Network, YouTube.
41. "The End of the Roosevelt Era: 1948," Roosevelt House, Hunter College, CUNY.
42. James MacGregor Burns, *Roosevelt: The Lion and the Fox* (New York: Harcourt, Brace, 1956), 156–57.
43. William A. Degregorio, *The Complete Book of U.S. Presidents* (New York: Barricade Books, 1993), 731.
44. "Statistics of the Presidential and Congressional Election of November 2, 1948," GPO, March 1, 1949.
45. "Adlai Stevenson (1900–1965)," ERPP.
46. Lash, *Eleanor,* 149.
47. "Adlai Stevenson (1900–1965)," ERPP.
48. Barbara A. Perry, *Jacqueline Kennedy: First Lady of the New Frontier* (Lawrence, KS: University Press of Kansas, 2004), 188–89.
49. Rob Goodman, "What Happened to the Roosevelts?" *Politico,* October 7, 2014.
50. Lash, *Eleanor,* 173–78.
51. Barbara A. Perry, *Rose Kennedy: The Life and Times of a Political Matriarch* (New York: Norton, 2013); Wallace interview with Eleanor Roosevelt, 1957, C-SPAN 3, YouTube; "James Roosevelt Documentary Intro," YouTube.
52. Lash, *Eleanor,* 178–79; Curtis Roosevelt, *Too Close to the Sun: Growing Up in the Shadow of My Grandparents, Franklin and Eleanor* (New York: Public Affairs, 2008), 52–53.
53. 330 U.S. 1 (1947), Cornell University Law School, Legal Information Institute; Lash, *Eleanor,* 175–76; "Fast Facts: JFK: Voting Record and Stands on Issues," JFKL.
54. Perry, "The Kennedy Dynasty," 85.

55. Perry, "The Kennedy Dynasty," 85.
56. ER to Albert Harris, September 8, 1947, quoted in Black, *Courage in a Dangerous World*, 242–43.
57. Perry, "The Kennedy Dynasties," 85.
58. "FDR and the Wagner Act," FDRL; Blanche Wiesen Cook, *Eleanor Roosevelt, Vol. 2, 1933–1938: The Defining Years* (New York: Penguin, 1999), 266; ER, MD, June 14, 1947, ERPDE.
59. Esther E. Peterson, interview by Ann M. Campbell, January 20, 1970, pp. 24–25, JFKL OH.
60. ER, *AER*, 305.
61. ER, *AER*, 308.
62. ER, *AER*, chapter 32.
63. "Universal Declaration of Human Rights," December 10, 1948, UN.org, About Us.
64. Harris Wofford and Tad Daley, "JFK, *One World or None* and 'A New Effort to Achieve World Law,'" Federation of American Scientists, August 21, 2014.
65. Cook, *Eleanor Roosevelt*, 3:560–61.
66. "Executive Order 9835: Prescribing Procedures for the Administration of an Employees Loyalty Program in the Executive Branch of the Government," March 22, 1947, Harry S. Truman Presidential Library and Museum.
67. ER, MD, March 27, 1947, ERPDE.
68. "Truman's Loyalty Program," Harry S. Truman Library and Museum, citing Richard Kirkendall, ed., *Civil Liberties and the Legacy of Harry S. Truman* (Kirksville, MO: Truman State University Press, 2013), 70.
69. David McMillen, "JFK in Congress: Kennedy Develops Expertise on National Issues as He Prepares to Seek Presidency," *Prologue* 49, no. 1 (2017), Archives.gov.
70. "Presidential Approval Ratings—Gallup Historical Statistics Trends," Gallup Poll.
71. McCullough, *Truman*, 887–94.
72. Mark J. White, "Adlai Stevenson: Hamlet in New York," in White, *The Cuban Missile Crisis* (London: Palgrave Macmillan, 1996), https://doi.org/10.1057/9780230374508_7.
73. McCullough, *Truman*, 903.
74. Carl McGowan interview, Truman Presidential Library and Museum.
75. McCullough, *Truman*, 904.
76. ER, *AER*, 353.
77. "Speech to the Democratic National Convention Urging Support for the United Nations," July 22, 1952, Democratic National Convention, Chicago, ERPP.
78. ER, *AER*, 353.

79. Perry, "The Kennedy Dynasty," 88.
80. Perry, "The Kennedy Dynasty," 88–89.
81. Perry, "The Kennedy Dynasties," 89.
82. Perry, *Rose Kennedy*, 203.
83. Perry, *Jacqueline Kennedy*, 33, 37.
84. Perry, "The Kennedy Dynasties," 89; see a video of JFK and Stevenson campaigning together in Massachusetts for the 1952 election, "September 19, 1952—Congressman John F. Kennedy campaigning with Adlai Stevenson in Massachusetts," YouTube.
85. ER, MD, September 27, 1952, ERPDE.
86. ER, MD, September 27, 1952, ERPDE.
87. Dallek, *Unfinished Life*, 175.
88. Michael O'Brien, *John F. Kennedy: A Biography* (New York: Thomas Dunne Brooks, 2005), 250.
89. ER, *AER*, 353–54.
90. ER, MD, April 9, 1953, quoted in Black, *Courage in a Dangerous World*, 189–90.
91. ER, MD, May 20, 1954, ERPDE.
92. 347 U.S. 483 (1954), Cornell University Law School, Legal Information Institute.
93. ER, MD, May 20, 1954, ERPDE.
94. "Eleanor's Commitment to African Americans," interview with Vernan Jarrett, PBS.org.
95. *Brown v. Board of Education of Topeka II*, 394 U.S. 295 (1955), U.S. Supreme Court Resources, Justia Supreme Court Center.
96. Stephen Heard, "Adlai and Eleanor: Progressives Who Shaped the World," April 14, 2017, FDR Foundation.
97. ER, *AER*, 354.
98. Degregorio, *Complete Book of U.S. Presidents*, 732.
99. "James Roosevelt (1907–1991)," ERPP.
100. "Longines Chronoscope with James Roosevelt," CBS [1955?], available at YouTube.
101. ER, *AER*, 354.

3. THE GRAND DAME AND "MY DEAR BOY"

1. David G. McCullough, *Truman* (New York: Simon and Schuster, 1992), 889; ER, *AER*, 355.
2. McCullough, *Truman*, 959.
3. "1956 Democratic Platform," American Presidency Project, UC Santa Barbara, https://www.presidency.ucsb.edu/.

4. ER, *AER*, 355–56.
5. ER, MD, August 16, 1956, ERPDE.
6. Barbara A. Perry, *Jacqueline Kennedy: First Lady of the New Frontier* (Lawrence, KS: University Press of Kansas, 2004), 46–47.
7. Joseph P. Lash, *Eleanor: The Years Alone* (New York: Norton, 1962), 285. Allida Black notes that Mrs. Roosevelt only supported JFK after he won the Massachusetts Democratic primary to oppose Lodge: see Black *Casting Her Own Shadow: Eleanor Roosevelt and the Shaping of Postwar Liberalism* (New York: Columbia University Press, 1996), 175.
8. Tom Arnold-Forster, "JFK: A Moving Target," *Prospect,* November 12, 2013.
9. Larry Tye, *Bobby Kennedy: The Making of a Liberal Icon* (New York: Random House, 2016), 24–28; Black, *Casting Her Own Shadow,* 172–73.
10. Thomas Maier, *The Kennedys: America's Emerald Kings* (New York: Basic Books, 2003), 276.
11. James MacGregor Burns, *John Kennedy: A Political Profile* (New York: Harcourt, Brace, 1961), 154.
12. Burns, *John Kennedy,* 143–50.
13. Robert Dallek, *An Unfinished Life: John F. Kennedy, 1917–1963* (Boston: Little, Brown, 2003), 189–92.
14. Burns, *John Kennedy,* 150.
15. Black, *Casting Her Own Shadow,* 172.
16. Black, *Casting Her Own Shadow,* 176; Thomas Oliphant and Curtis Wilkie, *The Road to Camelot: Inside JFK's Five-Year Campaign* (New York: Simon and Schuster, 2017), 41.
17. ER, *AER,* 356.
18. ER, *AER,* 356.
19. Oliphant and Wilkie, *Road to Camelot,* 41.
20. Oliphant and Wilkie, *Road to Camelot,* 41.
21. Arthur M. Schlesinger Jr., *Journals: 1952–2000* (New York: Penguin, 2007), 179.
22. Michael R. Beschloss, *Kennedy and Roosevelt: The Uneasy Alliance* (New York: Harper & Row, 1980), 263.
23. Arthur M. Schlesinger Jr., *A Thousand Days: John F. Kennedy in the White House* (Greenwich, CT: Fawcett, 1967), 23.
24. David Nasaw, *The Patriarch: The Remarkable Life and Turbulent Times of Joseph P. Kennedy* (New York: Penguin Press, 2012), 207–8.
25. ER, *AER,* 357.
26. ER, "Stevenson Campaign Address," Charleston, West Virginia, October 1956, quoted in Black, *Courage in a Dangerous World,* 273–77.
27. "A Conversation with George Takei: Meeting Eleanor Roosevelt," FDRL.

28. Arthur M. Schlesinger Jr., *Robert Kennedy and His Times* (New York: Ballentine Books, 1978), 143–47; Chris Matthews, *Bobby Kennedy: A Raging Spirit* (New York: Simon & Schuster, 2017), 141–43; Oliphant and Wilkie, *Road to Camelot*, 57–59.
29. Schlesinger, *Robert Kennedy and His Times*, 145.
30. Schlesinger, *Robert Kennedy and His Times*, 146.
31. Matthews, *Bobby Kennedy*, 143.
32. Mike Wallace interview with ER, 1957, C-SPAN 3, YouTube.
33. JFK, "Where Democrats Should Go From Here," *Life*, March 11, 1957, 166.
34. ER, *On My Own* (New York: Harper and Brothers, 1958), in *AER*, 356.
35. "Excerpts from CBS-TV Broadcast of 'Face the Nation,'" March 30, 1958; *Eleanor Roosevelt, John Kennedy, and the Election of 1960: A Project of The Eleanor Roosevelt Papers*, eds. Allida Black et al. (Columbia, SC: Model Editions Partnership, 2003), ERPP.
36. Alan Brinkley, *John F. Kennedy* (New York: Times Books, 2012), 29–30; John T. Shaw, *JFK in the Senate: Pathway to the Presidency* (New York: Palgrave Macmillan, 2013), 64; Schlesinger, *A Thousand Days*, 23.
37. *Palko v. Connecticut*, 302 U.S. 319 (1937), Cornell Law School, Legal Information Institute.
38. ER, MD, May 22, 1952, ERPDE.
39. Blanche Wiesen Cook, *Eleanor Roosevelt, Vol. I, 1884–1933* (New York: Penguin, 1992), 239.
40. Cook, *Eleanor Roosevelt*, 1:244.
41. Barbara A. Perry, *Rose Kennedy: The Life and Times of a Political Matriarch* (New York: Norton, 2013), 53–54.
42. Joseph P. Lash, *Eleanor and Franklin: The Story of Their Relationship, Based on Eleanor Roosevelt's Private Papers* (New York: New American Library, 1972), 755.
43. ER, *This I Remember* (New York: Harper & Row, 1949), 199–205.
44. Blanche Wiesen Cook, *Eleanor Roosevelt, Vol. 3, 1939–1962: The War Years and After* (New York: Penguin, 2016), 172–75.
45. ER, FBI Records: The Vault, FBI, https://vault.fbi.gov/Eleanor%20Roosevelt.
46. Burns, *John Kennedy*, 154.
47. Burns, *John Kennedy*, 154.
48. Tye, *Bobby Kennedy*, 48.
49. Cass Canfield to ER, in Black, *Eleanor Roosevelt, John Kennedy, and the Election of 1960*, ERPP.
50. ER to Cass Canfield, May 3, 1958, in Black, *Eleanor Roosevelt, John Kennedy, and the Election of 1960*.

51. JFK to ER, May 29, 1958; ER to JFK, June 2, 1958, JFKPOF-032-JFKPOF-032-006, ER, June 1958–November 1960, JFKL.
52. Black, *Casting Her Own Shadow,* 181.
53. Lash, *Eleanor,* 285.
54. Lash, *Eleanor,* 286.
55. Fredrik Logevall, *JFK: Coming of Age in the American Century, 1917–1956* (New York: Random House, 2020), 617.
56. JFK to ER, December 11, 1958, JFKPOF-032-JFKPOF-032-006, ER, June 1958–November 1960, JFKL.
57. ER to JFK, December 18, 1958, JFKPOF-032-JFKPOF-032-006, ER, June 1958–November 1960, JFKL.
58. JFK to ER, December 29, 1958, JFKPOF-032-JFKPOF-032-006, ER, June 1958–November 1960, JFKL, original emphasis.
59. Merle Miller, *Plain Speaking: An Oral Biography of Harry S. Truman* (New York: Berkeley Publishing, 1974), 199.
60. "A Conversation with Eleanor Roosevelt," with Robert Atwood, NBC, 1958, FDRL, YouTube.
61. "A Conversation with ER," FDRL, YouTube.
62. "Excerpt from Column Dated January 6, 1959"; ER to JFK, January 6, 1959, JFKPOF-032-JFKPOF-032-006, ER, June 1958–November 1960, JFKL.
63. JFK to ER, January 10, 1959, JFKPOF-032-JFKPOF-032-006, ER, June 1958–November 1960, JFKL.
64. ER to JFK, January 20, 1959, JFKPOF-032-JFKPOF-032-006, ER, June 1958–November 1960, JFKL.
65. JFK to ER, January 22, 1959, JFKPOF-032-JFKPOF-032-006, ER, June 1958–November 1960, JFKL.
66. Cook, *Eleanor Roosevelt,* 3:364–65.
67. ER, January 29, 1959, JFKPOF-032-JFKPOF-032-006, ER, June 1958–November 1960, JFKL.
68. Ted Sorensen, *Counselor: A Life at the Edge of History* (New York: Harper, 2008), 108.
69. "A Majority of Minorities: Eleanor Roosevelt Supports John F. Kennedy in the 1960 Presidential Election," FDRL.

4. CLASHING OVER RACE

1. Mark White, *Icon, Libertine, Leader: The Life and Presidency of John F. Kennedy* (London: Bloomsbury Academic 2024), 136.

2. "After Abolition: Where's Black Boston?" Boston Black History, http://academics.wellesley.edu/AmerStudies/BostonBlackHistory/history/where.html.
3. Geoffrey Perret, *Jack: A Life Like No Other* (New York: Random House, 2001), 67. Perret mistakenly lists the valet as George Thomas, who didn't join Jack's household until 1946. His "gentleman's gentleman" at Harvard and after the war was George Taylor.
4. George H. Taylor, interview by Sheldon Stern, August 12, 1977, JFKL OH.
5. Christopher Anderson, *These Few Precious Days: The Final Year of Jack and Jackie* (New York: Gallery Books, 2013), 19.
6. Jim Bishop, *A Day in the Life of President Kennedy* (New York: Random House, 1964), 8, 12.
7. Robert Dallek, *An Unfinished Life: John F. Kennedy, 1919–1963* (Boston: Little, Brown, 2003), 76–77. Barbara A. Perry and Alfred Reaves IV, "JFK's White House Valet," *White House Historical Journal* 63 (2021): 88–95.
8. Ted Sorensen, *Kennedy* (New York: Harper and Row, 1965), 49.
9. Nick Bryant, *The Bystander: John F. Kennedy and the Struggle for Black Equality* (New York: Basic Books, 2006), 66.
10. James Giglio, *The Presidency of John F. Kennedy*, 2nd ed. (Lawrence: University Press of Kansas, 2006), 14.
11. Sorensen, *Kennedy*, 49; Burns, *John Kennedy*, xi, 200.
12. *Brown v. Board of Education I*, 347 U.S. 483 (1954), Cornell Law School, Legal Information Institution; *Brown v. Board of Education II*, 349 U.S. 294 (1955), Cornell Law School, Legal Information Institution.
13. Dallek, *Unfinished Life*, 215.
14. Allida Black, *Casting Her Own Shadow: Eleanor Roosevelt and the Shaping of Postwar Liberalism* (New York: Columbia University Press, 1996), 177.
15. Burns, *John Kennedy*, 201–2.
16. Sorensen, *Kennedy*, 51.
17. Dallek, *Unfinished Life*, 216.
18. Burns, *John Kennedy*, 203; Giglio, *Presidency of John F. Kennedy*, 14.
19. Donald A. Ritchie, "Kennedy in Congress," in *A Companion to John F. Kennedy*, ed. Marc J. Selverstone (Chichester, UK: Wiley Blackwell, 2014), 41; Barbara A. Perry, "John F. Kennedy," in *The Presidents and the Constitution: A Living History*, ed. Ken Gormley (New York: NYU Press, 2016), chapter 35.
20. Burns, *John Kennedy*, 203–4.
21. "Civil Rights: The Little Rock School Integration Crisis," Dwight D. Eisenhower Library, Museum, and Boyhood Home; Dallek, *Unfinished Life*, 217–18.

22. Burns, *John Kennedy,* 204.
23. ER, interview with Arnold Michaelis, December 1956, C-SPAN Radio.
24. Joseph P. Lash, *Eleanor and Franklin: The Story of Their Relationship, Based on Eleanor Roosevelt's Private Papers* (New York: New American Library, 1972), 4.
25. Black, *Casting Her Own Shadow,* 203.
26. David B. Roosevelt, with Manuela Dunn-Mascetti, *Grandmère: A Personal History* (New York: Warner Books, 2002), 191.
27. Lash, *Eleanor and Franklin,* 660.
28. "Demographic History of New York City," Wikipedia, last updated October 26, 2025.
29. Lash, *Eleanor and Franklin,* 225.
30. Blanche Wiesen Cook, *Eleanor Roosevelt, Vol. 3, 1939–1962: The War Years and After* (New York: Penguin, 2016), 177.
31. David Michaelis, *Eleanor* (New York: Simon & Schuster, 2020), 340.
32. Lash, *Eleanor and Franklin,* 61.
33. D. Michaelis, *Eleanor,* 119–21; ER, *AER,* 68.
34. "Demographics of Washington, D.C.," Wikipedia, last updated October 24, 2025.
35. Cook, *Eleanor Roosevelt,* 3:203.
36. ER, *AER,* 72.
37. ER, *AER,* 75–76, 86–87.
38. D. Michaelis, *Eleanor,* 150–54; Lash, *Eleanor and Franklin,* 267–69.
39. D. Michaelis, *Eleanor,* 184–86; Lash, *Eleanor and Franklin,* 294.
40. James Tobin, *The Man He Became: How FDR Defied Polio to Win the Presidency* (New York: Simon & Schuster, 2013).
41. Lash, *Eleanor and Franklin,* 367–68.
42. Blanche Wiesen Cook, *Eleanor Roosevelt, Vol. 2, 1933–1938: The Defining Years* (New York: Penguin, 1999), 155.
43. Lash, *Eleanor and Franklin,* 380–81.
44. Lash, *Eleanor and Franklin,* 406.
45. Lash, *Eleanor and Franklin.*
46. Lash, *Eleanor and Franklin,* 429.
47. Cook, *Eleanor Roosevelt,* 2:156–57.
48. Lash, *Eleanor and Franklin,* 459–60.
49. Elaine Smith, introduction to the *Mary McLeod Bethune Papers: The Bethune Cookman College Collection, 1922–1955,* Black Studies Research Sources microfilm project (Bethesda, MD: University Publications of America, 1995).

50. Maurine H. Beasley, *Eleanor Roosevelt: Transformative First Lady* (Lawrence, KS: University Press of Kansas, 2010), 154–55; Cook, *Eleanor Roosevelt,* 3:357–58.
51. Lash, *Eleanor and Franklin,* 647–57; Jill Abraham Hemmer, *First Ladies and the American Woman: In Politics and at Home* (Lawrence, KS: University Press of Kansas, 2017), 61–64. Lynching statistics are compiled from Tuskegee Institute's archives, found at the University of Missouri, Kansas City.
52. "A Conversation with ER," with Robert Atwood, NBC, 1958, FDRL, YouTube.
53. Lash, *Eleanor and Franklin,* 650.
54. Lash, *Eleanor and Franklin,* 662–63.
55. Patricia Bell-Scott, *The Firebrand and the First Lady: Portrait of Friendship: Pauli Murray, Eleanor Roosevelt, and the Struggle for Social Justice* (New York: Knopf, 2016), 29.
56. The most recent and accurate portrayal of this historic episode can be found in the two-part PBS *American Experience* documentary *Voice of Freedom,* February 2021, PBS.org. See also Allida Black, "Championing a Champion: Eleanor Roosevelt and the Marian Anderson 'Freedom Concert,'" *Presidential Studies Quarterly* 20, no. 4 (1990): 719–36.
57. "Eleanor Roosevelt and Marian Anderson," FDRL; "I regret exceedingly that Washington is to be deprived of hearing Marian Anderson, a great artist," *American Originals,* Archives.gov; Black, "Championing a Champion," 722.
58. Black, "Championing a Champion," 724.
59. "Eleanor Roosevelt and Marian Anderson," *American Originals,* Archives .gov.
60. ER, "I Have, as a Rule, Accepted My Defeat," MD, *Washington Daily News,* February 27, 1939.
61. Lash, *Eleanor and Franklin,* 66.
62. Black, "Championing the Champion," 724.
63. "Marian Anderson Performs on the Steps of the Lincoln Memorial, with an Introduction by Harold Ickes, 04/09/1939"; "Marian Anderson Sings at Lincoln Memorial," Robert H. Jackson Center, YouTube.
64. "ER and Marian Anderson," FDRL; "Echoes from Marian Anderson's Defiant Performance," *PBS NewsHour,* April 9, 2014, YouTube.
65. "ER and Marian Anderson," FDRL.
66. "Marian Anderson's Defiant Performance," *PBS NewsHour,* April 9, 2014, YouTube.
67. "Marian Anderson: Musical Icon," *American Experience,* PBS.org.

68. Vincent Dowd, "The Opera Singer Who Changed the Civil Rights Movement," BBC, April 9, 2014.
69. Cook, *Eleanor Roosevelt,* 3:358.
70. See Isabel Wilkerson's brilliant description of this history in her book *Caste: The Origins of Our Discontent* (New York: Random House, 2020) and her interview "It's More Than Racism: Isabel Wilkerson Explains America's 'Caste' System," *Fresh Air,* NPR, August 4, 2020.
71. "Research Starters: The Draft and World War II," National WWII Museum, New Orleans (emphasis added); "African Americans in World War II," National WWII Museum.
72. Lash, *Eleanor and Franklin,* 670.
73. Cook, *Eleanor Roosevelt,* 3:11.
74. Lash, *Eleanor and Franklin,* 672.
75. James MacGregor Burns, *Roosevelt: The Lion and the Fox* (New York: Harcourt, Brace, 1956), 338–39.
76. Harvard Sitkoff, *Toward Freedom Land: The Long Struggle for Racial Equality in America* (Lexington: University Press of Kentucky, 2010).
77. Brooks Jackson, "Blacks and the Democratic Party," April 18, 2008, FactCheck.org, Annenberg Public Policy Center.
78. Lash, *Eleanor and Franklin,* 669.
79. Lash, *Eleanor and Franklin,* 674.
80. Lash, *Eleanor and Franklin,* 676–77.
81. "African Americans in World War II," National WWII Museum, https://www.nationalww2museum.org/.
82. "Mark F. Ethridge, Journalist, Dies at 84," *New York Times,* April 7, 1981.
83. "Eleanor Roosevelt and the Tuskegee Airmen," FDRL.
84. "The Double V Victory: African Americans on the Home Front During World War II," National WWII Museum, https://www.nationalww2museum.org/.
85. Lash, *Eleanor and Franklin,* 850, 853.
86. Cook, *Eleanor Roosevelt,* 3:431.
87. Curtis Roosevelt, *Too Close to the Sun: Growing Up in the Shadow of My Grandparents, Franklin and Eleanor* (New York: Public Affairs, 2008).
88. ER, interview with Arnold Michaelis, December 1956, C-SPAN Radio.
89. Bell-Scott, *Firebrand and First Lady,* 93.
90. Beasley, *Eleanor Roosevelt,* 193; Cook, *Eleanor Roosevelt,* 3:433–34.
91. Beasley, *Eleanor Roosevelt,* 196–97.
92. Cook, *Eleanor Roosevelt,* 3:435–36.
93. Lash, *Eleanor and Franklin,* 855–58.
94. Lash, *Eleanor and Franklin,* 858.

95. Randall L. Patton, "Southern Regional Council," *New Georgia Encyclopedia* online.
96. Beasley, *Eleanor Roosevelt,* 207.
97. Lash, *Eleanor and Franklin,* 868–81; Beasley, *Eleanor Roosevelt,* 198–99.
98. Lash, *Eleanor and Franklin,* 881.
99. Jill Cowen, "How a Bay Area Explosion Pushed the Military to Desegregate," *New York Times,* July 17, 2019. Most recently, the United States finally offered justice to Black servicemen accused in this disaster: see "Navy Exonerates 256 Black Sailors Punished after 1944 Port Chicago Explosion," July 18, 2024, National WWII Museum, https://www.nationalww2museum.org/.
100. Roosevelt and Dunn-Mascetti, *Grandmère,* 198.
101. Casey Gauntt, "Remembering Port Chicago," Write Me Something Beautiful, https://www.writemesomethingbeautiful.com/2019/07/04/remembering-port-chicago/.
102. Cook, *Eleanor Roosevelt,* 3:12–13.
103. Beasley, *Eleanor Roosevelt,* 218.
104. Roosevelt and Dunn-Mascetti, *Grandmère,* 195.
105. "Conversation with Pierre Salinger," Secret White House Tapes, Lyndon B. Johnson Presidency, UVA Miller Center; Beasley, *Eleanor Roosevelt,* 218–19.
106. Cook, *Eleanor Roosevelt,* 3:13.
107. Bill Carey, "The Highlander Folk School," *Tennessee Magazine,* February 2013; Beasley, *Eleanor Roosevelt,* 218; "The Civil Rights Movement: 1954," Civil Rights Movement Archive, https://www.crmvet.org/; Patrick Kiger, "Did Eleanor Roosevelt Really Pack a Pistol at 72?," AARP blog, May 20, 2013; ER, *This I Remember* (New York: Harper & Row, 1949), 120–21.
108. ER, *This I Remember.*
109. ER, *AER;* King photo opposite p. 269.
110. ER, *Tomorrow Is Now* (New York: Harper and Row, 1963), 50–66.
111. Cook, *Eleanor Roosevelt,* 3:565–66; "Southern Conference Education Fund (SCEF)," SNCC Digital Gateway, https://snccdigital.org/.

5. RIVALS TO ALLIES

1. Allida Black, *Casting Her Own Shadow: Eleanor Roosevelt and the Shaping of Postwar Liberalism* (New York: Columbia University Press, 1996), 181.
2. Esther Peterson, interview with Campbell, January 20, 1970, 26, JFKL OH.
3. Katie Scofield Louchheim, interview with Larry J. Hackman, June 14, 1968, JFKL OH.

4. Joseph P. Lash, *Eleanor: The Years Alone* (New York: Norton, 1962), 287; Mary Ann Glendon, "God and Mrs. Roosevelt," *First Things*, May 2010, 7–8.
5. Chris Matthews, *Jack Kennedy: Elusive Hero* (New York: Simon and Schuster, 2011), 276.
6. Arthur M. Schlesinger Jr., *A Thousand Days: John F. Kennedy in the White House* (Greenwich, CT: Fawcett, 1967), 22.
7. Merle Miller, *Plain Speaking: An Oral Biography of Harry S. Truman* (New York: Berkeley Publishing, 1974), 199.
8. ER, *AER*, 346–47
9. Lash, *Eleanor*, chapter 7, "Cardinal and Former First Lady," 151–63.
10. Barbara A. Perry, *Rose Kennedy: The Life and Times of a Political Matriarch* (New York: Norton, 2013), 177.
11. Lash, *Eleanor*, 151.
12. "April 1939," Timeline: FDR Day by Day, FDRL. See also ER, MD, November 2, 1960, fn. 2, ERPDE.
13. Lash, *Eleanor*, 151–52.
14. ER, MD, June 23, 1949, ERPDE.
15. Lash, *Eleanor*, 153–54.
16. ER, MD, August 24, 1949, ERPDE.
17. "April 1939," Timeline: FDR Day by Day, FDRL.
18. ER to George Fischer, September 5, 1949, quoted in Lash, *Eleanor*, 162.
19. Jacqueline Kennedy Onassis, Arthur M. Schlessinger Jr., Michael Beschloss, *Jacqueline Kennedy: Historic Conversations on Life with John F. Kennedy, Interviews with Arthur M. Schlesinger, Jr., 1964*, foreword by Caroline Kennedy (New York: Hyperion, 2011), 104–5.
20. ER, MD, April 22, 1960, ERPDE.
21. Allida Black provides the most detailed account of Eleanor's approach to the 1960 presidential nomination, especially her relationship with Stevenson, in *Casting Her Own Shadow*, 182–87; ER, "The Democratic Convention of 1960," *AER*, chapter 42, n1; *Eleanor Roosevelt, John Kennedy, and the Election of 1960: A Project of the Eleanor Roosevelt Papers*, eds. Allida Black et al. (Columbia, SC: Model Editions Partnership, 2003), ERPP; Schlesinger, *Thousand Days*, 23.
22. ER, "Democratic Convention of 1960," *AER*.
23. ER, MD, May 13, 1960, ERPDE.
24. Black, *Casting Her Own Shadow*, 183–84; Edna Gurewitsch, *Kindred Souls: The Devoted Friendship of Eleanor Roosevelt and Dr. David Gurewitsch* (New York: Open Road Integrated Media, 2014), 228; Thomas B. Morgan, "Madly for Adlai," *American Heritage* 35, no. 5 (1984): 7.

25. ER, MD, June 11, 1960, ERPDE.
26. ER, "Democratic Convention of 1960," *AER*.
27. Thomas Oliphant and Curtis Wilkie, *The Road to Camelot: Inside JFK's Five-Year Campaign* (New York: Simon and Schuster, 2017), 204.
28. ER, "Democratic Convention of 1960," *AER*.
29. "1960 Democratic Convention," YouTube.
30. Oliphant and Wilkie, *Road to Camelot,* 246 (emphasis added).
31. Theodore H. White, *The Making of the President, 1960* (New York: Atheneum, 1961), 166.
32. Arthur M. Schlesinger Jr., *Journals: 1952–2000* (New York: Penguin, 2007), 72–73.
33. Oliphant and Wilkie, *Road to Camelot,* 247.
34. Gurewitsch, *Kindred Souls,* 229–30.
35. "Senator Gene McCarthy Nominating Adlai Stevenson II at the 1960 Democratic Convention," YouTube.
36. Oliphant and Wilkie, *Road to Camelot,* 248–49.
37. Gurewitsch, *Kindred Souls,* 229–30.
38. Lash, *Eleanor,* 302.
39. ER, "The Democratic Convention of 1960," *AER;* Barbara A. Perry, *Edward M. Kennedy: An Oral History* (New York: Oxford University Press, 2018), chapter 2.
40. ER, MD, July 16, 1960, ERPDE.
41. Lash, *Eleanor,* 503.
42. ER to Mary D. Lasker, August 15, 1960, n.5, ERPDE.
43. Robert Dallek, *An Unfinished Life: John F. Kennedy, 1919–1963* (Boston: Little, Brown, 2003), 259; Oliphant and Wilkie, *Road to Camelot,* 244.
44. ER to JFK August 16, 1960, Black, *Eleanor Roosevelt, John Kennedy, and the Election of 1960,* ERPP.
45. All of William Walton's references to JFK and ER come from his 1993 oral history, "Walton, William: OH—JFK #1, 3/3/1993," JFKOH-WW-01, JFKL OH.
46. John W. Barry, "Remembering John F. Kennedy's Visits to Dutchess County," *Democrat and Chronicle,* November 21, 2013.
47. Barry, "Remembering JFK's Visits."
48. Gurewitsch, *Kindred Souls,* 231.
49. Jennifer Lind, "When Camelot Went to Japan," *National Interest,* June 25, 2013; "Commander Hamani's Letter to JFK," *U.S. Embassy in Japan Official Magazine,* April 5, 2015.
50. Gurewitsch, *Kindred Souls,* 232–33.

51. Gurewitsch, *Kindred Souls,* 230.
52. "JFK: A Vision for America," JFKL Forum, May 15, 2017.
53. Edward Kennedy's Republican colleague and friend Sen. Alan Simpson of Wyoming made this observation in a panel celebrating the release of the Edward M. Kennedy Oral History Project, September 30, 2015, C-SPAN. See also Perry, *Edward M. Kennedy,* for numerous examples of Senator Ted Kennedy's fighting for principles but compromising with Republicans to achieve a partial policy goal.
54. "25th Anniversary of the Signing of the Social Security Act," Hyde Park, New York, 14 August 1960, JFKL, Papers of JFK, Pre-Presidential Papers, Senate Files, Series 12, Speeches and the Press, Box 910.
55. "25th Anniversary of the Signing of the SSA."
56. Gurewitsch, *Kindred Souls,* 234.
57. Perry, *Rose Kennedy,* 239.
58. Esther Peterson, interview with Campbell, January 20, 1970, p. 26, JFKL OH.
59. All references to the letter may be found in ER to Mary D. Lasker, August 15, 1960, ERPDE.
60. JFK, "Where Democrats Should Go from Here," *Life,* March 11, 1957, 164–79.
61. ER, MD, August 17, 1960, ERPDE.
62. Black, *Eleanor Roosevelt, John Kennedy, and the Election of 1960,* ERPP.
63. JFK to ER, August 26, 1960, Black, *Eleanor Roosevelt, John Kennedy, and the Election of 1960,* ERPP.
64. ER to Mary D. Lasker, August 15, 1960, n5, ERPDE. Kennedy biographer Robert Dallek reports that at their July 1960 meeting in Hyannis Port, Stevenson had suggested the foreign policy task force to prepare JFK for transitioning to the presidency. Kennedy agreed and asked Adlai to chair it: see Dallek, *Unfinished Life,* 278.
65. Gurewitsch, *Kindred Souls,* 254.
66. JFK to ER, n.d. [ca. summer, fall 1960], JFKL.
67. ER, MD, August 17, 1960, ERPDE.
68. ER, *AER,* chapter 43.

6. ELEANOR BACKS JACK

1. ER, MD, August 20, 1960, ERPDE.
2. Ted Sorensen, *Kennedy* (New York: Harper and Row, 1965), 188–95.
3. All quotes from JFK's church-state speech may be found at "Address to the Greater Houston Ministerial Association," September 12, 1960, IFP-140, JFKL.

4. Rick Warren, "Not the Catholic Candidate," in *A Vision for America: JFK in Words and Pictures,* eds. Stephen Kennedy Smith and Douglas Brinkley (New York: Harper, 2017), 138.
5. ER, Excerpt, MD, September 21, 1960, ERPP.
6. ER, MD, November 2, 1960, n2, ERPP.
7. ER, *AER,* 439.
8. ER, *AER,* 437.
9. ER, *AER,* 437.
10. "Battleground West Virginia: Electing the President in 1960"; "Eleanor Roosevelt campaigning in Fayette and Kanawha counties for John F. Kennedy, October 19, 1960, during the 1960 presidential campaign," West Virginia Archives and History Online Exhibit, West Virginia Culture Center, wvculture.org; "Daily Campaign Stops," October 19, 1960; "Mrs. Eleanor Roosevelt Draws Large Crowds in Fayette County," *Fayette Tribune,* October 20, 1960.
11. "Battleground West Virginia": "Hundred Line Caravan Route to Welcome Mrs. Roosevelt," *Hinton Daily News,* October 19, 1960, wvculture.org.
12. "Battleground West Virginia"; "ER campaigning in Fayette and Kanawha counties."
13. Chris Matthews, *Jack Kennedy: Elusive Hero* (New York: Simon and Schuster, 2011), 267.
14. All of William Walton's references to JFK and ER come from his 1993 oral history, "Walton, William: OH—JFK #1, 3/3/1993," JFKOH-WW-01, JFKL OH.
15. ER to Mary D. Lasker, August 15, 1960, n2, ERPDE.
16. Robert Dallek, *An Unfinished Life: John F. Kennedy, 1919–1963* (Boston: Little, Brown, 2003), 292–93; Sorensen, *Kennedy,* 158, 188, 215–16; Taylor Hiegel, "Remembering Kennedy's Micro-Targeting in the 1960 Election," NBC News, November 22, 2013.
17. "Walton, William: OH—JFK#1, 3/3/1993," JFKOH-WW-01, JFKL.
18. Sorensen, *Kennedy,* 208–9.
19. *FDR Speaks: 1933–1945,* ed. Henry Steele Commager, introduction by ER (Washington Records, n.d.).
20. "John F. Kennedy Presidential Campaign in Harlem, New York," *Harlem World Magazine,* February 2, 2019; Andrew Cohen, *Two Days in June: John F. Kennedy and the 48 Hours That Made History* (Toronto: Signal, 2014); "Televised Address to the Nation on Civil Rights," June 11, 1963, JFKL.
21. ER press conference, JFK Campaign, Washington, DC, n.d., Black, *Eleanor Roosevelt, John Kennedy, and the Election of 1960,* ERPP.
22. ER press conference, n1. Alabama Governor John Patterson had endorsed Kennedy in 1959, although, according to Sorensen, an embarrassed JFK

had asked him not to do so. Kennedy was walking a fine line, as he had throughout his legislative career, of trying not to put off either bloc (white Southerners or African Americans) in the Democratic coalition. See Sorensen, *Kennedy*, 215–16.

23. ER speech, Chevy Chase, Maryland, or Washington, DC, n.d., Papers of Abba P. Schwartz, Publications, 1966 Campaigns, 1960–1980, Box 15, JFKL.
24. ER, MD, October 19, 1960, n1, ERPDE.
25. ER speech, Indianapolis, Indiana, October 24, 1960, Schwartz Papers, JFKL.
26. ER press conference, n.d., Schwartz Papers, JFKL.
27. ER press conference, October 28, 1960, Chicago, Schwartz Papers, JFKL.
28. ER to JFK, September 27, 1960, in Rebecca Onion, "Pointers Eleanor Roosevelt Gave to JFK After His First Televised Debate With Nixon," *Slate*, October 7, 2014.
29. Barbara A. Perry, *Rose Kennedy: The Life and Times of a Political Matriarch* (New York: Norton, 2013), 241.
30. ER, MD, September 28, 1960, ERPDE.
31. ER, MD, October 12, 1960, ERPDE.
32. ER to JFK, October 24, 1960; Dr. Philip S. Herbert Jr. to ER, October 21, 1960, both in Black *Eleanor Roosevelt, John Kennedy, and the Election of 1960*, ERPP.
33. ER press conference, JFK Campaign, Washington, DC, n.d., in Black, *Eleanor Roosevelt, John Kennedy, and the Election of 1960*, ERPP.
34. ER, speech, October 26, 1960, New York, Schwartz Papers, JFKL.
35. ER speech before Kennedy for President Rally, St. Louis, Missouri, October 27, 1960, in Black, *Eleanor Roosevelt, John Kennedy, and the Election of 1960*, ERPP.
36. Edna Gurewitsch, *Kindred Souls: The Devoted Friendship of Eleanor Roosevelt and Dr. David Gurewitsch* (New York: Open Road Integrated Media, 2014), 219.
37. ER speech before Kennedy for President rally, in Black, *Eleanor Roosevelt, John Kennedy, and the Election of 1960*, ERPP.
38. ER, MD, October 10, 1960, ERPDE.
39. ER press conference, Kennedy for President Campaign, Chicago, October 28, 1960, in Black, *Eleanor Roosevelt, John Kennedy, and the Election of 1960*, ERPP.
40. ER, MD, November 2, 1960, n1, ERPDE.
41. ER, MD, November 2, 1960, n1, ERPDE.
42. ER, MD, November 2, 1960, n1, ERPDE.
43. ER for JFK, IFP:135 F42–1M, JFK, YouTube.
44. ER, JFK campaign ad, in Black, *Eleanor Roosevelt, John Kennedy, and the Election of 1960*, ERPP.

45. Jacqueline Kennedy Onassis, Arthur M. Schlessinger Jr., Michael Beschloss, *Jacqueline Kennedy: Historic Conversations on Life with John F. Kennedy, Interviews with Arthur M. Schlesinger, Jr., 1964,* foreword by Caroline Kennedy (New York: Hyperion, 2011), 97.
46. Gurewitsch, *Kindred Souls,* 242–43.
47. Glenn Fowler, "Abba Schwartz Dies at Age 73," *New York Times,* September 15, 1989; Abba Schwartz memorandum of conversation with ER, November 18, 1960, in Black, *Eleanor Roosevelt, John Kennedy, and the Election of 1960,* ERPP.
48. ER, MD, November 11, 1960, ERPDE.
49. Larry Tye, *Bobby Kennedy: The Making of a Liberal Icon* (New York: Random House, 2016), 139.
50. ER, MD, December 27, 1960, ERPDE.
51. Schwartz memorandum of conversation with ER, November 18, 1960, in Black, *Eleanor Roosevelt, John Kennedy, and the Election of 1960,* ERPP.
52. "January 10, 1961—Eleanor Roosevelt Meets President-Elect John F. Kennedy at Hotel Carlyle, New York," YouTube.
53. ER to JFK, January 17, 1961, JFKPOF-032-007-p0004, ER, 1961, JFKL.
54. Fred Dutton to Evelyn Lincoln, n.d., JFKPOF-032-007-p0003, ER, 1961, JFKL.

7. ELEANOR ROOSEVELT AND JOHN F. KENNEDY ON THE NEW FRONTIER

1. Carl Anthony Online, "Former Presidents Who Attended Inaugurations—and Didn't," January 13, 2017; Edna Gurewitsch, *Kindred Souls: The Devoted Friendship of Eleanor Roosevelt and Dr. David Gurewitsch* (New York: Open Road Integrated Media, 2014), 244–46.
2. ER to JFK, January 29, 1961, JFKPOF-032-007-p0009, ER, 1961, JFKL.
3. ER to JFK, March 2, 1961, JFKPOF-032-007-p0014, ER, 1961, JFKL.
4. ER to JFK, April 10, 1961, JFKPOF-032-007-p0019, ER, 1961, JFKL.
5. JFK's 1961 State of the Union Address, January 30, 1961, Miller Center, YouTube.
6. ER to JFK, February 6, 1961, JFK Papers, White House Central Files, Subject File, Box No. 111, File: FG 2/Roosevelt, JFKL.
7. Gurewitsch, *Kindred Souls,* 249.
8. "Ep. 207: *Prospects of Mankind,*" GW Scholar Space, PDF transcript, https://scholarspace.library.gwu.edu/concern/gw_works/zp38wc93h.
9. "Teaching Eleanor Roosevelt Glossary: Peace Corps," ERPP; ER to JFK, April 13, 1961, JFKPOF-032-007-p0020, ER, 1961, JFKL.

10. For an excellent historiography of the Peace Corps, see Nicole L. Anslover's "The Peace Corps," in *A Companion to John F. Kennedy,* ed. Marc J. Selverstone (Chichester, UK: John Wiley and Sons, 2014), 422–33.
11. ER interviews JFK, *Prospects of Mankind,* YouTube.
12. "Ep. 207: *Prospects of Mankind,*" GW Scholar Space, PDF transcript.
13. "Ep. 207: *Prospects of Mankind,*" GW Scholar Space, PDF transcript.
14. "Ep. 207: *Prospects of Mankind,*" GW Scholar Space, PDF transcript.
15. Henry Morgenthau III, "Eleanor Roosevelt at Brandeis: A Personal Memoir," *Brandeis Alumni Journal,* 1984, p. 4.
16. Gurewitsch, *Kindred Souls,* 249.
17. Gurewitsch, *Kindred Souls,* 264.
18. ER to JFK, March 2, 1961, JFKPOF-032-007-p0014, ER, 1961, JFKL.
19. Hartford N. Gunn Jr. to President and Mrs. JFK, February 24, 1961, JFKPOF-032-007-p0017, JFKL; and note by Evelyn Lincoln, March 4, 1961, JFKPOF-032-007-p0016, ER, 1961, JFKL.
20. JFK to ER, March 14, 1961, Papers of John F. Kennedy, White House Central Files, Subject File, Box No. 111, File: FG 2/Roosevelt, JFKL.
21. ER to JFK, February 19, 1961, JFKPOF-032-007-p0013, ER, 1961, JFKL.
22. ER to JFK, 1961, JFKPOF-032-007-p0021, ER, 1961, JFKL.
23. A superb historiographic review of Kennedy's Cuba policy is by Alan McPherson, in Selverstone, *Companion to John F. Kennedy,* chapter 12.
24. "Teaching ER Glossary: Tractors for Freedom Committee," ERPP; Arthur M. Schlesinger Jr., *A Thousand Days: John F. Kennedy in the White House* (Greenwich, CT: Fawcett, 1967), 766; Thomas G. Smith, "Negotiating with Fidel Castro: The Bay of Pigs Prisoners and a Lost Opportunity," *Diplomatic History* 19, no. 1 (1995): 59–86.
25. ER, MD, June 23, 1961, ERPDE.
26. Schlesinger, *Thousand Days,* 766; "Teaching ER," ERPP.
27. News conference 13, June 28, 1961, President JFK, JFKL.
28. Harold W. Chase and Allen H. Lerman, eds., *Kennedy and the Press: The News Conferences* (New York: Thomas Y. Crowell Co., 1965), 88; News conference 13, June 28, 1961, President JFK, JFKL; Barbara A. Perry, *Edward M. Kennedy: An Oral History* (New York: Oxford University Press, 2019), 39n20; Jacqueline Kennedy Onassis, Arthur M. Schlessinger Jr., Michael Beschloss, *Jacqueline Kennedy: Historic Conversations on Life with John F. Kennedy, Interviews with Arthur M. Schlesinger, Jr., 1964,* (New York: Hyperion, 2011), 191–94, nn28, 35; President JFK's remarks on presenting Cuban Invasion Brigade flag, December 29, 1962, YouTube.
29. ER to JFK, September 9, 1961, JFKPOF-032-007-p0045, ER, 1961, JFKL.

30. Allida Black, *Casting Her Own Shadow: Eleanor Roosevelt and the Shaping of Postwar Liberalism* (New York: Columbia University Press, 1996), 193. A self-described "harsh" assessment of Kennedy's failure to lead on civil rights is political scientist Bruce Miroff's *Pragmatic Illusions: The Presidential Politics of John F. Kennedy* (New York: David McKay Co., 1976), chapter 6. See also Nick Bryant's book-length treatment of what he deems as JFK's failure to lead on civil rights: *The Bystander: John F. Kennedy and the Struggle for Black Equality* (New York: Basic Books, 2006).
31. Remarks at ER's Cancer Foundation Dinner, New York, May 30, 1961, JFKPOF-035-003-p0022, JFKL.
32. ER to JFK, July 22, 1961, JFKPOF-032-007-p0042, ER, 1961, JFKL.
33. ER to JFK, July 22, 1961, JFKPOF-032-007-p0042, JFKL; Chase and Lerman, eds., *Kennedy and the Press*, 96–102.
34. ER to JFK, July 22, 1961, JFKPOF-032-007-p0042, ER, 1961, JFKL.
35. ER to JFK, July 22, 1961, JFKPOF-032-007-p0042, ER, 1961, JFKL.
36. ER to JFK, July 26, 1961, JFKPOF-032-007-p0037, ER, 1961, JFKL.
37. JFK to ER, July 28, 1961, JFKPOF-032-007-p0036, ER, 1961, JFKL.
38. ER to JFK, July 26, 1961, JFKPOF-032-007-p0037, ER, 1961, JFKL; ER, MD, July 27, 1961, JFKPOF-032-007-p0038, ER, 1961, JFKL.
39. JFK to ER, July 28, 1961, JFKPOF-032-007-p0036, ER, 1961, JFKL.
40. Tim Soutphommasane and Shaun Chau, "Talking Power," *Oxonian Review* 4, no. 2 (2005).
41. Mary Ann Glendon, "God and Mrs. Roosevelt," *First Things*, May 2010, 7–8.
42. Mrs. Earl Norris to ER, August 23, 1961, and enclosed unidentified newspaper clipping, "For Slaying White Man: Georgia Boy, 15, To Get 'Chair,'" n.d., JFKPOF-032-007-p0048 and p0049, ER, 1961, JFKL.
43. "Teaching ER Glossary: Wiltwyck School for Boys," ERPP; David B. Roosevelt, with Manuela Dunn-Mascetti, *Grandmère: A Personal History* (New York: Warner Books, 2002), 14–16.
44. ER to JFK, September 10, 1961, JFKPOF-032-007-p0046, ER, 1961, JFKL.
45. Clemency Statistics, FDR, US DOJ, https://www.justice.gov/pardon/clemency-statistics.
46. ER, MD, September 11, 1961, ERPDE.
47. JFK to ER, October 16, 1961, JFKPOF-032-007-p0052, ER, 1961, JFKL.
48. *Ex Rel. Preston Cobb, Jr. v. R. P. Balkcom, Jr., Warden*, 339 F.2d 95 (5th Cir. 1964), Court Listener.com.
49. "Questionable Verdict Reminds Some of Ga.'s Flawed Judicial Past," September 22, 2011, Auburn Avenue Research Library on African American Culture and History.

50. Jerold L. Simmons, "Smith Act," in *Oxford Companion to the Supreme Court,* ed. Kermit L. Hall (New York: Oxford University Press, 1992), 799–800.
51. Ari L. Goldman, "Junius Scales, Communist Sent to U.S. Prison, Dies at 82," *New York Times,* August 7, 2002.
52. Milton Kovitz, "*Scales v. United States,*" in Hall, *Oxford Companion to the Supreme Court,* 756.
53. Goldman, "Junius Scales."
54. ER to JFK, December 12, 1961, JFKPOF-032-007-p0054, ER, 1961, JFKL.
55. Goldman, "Junius Scales."
56. ER, MD, October 11, 1961, ERPDE.
57. ER to JFK, October 18, 1961, JFKPOF-032-007-p0053, ER, 1961, JFKL.
58. ER to JFK, December 18, 1961, JFKPOF-032-007-p0057, ER, 1961, JFKL.
59. "Forging the Alliance—President Kennedy Visits Venezuela and Colombia, December 1961: 15–18," USG-01-A, JFKL; Kennedy et al., *Jacqueline Kennedy: Historic Conversations,* 176–94, 722–26; "Jacqueline Kennedy's Speech in Spanish at La Morita, Venezuela," December 16, 1961, YouTube.
60. "The Day Venezuelans Attacked Nixon," Foreign Affairs OH, Association for Diplomatic Studies and Training, https://adst.org/.
61. JFK to ER, December 28, 1961, JFKPOF-032-007-p0056, ER, 1961, JFKL.
62. Perry, *Edward M. Kennedy,* 39n20; Kennedy et al., *Jacqueline Kennedy: Historic Conversations,* 191–94nn28, 35; JFK's remarks on presenting Cuban Invasion Brigade flag, December 29, 1962, YouTube.
63. Jeffrey F. Taffet, "Latin America," in Selverstone, *Companion to John F. Kennedy,* 307–27; Jorge I. Dominguez, "A Plan for Latin America," in *A Vision for America: JFK in Words and Pictures,* eds. Stephen Kennedy Smith and Douglas Brinkley (New York: Harper, 2017), 225–27.
64. Esther Peterson, interview by Campbell, January 20, 1970, p. 26, JFKL OH.
65. ER to JFK, December 27, 1961, JFKPOF-032-007-p0059, ER, 1961, JFKL.

8. FIGHTING FOR WOMEN'S RIGHTS

1. ER to JFK, January 26, 1962, JFKPOF-032-008-p0003, ER, 1962, JFKL.
2. Radio and television address to the American people: "Nuclear Testing and Disarmament," March 2, 1962, JFK HA-076-001, JFKL.
3. JFK to ER, June 16, 1962, JFKPOF-032-008-p0003, ER, 1962, JFKL.
4. ER to JFK, June 20, 1962, JFKPOF-032-008-p0003, ER, 1962, JFKL.
5. David B. Roosevelt, with Manuela Dunn-Mascetti, *Grandmère: A Personal History* (New York: Warner Books, 2002), 207; Joseph P. Lash, *Eleanor: The Years Alone* (New York: Norton, 1962), 341.

6. ER to JFK, February 1, 1962, JFKPOF-032-008-p0003, ER, 1962, JFKL.
7. "1960 Democratic Party Platform," American Presidency Project, UC Santa Barbara, https://www.presidency.ucsb.edu/.
8. Lisa Des Jardins, *American Queenmaker: How Missy Meloney Brought Women into Politics* (New York: Basic Books, 2020), 210.
9. Joseph P. Lash, *Eleanor and Franklin: The Story of Their Relationship, Based on Eleanor Roosevelt's Private Papers* (New York: New American Library, 1972), 120–22.
10. Lash, *Eleanor and Franklin*, 206–7.
11. John Gable, "Theodore Roosevelt and Women's Suffrage," *American Experience*, PBS.org; ER, *AER*, 68.
12. Blanche Wiesen Cook, *Eleanor Roosevelt, Vol. I, 1884–1933* (New York: Penguin, 1992), 239–40; Lash, *Eleanor and Franklin*, 289.
13. ER, interview with Arnold Michaelis, December 1956, C-SPAN Radio.
14. "A Conversation with ER," with Robert Atwood, NBC, 1958, FDRL, YouTube.
15. Lash, *Eleanor and Franklin*, 289–90, 315, 318.
16. ER, *AER*, 103.
17. Renee Davidson, "Eleanor Roosevelt: First Lady, League Leader, Pioneer," LWV.org, March 13, 2014.
18. Lash, *Eleanor and Franklin*, 320–22; ER, *AER*, 112; Maurine H. Beasley, *Eleanor Roosevelt: Transformative First Lady* (Lawrence, KS: University Press of Kansas, 2010), 29.
19. David Michaelis, *Eleanor* (New York: Simon & Schuster, 2020), 80.
20. ER, *AER*, 103.
21. ER, MD, March 31, 1953, ERPDE.
22. ER, MD, March 31, 1953, ERPDE.
23. Lash, *Eleanor and Franklin*, 236–37; Cook, *Eleanor Roosevelt*, 1:291–92. Cook believes that ER's comment to her husband constituted an effort to reassure him, rather than a genuine belief on her part. Written for a general audience, Jan Jarboe Russell's book *Eleanor in the Village: Eleanor Roosevelt's Search for Freedom and Identity in New York's Greenwich Village* (New York: Scribner's, 2021) offers an accessible and brief account of ER's meeting feminists who changed her view of politics and lifestyles in the early 1920s: see esp. chapter 8.
24. Lash, *Eleanor and Franklin*, 326–27, 344–45; ER, *This I Remember* (New York: Harper & Row, 1949), 30–32.
25. ER, interview with Arnold Michaelis, December 1956, C-SPAN Radio.
26. D. Michaelis, *Eleanor*, 389–90.
27. ER, interview with Arnold Michaelis, December 1956, C-SPAN Radio.

28. ER, *This I Remember,* 30–31; Cook, *Eleanor Roosevelt,* 1:292.
29. Barbara A. Perry and Alfred Reaves IV, "A Power Broker Like No Other: Stacey Abrams and the Democratic Party," *Thoughts from the Lawn,* December 15, 2020.
30. Cook, *Eleanor Roosevelt* 1:39–40.
31. Lash, *Eleanor and Franklin,* 346–47.
32. ER, "How to Interest Women in Voting," *Women's Democratic Campaign Manual, 1924* (Washington: Democratic Party National Committee 1924–1928, 1924), 102–3, ERPP.
33. Cook, *Eleanor Roosevelt* 1:38–40.
34. Lash, *Eleanor and Franklin,* 361–62.
35. Davidson, "Eleanor Roosevelt: First Lady, League Leader, Pioneer," LWV .org, March 13, 2014; "First Lady Biography: Eleanor Roosevelt," National First Ladies Library, http://www.firstladies.org/ .
36. "National Women's Trade Union League," VCU Libraries Social Welfare History Project, https://socialwelfare.library.vcu.edu/; Susan Amsterdam, "The National Women's Trade Union League," *Social Service Review* 56, no. 2 (1982): 259–60.
37. Cook, *Eleanor Roosevelt,* 1:356.
38. "The Most Popular Never-Ratified Amendment," National Archives, Education Updates, https://education.blogs.archives.gov/2013/12/05/the-equal-rights-amendment/.
39. Kathryn Kish Sklar, "Why Were Most Politically Active Women Opposed to the ERA in the 1920s?," in *Women and Power in American History,* eds. Kathryn Kish Sklar and Thomas Dublin (Upper Saddle River, NJ: Prentice Hall, 2009), 226.
40. In 2020, the Virginia legislature became the thirty-eighth and final state needed to ratify the ERA. Whether it would become an amendment to the Constitution, however, remained mired in controversy. The congressional deadline for ratifying the ERA (1982) had long passed, and several states that had initially voted for the amendment have rescinded their approval. Bill Chappell, "Virginia Ratifies The Equal Rights Amendment, Decades After The Deadline," NPR, January 15, 2020. As of 2024, supporters of the ERA tried unsuccessfully to have Congress vote to declare it ratified and recorded as the Twenty-Eighth Amendment.
41. ER MD, May 15, 1945, ERPDE.
42. ER, MD, May 14, 1945, ERPDE.
43. ER, MD, May 14, 1945, ERPDE.
44. "First Lady Biography: Eleanor Roosevelt," National First Ladies' Library, https://firstladies.org/.

45. Lash, *Eleanor and Franklin,* 387; "How the Leslie Bureau Educated America," from Rose Young's "Highlights from the Record of the Leslie Woman Suffrage Commission, Inc." (1922), the Liz Library, http://www.thelizlibrary.org/.
46. "How the Leslie Bureau Educated America."
47. ER, "Women Must Learn to Play the Game as Men Do," *Red Book Magazine* 50 (April 1928): 78–79, 141–42.
48. ER, "Women Must Learn to Play the Game."
49. ER, "Women Must Learn to Play the Game."
50. ER, "Women Must Learn to Play the Game."
51. Roosevelt, *This I Remember,* 44–47; David Michaelis, *Eleanor,* 262–63.
52. Cook, *Eleanor Roosevelt,* 1: chapter 1.
53. Lash, *Eleanor and Franklin,* 393.
54. ER, *This I Remember,* 46–47.
55. Lash, *Eleanor and Franklin,* 399.
56. Cook, *Eleanor Roosevelt,* 1:406–7.
57. "First Lady Biography: Eleanor Roosevelt," National First Ladies Library, https://firstladies.org/; Cook, *Eleanor Roosevelt,* 1:382–84.
58. "Triangle Shirtwaist Factory File," US Department of Labor, OSHA.
59. ER, "ER Talks with Rose Schneiderman on the Problems of the Modern Working Woman," May 12, 1937, GW ScholarSpace Library.
60. Lash, *Eleanor and Franklin,* 403.
61. "Frances Perkins," FDRL; "Frances Perkins (1880–1965)," ERPP; Lash, *Eleanor and Franklin,* 403–4.
62. "Mary (Molly) Williams Dewson (1874–1962)," ERPP.
63. "Frances Perkins," FDRL.
64. David Michaelis, *Eleanor,* 270–71; Lash, *Eleanor and Franklin,* 412–13.
65. ER, *This I Remember,* 56.
66. Cook, *Eleanor Roosevelt,* 1:392.
67. ER, *This I Remember,* 60–61, 69.
68. "First Lady Biography: Eleanor Roosevelt," National First Ladies Library, https://firstladies.org/; Lash, *Eleanor and Franklin,* 439–42.
69. ER, *This I Remember,* 69.
70. Lash, *Eleanor and Franklin,* 439–40.
71. "FDR's Flight to the Democratic National Convention, 1932," YouTube.
72. "FDR Democratic Convention 1932," YouTube; "Candidates' Wives at RNC, DNC Conventions," ABC News.
73. "The Promise of Change: ER on the Campaign Trail," FDRL; "First Lady Biography: Eleanor Roosevelt," National First Ladies Library, https://firstladies.org/.

74. All quotes from this program can be found at ER, *Pond's Dance Program,* January 20, 1933, "Woman's Home vs. Woman's Career," ERPP.
75. Betty Friedan, *The Feminine Mystique* (New York: Norton, 1963).
76. ER, *Pond's Dance Program,* March 3, 1933, "Eleanor Roosevelt's Closing Speech as a Special Recurring Guest on the *Pond's Dance Program,* on the Day Before FDR's Inauguration," ERPP.
77. "Eleanor Roosevelt: Her Life in Pictures," *McCall's* magazine editorial film, 1958, YouTube.
78. "ER: Her Life in Pictures," *McCall's* magazine editorial film, 1958, YouTube.
79. ER, *Pond's Dance Program,* March 3, 1933, "Eleanor Roosevelt's Closing Speech."
80. ER, *Pond's Dance Program,* March 3, 1933, ERPP.
81. ER, *Pond's Dance Program,* March 3, 1933, ERPP.
82. ER, *It's Up to the Women,* introduction by Jill Lepore (New York: Nation Books, 2017), x.
83. ER, *It's Up to the Women,* 1–4, 58.
84. ER, *It's Up to the Women,* 135, 139, 168, 204 (original emphasis).
85. ER, *It's Up to the Women,* 172–75.
86. Sarah Pruitt, "Is Marriage History?" History.com, August 22, 2018.
87. ER, *It's Up to the Women,* 196–97.
88. ER, *It's Up to the Women,* 183.
89. "Ep. 2: The Simmons Program, September 4, 1934," ERPP.
90. "Ep. 2: The Simmons Program," ERPP.
91. Blanche Weisen Cook, *Eleanor Roosevelt, Vol. 2, 1933–1938: The Defining Years* (New York: Penguin, 1999), 351–52; Lash, *Eleanor and Franklin,* 489.
92. Clare Malone, "From 1937 to Hillary Clinton, How Americans Have Felt About a Woman President," FiveThirtyEight.com, June 9, 2016. As of 2025, no woman has served as president, with both Hillary Clinton and Kamala Harris losing in 2016 and 2024, respectively. "Women in the U.S. Congress," Center for American Women and Politics.
93. ER, interview with Arnold Michaelis, December 1956, C-SPAN Radio.
94. ER, *It's Up to the Women,* 223–25.
95. Cook, *Eleanor Roosevelt,* 2:67, 69.
96. Cook, *Eleanor Roosevelt,* 2:70.
97. Beasley, *Eleanor Roosevelt,* 76; Cook, *Eleanor Roosevelt,* 2:84–85.
98. Cook, *Eleanor Roosevelt,* 2:347; Lash, *Eleanor and Franklin,* 485–87.
99. Cook, *Eleanor Roosevelt,* 2:72.
100. Cook, *Eleanor Roosevelt,* 2:70–74, 76–78, 88–91; Beasley, *Eleanor Roosevelt,* 153.
101. Beasley, *Eleanor Roosevelt,* 143, 150.

102. Cook, *Eleanor Roosevelt,* 1:360; ER, *This I Remember,* 102–6; Lash, *Eleanor and Franklin,* 453–55, 467–68; Beasley, *Eleanor Roosevelt,* 105–6.
103. Lash, *Eleanor and Franklin,* 875.
104. Lash, *Eleanor and Franklin,* 535.
105. Lash, *Eleanor and Franklin,* 548; Cook, *Eleanor Roosevelt,* 2:257.
106. ER, *Pond's Dance Program,* February 24, 1933, ERPP.
107. Cook, *Eleanor Roosevelt,* 2:347.
108. "A Conversation with ER," with Robert Atwood, 1958, FDRL, YouTube.
109. "Ep. 4: The Simmons Program, September 18, 1934," ERPP; Beasley, *Eleanor Roosevelt,* 84.
110. "Ep. 4: The Simmons Program, September 18, 1934," ERPP.
111. "Ep. 4, The Simmons Program, September 18, 1934," ERPP.
112. All material from this program can be found at "ER Talks with Rose Schneiderman," GW ScholarSpace Library.
113. "In Roosevelt History: 'This Is No Ordinary Time,'" FDRL (emphasis added). Note the reference to "men and women" coming to the aid of their country at a time when only the former were usually mentioned in public speeches by male politicians.
114. Beasley, *Eleanor Roosevelt,* 205.
115. Beasley, *Eleanor Roosevelt,* 206–7.
116. D. Michaelis, *Eleanor,* 428–30; Lash, *Eleanor and Franklin,* 919–20.
117. Beasley, *Eleanor Roosevelt,* 220.

9. ER AND JFK'S LAST ALLIANCE

1. *Muller v. Oregon,* 208 U.S. 412 (1908), Legal Information Institute, Cornell Law School; "The Brandeis Brief," Louis D. Brandeis School of Law, University of Louisville.
2. Allida Black, *Casting Her Own Shadow: Eleanor Roosevelt and the Shaping of Postwar Liberalism* (New York: Columbia University Press, 1996), photo caption.
3. MaryAnne Borrelli, "The Status of Women," in *A Companion to John F. Kennedy,* ed. Marc J. Selverstone (Chichester, UK: John Wiley and Sons, 2014), 519–20.
4. Esther Peterson, interview with Campbell, January 20, 1970, p. 30, JFKL OH.
5. Esther Peterson, interview with Campbell, January 20, 1970, pp. 54–55, JFKL OH.
6. "1960 Democratic Party Platform," July 11, 1960, American Presidency Project, UC Santa Barbara, https://www.presidency.ucsb.edu/.

7. "U.S. PCSW Records," JFKL.
8. Esther Peterson, interview with Campbell, January 20, 1970, pp. 55–56, JFKL OH.
9. Esther Peterson, interview with Campbell, January 20, 1970, pp. 56–57, JFKL OH.
10. Esther Peterson, interview with Campbell, January 20, 1970, pp. 56–57, JFKL OH.
11. Richard A. Lester, interview with Campbell, December 24, 1970, p. 19, JFKL OH.
12. PCSW, "Committee on Political and Civil Rights," USPCSW-001-008 Folder Title: Executive letters: #1–5, JFKL; Black, *Casting Her Own Shadow*, 193; Patricia Bell-Scott, *The Firebrand and the First Lady: Portrait of Friendship: Pauli Murray, Eleanor Roosevelt, and the Struggle for Social Justice* (New York: Knopf, 2016).
13. Esther Peterson, interview with Campbell, January 20, 1970, p. 30, JFKL OH.
14. JFK, "Executive Order 10980—Establishing PCSW," American Presidency Project, UC Santa Barbara, https://www.presidency.ucsb.edu/.
15. JFK, "Executive Order 10980," American Presidency Project, UC Santa Barbara, https://www.presidency.ucsb.edu/.
16. Borrelli, "Status of Women," 521.
17. Esther Peterson, interview with Campbell, January 20, 1970, p. 58, JFKL OH.
18. JFK, "Executive Order 10980," American Presidency Project, UC Santa Barbara, https://www.presidency.ucsb.edu/.
19. "Statement by the President of the Establishment of SCSW," December 14, 1961, JFKPOF-093-004-p0001, JFKL.
20. Esther Peterson, interview with Campbell, January 20, 1970, p. 63, JFKL OH. The JFKL and Schlesinger Library at Harvard house the commission's archived records, a few of which have been digitized at the JFKL. The main page for the PCSW records at the Kennedy Library is https://www.jfklibrary.org/asset-viewer/archives/USPCSW#admininfo. The COVID panedemic prevented in-person research at Schlesinger.
21. David Michaelis, *Eleanor* (New York: Simon & Schuster, 2020), 365.
22. PCSW, first meeting minutes, February 12–13, 1962, PCSW Document 18, USPCSW-001-008-p0001, Folder Title: Executive letters: #1–5, JFKL.
23. Esther Peterson, interview with Campbell, January 20, 1970, JFKL OH.
24. "What Status for Women?," *Prospects of Mankind,* season 3, episode 10, National Educational Television, WGBH TV, June 3, 1962.
25. "What Status for Women?," *Prospects of Mankind,* season 3, episode 10.

26. All material and quotations from "What Status for Women?" may be found at "Ep. 207: *Prospects of Mankind,*" GW ScholarSpace, PDF transcript.
27. Borrelli, "Status of Women," 521–22.
28. *American Women: Report of the President's Commission on the Status of Women,* 1963, HathiTrust.org.
29. Esther Peterson, interview with Campbell, January 20, 1970, p. 62, JFKL OH.
30. Richard A. Lester, interview with Campbell, December 24, 1970, p. 26, JFKL OH.
31. Esther Peterson, interview with Campbell, January 20, 1970, p. 62, JFKL OH.
32. Esther Peterson, interview with Campbell, January 20, 1970, p. 63, JFKL OH.
33. Esther Peterson, interview with Campbell, January 20, 1970, p. 63, JFKL OH.
34. Esther Peterson, interview with Campbell, January 20, 1970, p. 63, JFKL OH.
35. ER to JFK, August 24, 1962, JFKPOF-032-008-p0003, ER, 1962, JFKL.
36. "Progress Report to the President on PCSW," JFKPOF-032-008-p0003, ER, 1962, JFKL.
37. "Progress Report on PCSW," JFKPOF-032-008-p0003, ER, 1962, JFKL.
38. JFK to ER, August 26, 1962, JFKPOF-032-008-p0003, ER, 1962, JFKL.
39. Edmond S. Muskie to JFK, July 1962, August 15, 1962, Dedication, FDR Memorial Bridge, White House Central Files, Subject File, Box No. 111, File: FG 2/Roosevelt, Franklin D., JFKL.
40. JFK to ER, August 2, 1962, Papers of John F. Kennedy, White House Central Files, Subject File, Box No. 111, File: FG 2/Roosevelt, Franklin D., JFKL.
41. Edna Gurewitsch, *Kindred Souls: The Devoted Friendship of Eleanor Roosevelt and Dr. David Gurewitsch* (New York: Open Road Integrated Media, 2014), 281; Jonas Klein, *Beloved Island: Franklin and Eleanor and the Legacy of Campobello* (Forest Dale, VT: Eriksson, 2000), 231–40.
42. ER, MD, September 26, 1962, ERPDE.
43. ER to JFK, September 27, 1962, JFKPOF-032-008-p0003, ER, 1962, JFKL.
44. ER to JFK, October 2, 1962, JFKPOF-032-008-p0003, ER, 1962, JFKL.
45. JFK to ER, October 11, 1962, JFKPOF-032-008-p0003, ER, 1962, JFKL.
46. Anna Roosevelt Halstead to JFK, October 25, 1962, JFKPOF-032-008-p0003, ER, 1962, JFKL.
47. Joseph P. Lash, *Eleanor: The Years Alone* (New York: Norton, 1972), 324.
48. Gurewitsch, *Kindred Souls,* 83–99. For a modern analysis of ER's medical condition and the tortuous treatment she received but wished to avoid, see Daniel P. Sulmasy, Christopher Brick, and Philip A. Mackowiak, "Eleanor Roosevelt's Last Days: A Bioethical Case Study," *American Journal of Medicine* 128, no. 4 (2015): 437–40.
49. D. Michaelis, *Eleanor,* 533.

50. Gurewitsch, *Kindred Souls.*
51. Lash, *Eleanor,* 338–40.

EPILOGUE

1. "Executive Order 11061, Mrs. Anna Eleanor Roosevelt, November 8, 1962," JFK Papers, White House Central Files, Subject File, Box No. 111, File: FG 2/Roosevelt, JFKL.
2. The Roosevelt Family to President and Mrs. JFK, November 8, 1962, DJFKPOF-032-008-p0003, ER, 1962, JFKL.
3. "Eleanor Roosevelt Funeral (1962)," *News of the Day,* British Pathé, YouTube; David B. Roosevelt, with Manuela Dunn-Mascetti, *Grandmère: A Personal History* (New York: Warner Books, 2002), 14–16.
4. David Michaelis, *Eleanor* (New York: Simon & Schuster, 2020), 491, 535.
5. "ER Funeral (1962)," *News of the Day,* British Pathé, YouTube.
6. ER, *AER,* 287–88.
7. Press release, White House Press Secretary Office, November 14, 1962, White House Central Files, Subject File, Box No. 200, File: FG652 Eleanor Roosevelt Committee, JFKL.
8. Press release, White House Press Secretary Office, April 23, 1963, White House Central Files, Subject File, Box No. 200, File: FG652 ER Committee; "Jacqueline and John F. Kennedy Attending the Funeral of Eleanor Roosevelt," November 10, 1962, JFKL, also includes Adlai Stevenson's and President Kennedy's remarks on April 23, 1963, at creation of Eleanor Roosevelt Foundation, YouTube.
9. Certificate of JFK, ER Foundation, JFKPOF-032-008-p0003, ER, 1962, JFKL.
10. "ADA History," Americans for Democratic Action, https://adaction.org/ada-history/.
11. JFK's remarks sent to FDR Day diners, January 1963, JFK Papers, White House Central Files, Subject File, Box No. 11, File: FG 2/Roosevelt, Franklin D., JFKL.
12. James Roosevelt to Rose Kennedy, November 19, 1962, JFKPOF-032-008-p0032, JFKL.
13. Esther Peterson, interview with Campbell, January 20, 1970, pp. 45–47, JFKL OH.
14. Esther Peterson, interview with Campbell, January 20, 1970, p. 45, JFKL OH.
15. *American Women: Report of the President's Commission on the Status of Women* (1963), 53, HathiTrust.org; Esther Peterson, interview with Campbell, January 20, 1970, p. 45, JFKL OH.

16. Lily Rothman, "How *Time* Once Mansplained Why Equal Pay for Women Wouldn't Work," *Time,* June 10, 2015; "Equal Pay Act of 1963," Andrew Walton, NC Media Services, https://vimeo.com/441674667; "June 10, 1963—President John F. Kennedy signs the Equal Pay Act in the Oval Office," YouTube.
17. *American Women: Report of the PCSW.*
18. Esther Peterson, interview with Campbell, February 11, 1970, p. 72, JFKL OH.
19. "Remarks at Presentation of Final Report of PCSW, 11 October 1963," JFKWHA-230-007, JFKL.
20. "Remarks at the Presentation," JFKWHA-230-007, JFKL.
21. William Turner Levy, with Cynthia Eagle Russett, *The Extraordinary Mrs. R: A Friend Remembers Eleanor Roosevelt* (New York: John Wiley and Sons, 1999), xiii–xvi.
22. Cynthia Harrison, "A 'New Frontier' for Women: The Public Policy of the Kennedy Administration," *Journal of American History* 67, no. 3 (1980): 631.
23. "Hall of Honor Inductee: Esther Peterson," US Department of Labor, https://www.dol.gov/general/aboutdol/hallofhonor/2013_peterson.
24. "Equal Pay Act of 1963 and Lily Ledbetter Equal Pay Act of 2009," US Equal Employment Opportunity Commission.
25. *Ledbetter v. Goodyear Tire and Rubber Co.,* 550 U.S. 15 (2007).
26. "The State of the Gender Pay Gap 2020," Payscale.com.
27. Melanie Hanson, "College Enrollment and Student Demographic Statistics," March 1, 2021, educationdata.org.
28. Jon Marcus, "The Pandemic Is Speeding Up the Mass Disappearance of Men from College," Hechinger Report, January 19, 2021.
29. "Executive Order 11126—Establishing Committee and Council Relating to Status of Women," November 1, 1963, American Presidency Project, UC Santa Barbara, https://www.presidency.ucsb.edu/.
30. Harrison, "'New Frontier' for Women," 645–46; Maureen Mann Tannetta, "GBH and the President's Commission on the Status of Women," https://openvault.wgbh.org/; "Betty Friedan and the President's Commission on the Status of Women," Radcliffe Institute for Advanced Study, Harvard University.
31. "PCSW," October 14, 2013, C-SPAN.org.; see also Dorothy Sue Cobble's *The Other Women's Movement: Workplace Justice and Social Rights in Modern America* (Princeton: Princeton University Press, 2011); and her coauthored book, with Linda Gordon and Astrid Henry, *Feminism Unfinished: A Short, Surprising History of American Women's Movements* (New York: Liveright, 2014).
32. "Inaugural Address 1981," Ronald Reagan Presidential Library and Museum (original emphasis).

33. *American Women: Report of the PCSW,* 62 (emphasis added); the word "now" in the final draft provided a compromise, holding open the possibility that the ERA might be required in the future.
34. Barbara A. Perry, "Ruth Bader Ginsburg," in *"The Supremes": An Introduction to the U.S. Supreme Court Justices* (New York: Peter Lang, 2009), 104–5; Linda Hirshman, *Sisters in Law: How Sandra Day O'Connor and Ruth Bader Ginsburg Went to the Supreme Court and Changed the World* (New York: Harper, 2015), 57–58.
35. MaryAnne Borrelli, "The Status of Women," in *A Companion to John F. Kennedy,* ed. Marc J. Selverstone (Chichester, UK: John Wiley and Sons, 2014), 523.
36. Jo Freeman, "Gender Gaps in Presidential Elections," letter to the editor, *P.S.: Political Science and Politics* 32, no. 2 (1999): 191–92.
37. See Professor Ellen Fitzpatrick's comments on the 2013 panel, "PCSW," October 14, 2013, C-SPAN.org.
38. Arthur M. Schlesinger Jr., *Journals: 1952–2000* (New York: Penguin, 2007), 181.

INDEX

Page numbers in italics refer to illustrations.

MILLER CENTER STUDIES ON THE PRESIDENCY

The Elections of 2024
MICHAEL NELSON, EDITOR

Watchdogs: Inspectors General and the Fight for Honest and Accountable Government
GLENN A. FINE

Diplomats at War: Friendship and Betrayal on the Brink of the Vietnam Conflict
CHARLES TRUEHEART

Year Zero: The Five-Year Presidency
CHRISTOPHER P. LIDDELL

The Presidency and the American State: Leadership and Decision Making in the Adams, Grant, and Taft Administrations
STEPHEN J. ROCKWELL

Mourning the Presidents: Loss and Legacy in American Culture
LINDSAY M. CHERVINSKY AND MATTHEW R. COSTELLO, EDITORS

The Peaceful Transfer of Power: An Oral History of America's Presidential Transitions
DAVID MARCHICK AND ALEXANDER TIPPETT, WITH A. J. WILSON

Averting Doomsday: Arms Control During the Nixon Presidency
PATRICK J. GARRITY AND ERIN R. MAHAN

The Presidency: Facing Constitutional Crossroads
MICHAEL NELSON AND BARBARA A. PERRY, EDITORS

Trump: The First Two Years
MICHAEL NELSON

Broken Government: Bridging the Partisan Divide
WILLIAM J. ANTHOLIS AND LARRY J. SABATO, EDITORS

Race: The American Cauldron
DOUGLAS A. BLACKMON, EDITOR

Communication: Getting the Message Across
NICOLE HEMMER, EDITOR

American Dreams: Opportunity and Upward Mobility
GUIAN MCKEE AND CRISTINA LOPEZ-GOTTARDI CHAO, EDITORS

Immigration: Struggling over Borders
SIDNEY M. MILKIS AND DAVID LEBLANG, EDITORS

Crucible: The President's First Year
MICHAEL NELSON, JEFFREY L. CHIDESTER, AND STEFANIE GEORGAKIS ABBOTT, EDITORS

The Dangerous First Year: National Security at the Start of a New Presidency
WILLIAM I. HITCHCOCK AND MELVYN P. LEFFLER, EDITORS

The War Bells Have Rung: The LBJ Tapes and the Americanization of the Vietnam War
GEORGE C. HERRING